The C. S. Lewis Handbook

The
C. S. Lewis
Handbook

Colin Duriez

BAKER BOOK HOUSE
Grand Rapids, Michigan 49516

Library of Congress Cataloging-in-Publication Data

Duriez, Colin.
    The C.S. Lewis handbook / Colin Duriez.
        p.   cm.
    Includes bibliographical references.
    ISBN 0-8010-3001-3
    1. Lewis, C. S. (Clive Staples), 1898–1963—Dictionaries, indexes, etc.
I. Title.
PR6023.E926Z643   1990
828'.91209—dc20   90-20228
                                                       CIP

Printed in the United States of America

To Barbara, Ben and Emilia

Contents

Preface

C.S. Lewis is probably the greatest populariser of the Christian faith this century, and certainly one of the most widely read believers in the history of the church. His *Chronicles of Narnia* are consistently among the best-selling children's books, firmly established as classics along with *Alice in Wonderland, The Hobbit,* and *The Wind in the Willows.*

Yet how well is C.S. Lewis known? I suspect that many of his readers have only read one kind of his wide range of writings—his science fiction perhaps, or his children's stories, or his popular theology (especially *The Screwtape Letters* and *Mere Christianity*) or his literary criticism.

A C.S. Lewis Handbook has been written to encourage an exploration and discovery (or rediscovery) of the 'Christian world of C.S. Lewis', a phrase used as the title of a book by Clyde S. Kilby—a book which is very much the inspiration for my *Handbook*. As a young student, Clyde Kilby's book introduced me to a world that has been a permanent part of my life ever since, strengthening my Christian faith and opening both my mind and imagination.

The rich variety of C.S. Lewis' writings are part of an integrated whole. He was able to combine reasoning and imagination in a unified and bright vision of reality—and of the God who made a gift of the reality we inhabit.

I see C.S. Lewis as a twentieth-century John Bunyan,

9

even though the roots of the two men are very different. Both were concerned to capture the minds and imaginations of ordinary people and take them into a richer world of thought and experience, indeed, into a world unimaginable in depths and splendour. Both sensed the possibilities of ordinary humanity. Both employed folk traditions of fairy tale and myth as a vehicle for theological meanings, recognising the natural symmetry between story and theology. Both in their way defended the method of allegory and symbolism, and had deep insight into the psychology of human experience.

To allow readers to follow through themes and subjects that capture their interest I have used asterisks within articles to show other references. If this omits a significant cross-reference I give it at the article's end. Where appropriate, I have added further reading. At the end of the book is a list of C.S. Lewis' works (most of which are described within the *Handbook*). There is also a simple reference guide which groups together many of the related articles.

The A-to-Z character of this *Handbook* helps it to avoid the trap of becoming specialist, perpetrating the common separation of the different aspects of C.S. Lewis' thinking and imagination. My hope is that this book extends Lewis' own aims in the breadth of his writings.

A passage in one of his letters, written in 1932, encourages me to think that C.S. Lewis would not have been totally out of sympathy with my book, and the enjoyment that went into its writing, and, hopefully, will mark its reading.

> To enjoy a book . . . I find I have to treat it as a sort of hobby and set about it seriously. I begin by making a map on one of the end leafs; then I put in a genealogical tree or two; then I put a running headline at the top of each page; finally I index at the end all the passages I

have for some reason underlined. I often wonder—considering how people enjoy themselves developing photos or making scrapbooks—why so few people make a hobby of their reading in this way. Many an otherwise dull book which I had to read have I enjoyed in this way, with a fine-nibbed pen in my hand: one is *making* something all the time and a book so read acquires the charm of a toy without losing that of a book.

Parts of this book are greatly altered versions of material that has appeared as articles elsewhere or has been given as lectures. Comeback that I have received from readers of those articles and from those attending the lectures was a great help in preparing this *Handbook*. My particular thanks go to Dr Andrew Walker and Miss Elizabeth Fraser for reading the basic draft and providing helpful comments.

My thanks are also due to William Collins for permission to quote the poignant poem by C.S. Lewis on page 208, from the dedication page of *They Stand Together: The Letters of C.S. Lewis to Arthur Greeves (1914–1963)*, edited by Walter Hooper (1979).

Colin Duriez

The C.S. Lewis Handbook

A

The Abolition of Man (1943)   This powerful essay is concerned to defend the objectivity of values such as goodness and beauty against the modern view that they are merely in the mind of the beholder. C.S. Lewis gave a fictional expression to his case in his science fiction story, *That Hideous Strength*.★

If values are objective, argued Lewis, one person may be right and another wrong. If one says that a waterfall is beautiful, and another says that it is not, only one of them is right. A similar situation exists over the goodness or badness of an action. Judging goodness or badness is not simply a matter of opinion. Lewis argued that there is indeed a universal acknowledgement of good and bad over matters like theft, murder, rape, and adultery, a sense of what Lewis called the *Tao*. 'The human mind has no more power of inventing a new value than of imagining a new primary colour, or, indeed, of creating a new sun and a new sky for it to move in.'

Abandonment of the *Tao*, so much a characteristic of modern thought, spells disaster for the human race. Specifically human values like freedom and dignity become meaningless: the human being is merely part of nature.★ Nature, including humanity, is to be conquered by the technical appliance of science. Technology, with no limits upon it, becomes totalitarian—it is now technocracy. As technocracy advances, the control of the human race falls into fewer and fewer hands. The future generations are planned by an elite, and the present generation is cut off from the past. Such an elite is the most demonic example conceivable of what Lewis called the inner ring.*

As Clyde Kilby points out, a powerful passage Lewis wrote elsewhere sums up the urgency of the point he makes in *The Abolition of Man*:

> At the outset the universe appears packed with will, intelligence, life and positive qualities; every tree is a nymph and every planet a god. Man himself is akin to the gods. The advance of knowledge gradually empties this rich and genial universe: first of its gods, then of its colours, smells, sounds and tastes, finally of solidity itself as solidity was originally imagined. As these items are taken from the world, they are transferred to the subjective side of the account: classified as our sensations, thoughts, images or emotions. The Subject becomes gorged, inflated, at the expense of the Object. But the matter does not end there. The same method which has emptied the world now proceeds to empty ourselves. The masters of the method soon announce that we were just as mistaken (and mistaken in much the same way) when we attributed 'souls', or 'selves' or 'minds' to human organisms, as when we attributed Dryads to the trees. ... We, who have personified all other things, turn out to be ourselves personifications. ... And thus we arrive at a result uncommonly like zero.

Affection   *See THE FOUR LOVES.*
Ahoshta   In *The Horse and His Boy*,* an elderly Tarkaan

and Grand Vizier. He was due to marry Aravis★ in an arranged marriage.

Alambil In *The Chronicles of Narnia,*★ one of the Narnian stars, whose name means 'Lady of Peace'. When in conjunction with the star Tarva, it spells good fortune for Narnia.

See also NARNIA: Geography.

Alcasan, Francois In *That Hideous Strength,*★ a distinguished radiologist, an Arab by descent, who cut short an otherwise brilliant career in France by poisoning his wife. His severed head was rescued by the N.I.C.E.★ after his execution on the guillotine and kept alive perched on a metal bracket in a laboratory at Belbury.★ He is (in Lewis' grim joke) the Head of the Institute, embodying its belief that the human body is now an unclean irrelevance in mankind's evolutionary development, and revealing that physical immortality is a possibility. It is, in fact, uncertain that Alcasan himself has survived, because the macrobes, the bent eldila,★ speak through his head, needing human agents for their devilish activities. He parallels the dehumanisation of the Un-man★ of Perelandra, illustrating Lewis' belief in the gradual abolition of man in modern scientific society.

Alcasan's bearded head wore coloured glasses, making it impossible to see his tormented eyes. His skin was rather yellow, and he had a hooked nose. The top part of the skull had been removed, allowing the brain to swell out and expand. From its collar protruded tubes and bulbs necessary to keep it alive. The mouth had to be artificially moistened, and air pumped through in puffs to allow its laboured speech.

Mark Studdock★ is introduced to the Head as sign of his deeper initiation into the N.I.C.E. Dr Dimble★ speculates that its consciousness is one of agony and hatred.

See also THE ABOLITION OF MAN.

Alimash In *The Horse and His Boy*,★ Captain of the Chariots in Calormen and the cousin of Aravis.★

Allegory *See* ASLAN; THEOLOGY OF ROMANCE.

The Allegory of Love (1936) Subtitled 'A Study in Medieval Tradition'. This book is among the outstanding works of literary criticism of the century. 'To medieval studies in this country Lewis's logical and philosophical cast of mind gave a wholly new dimension,' commented Professor J. A. W. Bennett. This interest in ideas is shown in his concern with the philosophical and semantic development of the terms *phusis, natura,* and *kind.* Lewis traced these concepts from the beginnings of allegory★ through Chaucer and Spenser, turning to them again near the end of his life in his book *Studies in Words.*★

C. S. Lewis began work on *The Allegory of Love* in 1928, so it spans the period of his conversion to theism and then Christianity. He also wrote *The Pilgrim's Regress*,★ influenced both by his discoveries about the allegorical tradition and his conversion. Material he gathered while writing the study eventually led to his Oxford *Prolegomena* lectures, and ultimately a key book on the history of ideas, *The Discarded Image.*★ In a letter written in 1934, as *The Allegory of Love* neared completion, he suggested that the secret to understanding the Middle Ages, including its concern with allegory and courtly love, was to get to know thoroughly Dante's *The Divine Comedy, The Romance of the Rose,* the classics, and the Bible (including the apocryphal New Testament). The Middle Ages provide the key and the background to both Lewis' thought and fiction.

While in search of a publisher, he summarised the book to Oxford University Press, who accepted it for publication: 'The book as a whole has two themes: (1) The birth of allegory and its growth from what it is in Prudentius to what it is in Spenser. (2) The birth of the romantic conception of love and the long struggle between its earlier form (the romance of adultery) and its later form (the romance of marriage).'

Something of the intellectual excitement of the book can be conveyed by a small selection of statements from it: 'We shall understand our present, and perhaps even our future, the better if we can succeed, by an effort of the historical imagination, in reconstructing that long-lost state of mind for which the allegorical love poem was a natural mode of expression' (p 1). ' "Love", in our sense of the word, is as absent from the literature of the Dark Ages as from that of classical antiquity' (p 9). 'Allegory, besides being many other things, is the subjectivism of an objective age' (p 30). 'We have to inquire how something always latent in human speech [allegory] becomes, in addition, explicit in the structure of whole poems; and how poems of that kind come to enjoy an unusual popularity in the Middle Ages' (p 44). 'The allegorist leaves the given—his own passions—to talk of that which is confessedly less real, which is a fiction. The symbolist leaves the given to find that which is more real' (p 45). 'Symbolism is a mode of thought, but allegory is a mode of expression' (p 48). 'Men's gaze was turned inward. . . . The development of allegory [was] to supply the subject-ive element in literature, to paint the inner world' (p 113).

The content of the book is as follows: (1) Courtly love. (2) Allegory. (3) *The Romance of the Rose.* (4) Chaucer. (5) Gower; Thomas Usk. (6) Allegory as the dominant form. (7) *The Faerie Queene.* Appendix 1 ('Genius' and 'Genius'). Appendix 2 ('Danger').

Andrew, Uncle The Edwardian uncle of Digory Kirke★ in *The Magician's Nephew.*★ He is the uncle to which the title refers. An amateur magician, he forces Digory and his friend Polly Plummer★ into the Wood Between the Worlds by means of magic rings. He is tall, very thin,

17

with a long clean-shaven face and a sharply pointed nose, extremely bright eyes, and a great tousled mop of grey hair.

Annie, Aunt Anne Sargent Hamilton (1866–1930) was married to the brother of C.S. Lewis' mother, Flora Lewis.★ Both Jack and his brother, Warren Lewis,★ were very fond of her, especially after the loss of their own mother.

Anradin In *The Horse and His Boy*,★ a Tarkaan of Calormen, and master of Bree,★ the stolen talking horse of Narnia.★ He treated Bree badly and tried to buy Shasta.★

Ansit, Lady In *Till We Have Faces*,★ Bardia,★ the Captain of the King's Guard in Glome,★ marries her for love, and she bears him many children. After Bardia's death, Ansit tells Queen Orual★ how her possessiveness stole Bardia from his wife and family.

Anvard The capital of Archenland,★ the seat of King Lune★ in *The Horse and His Boy*.★ Anvard is a small, many-towered castle at the foot of the northern mountains. It is protected from the north wind by a wooded ridge. The ancient castle is built of a warm, reddish-brown stone. Pleasant green lawns extend to the front of the entrance gate.

See also NARNIA: Geography.

Aphallin Also called Abhalljin. A distant island beyond the seas of Lur in Perelandra,★ the Third Heaven. It is a cup-shaped land which contains the House of Kings, in which sits King Arthur, taken there by God to be in the body until the end of time, along with the Old Testament characters Enoch, Elijah, Moses and Melchisedec, the mystical King.

Aravir In *Prince Caspian*,★ the morning star of Narnia.★

See also NARNIA: Geography.

Aravis Only daughter of Kidrash Tarkaan, Lord of the

Calormene★ province of Calavar, and descended from the god Tash.★ She is the heroine of the Narnian Chronicle *The Horse and His Boy*.★ Aravis runs away from home when her mother arranges a marriage to Ahoshta— sixty years old, with a face like an ape. She meets up with and eventually marries Cor,★ and becomes Queen of Archenland.★

Archenland To Narnia's★ south, and connected by a high mountain pass, Archenland was ruled over by King Lune★ from Anvard★ during the time of the co-regency of Peter and Edmund, Susan and Lucy Pevensie.★ Leading to the high mountains are pine-covered slopes and narrow valleys. The highest peaks are Stormness Head and Mount Pire. In Archenlandian mythology the twin-peaked Mount Pire was once a two-headed giant who turned to stone. Archenland's southern boundary is marked by Winding Arrow River. Beyond this lies a vast desert which separates Archenland and the troublesome Calormen.★ Travellers en route to Archenland from Calormen could use the conspicuous double peak of Mount Pire as a landmark. Archenland's wine was highly regarded, and was so potent that water had to be mixed with it before drinking.

  See also NARNIA: Geography; NARNIA: History; *THE HORSE AND HIS BOY.*

Archon *See* Eldila.

Argan Prince of Phars★ in *Till We Have Faces,*★ and troublesome to neighbouring Glome.★ Eventually he is defeated in single combat by Queen Orual,★ allowing a peaceful alliance between the kingdoms. He had straw-coloured hair and beard, and was thin and yet somehow bloated, with pouting lips.

Argoz In *The Voyage of the 'Dawn Treader',*★ one of the seven Lords★ of Narnia sought by the Telmarine★ Caspian.★ He was eventually discovered slumbering a deep sleep of years at Ramandu's Island.★

19

Arlian   In *Prince Caspian*,★ one of the Telmarine★ Lords of Caspian★ IX, executed for treason by the usurper Miraz.★

Arnom   In *Till We Have Faces*,★ the progressive new priest of Ungit,★ whose 'new theology' takes in ideas from Greek rationalism. He was a dark man no older than Queen Orual,★ and 'smooth-cheeked as a eunuch'.

Arsheesh   In *The Horse and His Boy*,★ an unpleasant Calormene★ fisherman who raises the apparently orphaned Shasta.★

***Arthurian Torso* (1948)**   This book contains an unfinished prose work by Charles Williams★ on the figure of Arthur, and a commentary by C. S. Lewis on his friend's unfinished cycle of Arthurian poems, *Taliessin Through Logres* and *The Region of the Summer Stars*. The title refers to the geographical image of the human body that Williams employs in the poems. Lewis intended his commentary to be complementary to Williams' prose work in helping the reader to appreciate the difficult poetry. He also suggests an order for reading the poems that establishes a narrative continuity. Charles Williams' thought and poetry had a deep and lasting influence on C.S. Lewis' thinking and a number of his post-war writings. In 1974 William Eerdmans published, in one volume, *Arthurian Torso* and Williams' Arthurian poems.

Aslan   Narnia★ contains many talking lions, the kings of beasts. However, Aslan is not only this, but also the creator and ultimate sovereign of the land. His father is the Emperor-over-sea, dwelling beyond the Eastern Ocean, past Aslan's Country★ and the World's End. Aslan (Turkish for 'lion') is intended to be a symbol of Christ, Christ not as he appeared and will appear in our world (as a real man), but as he appears in Narnia (as a 'real' Narnian talking lion). The symbol of the lion (a traditional image of authority) perhaps owes something to the novel of Lewis' friend Charles Williams' *The Place of the Lion*.

C.S. Lewis, therefore, did not intend Aslan to be an allegory of Christ. He explained why in a letter written a few days after Christmas 1958: 'By an allegory I mean a composition (whether pictorial or literary) in which immaterial realities are represented as feigned physical objects; e.g. . . . in Bunyan, a giant represents Despair. If Aslan represented the immaterial Deity in the same way in which Giant Despair represents Despair, he would be an allegorical figure. In reality however he is an invention giving an imaginary answer to the question, "What might Christ become like, if there really were a world like Narnia and He chose to be incarnate and die and rise again in *that* world as he actually has done in ours?" This is not allegory at all.'

All seven of *The Chronicles of Narnia*★ teem with Christian meanings found also in Lewis' other writings, such as the true character of God,★ mankind, nature,★ heaven,★ hell, and joy★ (*sehnsucht*). The key to these meanings lies in the fact that Aslan is a figure of Christ, out of many possible figures of him. If a reader is unaware of this, he or she can still enjoy the stories in their own right; if he or she is aware, the meaning of Christian truths often comes strangely alive. Many readers who are so familiar with the Gospel narratives as to be unmoved by the accounts of Christ's death are, however, moved to tears at the death of Aslan, for instance.

See also THEOLOGY OF ROMANCE.

Aslan's Country This lies high up, beyond Narnia's★ Eastern Ocean. It features in *The Voyage of the 'Dawn Treader'*.★ Jill Pole★ and Eustace Scrubb★ arrive there when they are drawn out of our world in the story known as *The Silver Chair*.★ Seen from World's End Island,★ Aslan's Country appears to be made up of mountains of enormous height, yet for ever free of snow, clothed in grass and forests as far as the eye can glimpse. The highest peak is known as the Mountain of Aslan. Viewed from its summit, clouds above the Eastern Ocean look like small sheep. The distinctive water of Aslan's Country quenches hunger and thirst. Approaching visitors find a deepening and splendid brightness which confers increasing youthfulness to those long exposed to it. Its brightness is like that experienced by Elwin Ransom★ in Deep Heaven in Lewis' science fiction trilogy. The quality of light in Deep Heaven and near Aslan's Country reminds us that C.S. Lewis was very much inspired by the medieval imagination, with its marked response to brightness, rather than the modern imagination, with its awe at the vastness of deep space or large quantities.

In *The Voyage of the 'Dawn Treader'*, Aslan★ appears in his country to the children, Edmund and Lucy Pevensie★ and Eustace, first as a lamb and then as the familiar great lion.

Aslan's How   A huge mound, in the story *Prince Caspian*,★ which during the course of ages has been built over the Stone Table★ where Aslan,★ the great talking lion, was sacrificed. It is located in the Great Woods of Narnia,★ and has hollowed galleries and caves.

Atlantis   In *That Hideous Strength*,★ a lost world and origin of Logres, the spiritual and true Britain, established during the time of King Arthur and Merlin. Merlin's magical art was a last survival of the older and different realm of Atlantis, or Numinor, as it is sometimes called, which existed in the pre-glacial period before primitive Druidism. It was brought to Western Europe after the fall of Atlantis, and differed greatly from the Renaissance magic with which we are familiar. Merlin was a member of the Atlantian Circle and retained an instinctive feel for the powers of nature,★ lost to modern science.

The Atlantian heritage retains something of Eden, mankind's unfallen state, captured mythically in Lewis' planetary world of Perelandra.★ This heritage was passed on through the succession of the Pendragon of Logres to Elwin Ransom.★ It was also preserved in the language of Old Solar,★ spoken before the fall of mankind and beyond the moon's orbit. The N.I.C.E.★ wished to utilise this power through reviving the sleeping body of Merlin, preserved through the ages by a spell, for its own satanic ends.

In *The Magician's Nephew*,★ the magical rings which allowed Polly Plummer★ and Digory Kirke★ to travel to other worlds, including Narnia★ and Charn,★ were made from Atlantian dust.

See also WILLIAMS, CHARLES.

Further reading

J.R.R. Tolkien, *The Silmarillion* (1977); Charles Williams, *Taliessin Through Logres* (1938) and *The Region of the Summer Stars* (1944); Stephen Lawhead, *Taliesin* (1988); Plato, *Critias and Timaeus*; Pierre Benoit, *L'Atlantide* (1919); Sir Arthur Conan Doyle, *The Maracot Deep* (1929).

Augray In *Out of the Silent Planet*,★ a sorn★ whom Dr Elwin Ransom★ meets on his way across the high harandra★ to Meldilorn.★ Augray gives him oxygen, for the atmosphere on Malacandra is thin, and shelters him in his cave. Later Augray carries Ransom high on his shoulders to his destination.

Avra A sparsely inhabited island in *The Voyage of the 'Dawn Treader'*,★ the third of a group known as the Lone Islands, and the location of the estates of Lord Bern.★

  See also NARNIA: Geography.

Axartha In *The Horse and His Boy*,★ Grand Vizier of Calormen.★

Azim Balda   To the south of the capital of Calormen,★ a town at the junction of many roads. It was an important centre of communications and the core of the country's postal system. Letters were carried throughout the vast country by mounted messengers of the House of Imperial Posts.

See also NARNIA: Geography; *THE HORSE AND HIS BOY.*

B

Bar In *The Horse and His Boy*,★ the Chancellor of jolly King Lune.★ He turned traitor and kidnapped the infant Prince Cor★ when he heard that he would save Archenland.★ Later, Lord Bar was slain in battle.

Bardia In *Till We Have Faces*,★ the Captain of the King's Guard at the palace of Glome.★ He teaches Orual to use a sword, and Orual increasingly relies upon him when she becomes Queen. Unknowingly, her possessive love for him keeps him from his family, particularly his wife, Ansit.★

Barfield, Owen (*b* 1898) A lifelong friend of C.S. Lewis, Owen Barfield was the child of 'free-thinking' parents, one a London solicitor. After serving in World War I, he studied at Wadham College, Oxford, reading English, and later gaining a B Lit. At Oxford he met C.S. Lewis, and also became an anthroposophist, an advocate of the religious school of thought developed by Rudolf Steiner. For several years he was a free-lance writer, before joining his father's legal firm. His first book, *Poetic Diction* (1928), deeply influenced C.S. Lewis (see, for example, Chapter 10 of *Miracles*★). After thirty years in law, gradual retirement allowed him to publish a number of books influenced by anthroposophy. Barfield opposed many of Lewis' beliefs, including his early atheism and materialism. They called their intellectual battle 'the Great War'.

Further reading

Lionel Adey, *C.S. Lewis' 'Great War' with Owen Barfield* (1978).

Baron Corvo A jackdaw in *That Hideous Strength*★ who, along with Mr Bultitude★ the Bear and other animals, makes up the household of Elwin Ransom★ at St Anne's. 'Baron Corvo' was a pseudonym of Frederick Rolfe (1860–1913), one of the more unsavoury authors in English literature.

Batta In *Till We Have Faces*,★ the big-boned, fair-haired, hard-headed foreigner from the north who is the nurse of Orual★ and Redival.★ Because of her troublemaking, Orual has her hanged when she becomes Queen, as one of her reforms.

Baynes, Pauline (*b* 1922) C.S. Lewis chose her to illustrate his Narnia★ books after seeing her illustrations for a story by his friend, J.R.R. Tolkien,★ *Farmer Giles of Ham* (1949). Commenting on her work for *The Silver Chair*,★ Lewis observed: 'There is, as always, exquisite delicacy.' In Pauline Baynes C.S. Lewis found an illustrator whose imagination complemented his own, just as George MacDonald★ had done with the artist Arthur Hughes.

Beaver, Mr and Mrs Loyal Narnian talking beavers who lead Peter, Lucy and Susan to the meeting-point with Aslan in *The Lion, the Witch and the Wardrobe.*★
See also TALKING ANIMALS.

Belbury In *That Hideous Strength*,★ 'a florid Edwardian mansion which had been built for a millionaire who admired Versailles'. It was acquired by the N.I.C.E.★ for their headquarters, and contrasted directly with the household community run by Elwin Ransom★ at St Anne's. At its sides had sprouted a widespread outgrowth of newer and lower buildings, where a Blood Transfusion Office had been housed. Belbury had many opulent great rooms, including a large drawing-room, a library (the haunt of the inner ring★ of staff), a lounge where coffee was served, and a banqueting hall used for meals. Extending from the main building were laboratories, one of which housed the severed head of Alcasan,★ as well as outbuildings full of all varieties of animals due for experimentation and vivisection. There were also some prison cells in which convicts awaited scientific 'rehabilitation' in place of punishment. Near the garage at the back of the house was the objective room, used for psychological initiation into the abolition of human values and normal, 'outdated' responses. An old Roman road—Wayland Street—led to Edgestow.★ It was well known to Merlin,★ who regarded it as the obvious route.

Belisar In *Prince Caspian*,★ one of Caspian★ IX's Lords. The usurper King Miraz★ had him shot intentionally with arrows during a hunting party.

'Belsen' Wynward School, Watford, Hertfordshire, was so named by C.S. Lewis in his autobiography, *Surprised by Joy*.★ It was attended by the young Lewis brothers. C.S. Lewis was sent there immediately after his mother's untimely death. The brutal headmaster, Rev Robert Capron (1851–1911), was later certified insane. One speculation is that Uncle Andrew,★ the mad scientist in *The Magician's Nephew*,★ was based on him.

Bern In *The Voyage of the 'Dawn Treader'*★ one of the seven Lords★ of Caspian★ IX. He is discovered living on one of the Lone Islands,★ and Caspian X makes him a Duke.

Bernstead In *The Voyage of the 'Dawn Treader'*,★ the estates of Bern★ on Avra,★ one of the Lone Islands.★
    See also NARNIA: Geography.

Beruna, Fords of Fords over the River of Narnia,★ later bridged, near the Stone Table★ (Aslan's How★). During

27

the night of Aslan's★ terrible death his loyal forces encamp here. At the time of the events recorded in *Prince Caspian*★ there was a town here, named Beruna.

See also THE LION, THE WITCH AND THE WARDROBE.

The Bible, C.S. Lewis and The debate about the authority and infallibility of the Bible is a complex one. Generally, C.S. Lewis may be taken as orthodox in his high view of Scripture, but he offered some tentative views on inspiration and the Word of God, partly as a response to questions. Michael Christensen, in *C.S. Lewis on Scripture* (1979), has tried to extend these tentative observations logically to present what Lewis' views might have been on the inerrancy debate (the discussion about whether or not the Bible is always accurate where it touches on science or history). For Christensen, Lewis stands between the position of theological liberalism (which lessens biblical authority in favour of religious experience or rationalism) and evangelicalism (for which the Bible is the final authority on all of life).

Though Christensen's book contains many valuable insights, it is flawed in drawing Lewis into a debate he never addressed. An evangelical who was in correspondence with C.S. Lewis, Clyde S. Kilby, has commented helpfully on Lewis' view of Scripture in relation to evangelicalism. It is clear that while Lewis sharply attacked theological liberalism, he had little or nothing critical to say publically about evangelicalism. To Clyde Kilby, however, he offered a series of detailed difficulties that he had with an evangelical view of inspiration (letter, 7th May 1959). These were offered in a spirit of helpfulness, in the expectation that anyone grappling with the authority of Scripture must give honest answers to such questions. None of the questions is incapable of solution. Lewis, however, openly treated theological liberalism as the antithesis of all that he stood for as a supernaturalist and a 'mere Christian'. Thus it would be wrong to say that Lewis stood in opposition to both theological liberalism and evangelicalism.

For evangelicals and other orthodox groups, C.S. Lewis offers a great deal that is helpful to their positions. As a literary critic,★ Lewis' insights are valuable in approaching the Bible as a literary text (though Lewis was sceptical of 'the Bible as literature' approach). His book, *Reflections on the Psalms,*★ provides a useful model for how to read the Bible. Lewis' observation about inspiration, that truth is scattered in many stories around the world, and not only in the Bible, deserves attention. It bears similarity with Calvin's view that truth is to be welcomed where it is to be found in non-Christian thinking. Lewis' *Miracles*★ provides fascinating insights into the wider implications of the doctrine of incarnation, God's★ supreme revelation of himself. Lewis believed that language, story, and myth can, in God's grace, be incarnations of truth, anticipating or echoing the incarnation of truth himself. A seminal essay, *Transposition,*★ attempts to show the logic of incarnation, as the richer level of meaning is transposed or translated into a lower, poorer level. In the Gospel records, true history and the greatest of all stories are one; myth becomes fact.

See also THEOLOGY, C.S. LEWIS AND; MEANING AND IMAGINATION; MYTH.

Bism An underground world deep below Narnia,★ not to be confused with the Green Witch's★ perverted Underland★ which lies above Bism. The children in *The Silver Chair*★ catch a glimpse of Bism through a chasm in the earth. Here the bright gems of all colours are alive, and it is the home of gnomes. Through Bism runs a river of fire inhabited by salamanders.★

See also NARNIA: Geography.

Black Woods   In *Prince Caspian*,★ woods near the ruins of Cair Paravel★ and the sea. It was rumoured by the Telmarines★ that the woods were full of ghosts. Telmarines fear the sea and let the woods grow to protect them from it.

Boxen   An imaginary kingdom created by C.S. Lewis as a young child, in collusion with his brother, W.H. 'Warnie' Lewis.★ The stories have been collected and edited by Walter Hooper into a book of the same name (1985). In his autobiography, *Surprised by Joy*,★ C.S. Lewis describes the origin of Boxen. The first stories were written, and illustrated, 'to combine my two chief literary pleasures—"dressed animals" and "knights-in-armour". As a result, I wrote about chivalrous mice and rabbits who rode out in complete mail to kill not giants but cats.' In creating an environment for the tales, a medieval animal-land was born. In order to include Warnie in its creation and shaping, features of the modern world such as trains and steamships had to be included. Thus a history had to be created, and so on.

Bracton College   In *That Hideous Strength*,★ one of several university colleges at Edgestow,★ owning Bragdon Wood,★ later acquired by the N.I.C.E.★ for sinister purposes. Edgestow and its colleges is modelled on Durham, though C.S. Lewis disclaimed any definite connection. Lewis, in his preface to the book, tells us that he selected his own profession as the setting for his tale because he naturally knew it best, not because he thought Fellows of colleges more likely to be corrupted than anyone else! The other colleges were St Elizabeth's College, a nineteenth-century women's college beyond the railway, Northumberland, standing below Bracton on the River Wynd, and Duke's, opposite the Abbey. Jane Studdock★ had studied at St Elizabeth's, and was now a post-graduate at the university.

Bracton College took no undergraduates. It was founded in 1300 for the support of ten learned men whose duties were to pray for the soul of Henry de Bracton and to study the laws of England. At the time of the story there were forty Fellows, one of whom was Mark Studdock,★ a sociologist.

The college possessed a notable Newton quadrangle, overlooked by florid, but beautiful, Georgian buildings. Nearby was the medieval college, with its smaller Republic quadrangle and cloisters. Beyond and nearer Bragdon Wood and the River Wynd were the seventeenth-century buildings, and the Lady Alice quadrangle.

During the unrest that the N.I.C.E. brought to Edgestow, the famous east window in the common room was shattered, apparently by machine gun fire from the N.I.C.E. police.

Bragdon Wood Owned by Bracton College,★ in *That Hideous Strength*,★ the wood was enclosed by a high wall with only one entry, a gate by Inigo Jones within the college. The wood was perhaps a quarter of a mile broad and a mile from east to west, with the River Wynd flowing by it. In the centre of the wood was a well with worn steps going down to it and surrounded by the remains of an ancient pavement, built in the time of King Arthur. 'Merlin's Well' was situated by the subterranean tomb of Merlin, who lay in suspended animation. In the hope of arousing Merlin,★ and procuring his magical services, the N.I.C.E.★ claimed Bragdon Wood from the college and despoiled its beauty.

Bragdon Wood was destroyed at the same time as the Midland town of Edgestow,★ in which it was located.

Bramandin In *The Magician's Nephew*,★ an ancient dead world like Charn.★

Bree A dappled Narnian talking horse, he plays a leading part in the tale *The Horse and His Boy*,★ as he leads Shasta

(Cor★) to Narnia★ and the north. Bree escaped from service as a war-horse of Anradin's★ in Calormen,★ after previously being stolen from Narnia. Bree has a sceptical bent, needing proof that Aslan★ is a real talking lion. 'Bree' is the short form of the name 'Breehy-hinny-brinny-hoohy-hah'.

See also TALKING ANIMALS.

Brenn, Isle of   In *The Voyage of the 'Dawn Treader'*,★ one of the Seven Isles.★ Redhaven is located here, a major supply base for shipping in the area.

See also NARNIA: Geography.

Bricklethumb   In *The Horse and His Boy*,★ a red dwarf who, with his brother Duffle, feeds Shasta (Cor★) when he first comes into Narnia.★

***Brothers and Friends: The Diaries of Major Warren Hamilton Lewis* (1982)**   These diary extracts were edited by the late Clyde S. Kilby and Majorie Lamp Mead from over a million words filling twenty-three journals. The result is a fascinating and indispensable portrait of W.H. 'Warnie' Lewis which also vividly pictures the day-to-day life of C.S. Lewis and his household at The Kilns. Warnie's own biography of his brother was never published, and exists in typescript at The Marion E. Wade Center of Wheaton College.

As Warnie reread his journals up to 1949 on 6th September 1967, nearly four years after C.S. 'Jack' Lewis' death, he records: 'I find these notebooks do amount to something of a biography in which I see myself much as I have lived, and often with pangs of remorse for my own selfishness and ill-living. On the other hand with much vividly recalled happiness. . . . One thing that stands out from these books is that the great pleasures of my life have been J[ack]'s society, books and scenery in that order. . . . One thing I now bitterly regret about these diaries is that I preserved hardly any of my innumerable conversations with J. If only I had known that he was to leave me to end my life in loneliness, with what jealous care I would have Boswellised him.'

The diaries are also notable for the rare records of meetings of The Inklings,★ and of Lewis' friendship with and marriage to Joy Davidman,★ a person Warnie wholly and unjealously admired.

Bulgy Bears   In *Prince Caspian*,★ three sleepy bears who are among the loyal Old Narnians. They offer Caspian★ honey.

See also TALKING ANIMALS.

Mr Bultitude   A bear in *That Hideous Strength*★ who, along with a jackdaw and other animals, makes up the household of Elwin Ransom★ at St Anne's, into which he is welcomed after escaping from a provincial zoo after a fire. C.S. Lewis seems particularly fond of this character, basing him upon a bear at Whipsnade Zoo that his brother Warnie★ and he knew as 'Bultitude'. Lewis had, according to Warnie's diary, dreamed of adding a bear to their private 'menagerie' at The Kilns.

In the story, Jane Studdock★ encounters Mr Bultitude unexpectedly occupying most of her bathroom, 'a great, snuffly, wheezy, beady-eyed, loose-skinned, gor-bellied brown bear'. Later he was captured by the N.I.C.E.★ and narrowly escaped vivisection.

Burnt Island   In *The Voyage of the 'Dawn Treader'*,★ a low, green island within sight of Dragon Island.★ Here the only living creatures the travellers discover are rabbits and goats. Ruins of stone huts, several bones and broken weapons between the fire-blackened areas suggested that it had been inhabited fairly recently.

See also NARNIA: Geography.

C

Cabby   The name given to London horse-and-cab drivers. *See* FRANK THE CABBY; *THE MAGICIAN'S NEPHEW.*

Cair Paravel   Capital of Narnia,★ the beautiful castle stands on the estuary of the Great River. In *The Lion, the Witch and the Wardrobe,*★ it was the seat of High King Peter and the other ruling Kings and Queens. Originally it was situated between two streams, but erosion turned its location into a small island. When the children return to Narnia ages later (as told in *Prince Caspian*★) the castle is in ruins. Caspian★ X rebuilds it to its former splendour. In their subsequent visit, recounted in *The Silver Chair,*★ Eustace Scrubb★ and Jill Pole★ hear told the ancient tale of *The Horse and His Boy.*★

    See also NARNIA: Geography.

Calavar   In *The Horse and His Boy,*★ a province of Calormen★ ruled by Kidrash Tarkaan, Aravis' father.

Caldron Pool   In *The Last Battle,*★ a large pool under the cliffs at the western end of Narnia.★ It owes its name to the bubbling and dancing movement of its churning water.

    See also NARNIA: Geography.

Calormen   A huge land to the far south of Narnia,★ Calormen is ruled by a dark and cruel people. Its capital is Tashbaan, and it has many provinces, each ruled by a Tarkaan, or Lord. Calormen is the setting for *The Horse and His Boy.*★ To its north lies Archenland,★ from which it is isolated by a large desert.

Tashbaan city is one of the wonders of the world. It is situated on a river island, with a many-arched bridge leading to it from the southern river bank. The city is gated, with high walls. Within them, buildings are crowded together and climb to the top of a hill. At its summit is displayed the magnificent palace of the Tisroc★ and the great temple of Tash,★ with its silver-plated dome. From the city hill it is possible to see the masts of ships at anchor at the river's mouth. To the south of Tashbaan a range of low wooded hills is visible.

Unlike democratic Narnia and Archenland to its north, Calormen has a strictly hierarchical, caste-like society. The dark-skinned peasant majority have little or no rights and slavery is common. It is basically an agricultural society, though fishing, crafts and trade have an important place. A troublesome country, Calormen historically has coveted the northern lands of its peaceable neighbours, and particularly becomes a threat in the period described in *The Last Battle*.★

Calormen originated in the Narnian year 204, when outlaws fled south from Archenland.

See also NARNIA: History.

Calormene Inhabitant of Calormen.★

Caphad In *Till We Have Faces*,★ a kingdom south of Glome★ from which King Trom★ obtained his short-lived and delicate second wife, mother of Psyche.★

Caspian The name of the first ten of the Telmarine★ Kings. The story, *Prince Caspian*★ is of the Caspian who becomes Caspian X, after defeating the usurper Miraz.★ He appears also as a central figure in *The Voyage of the 'Dawn Treader'*,★ and, in old age, in *The Silver Chair*.★ He is succeeded by his son, Rilian.★ Caspian X married the daughter of Ramandu,★ later murdered by the Green Witch★ of the line of Jadis.★

Caspian, the first of the Kings of Telmar, conquered

Narnia★ and silenced the talking animals,★ its proper inhabitants. Caspian IX was murdered by his brother Miraz.

See also NARNIA: History.

Charn In *The Magician's Nephew*,★ a dead world which is the domain of Jadis,★ later known as the White Witch. Charn was once the city of the King of Kings, and wonder of all worlds. It was a gloomy world, dominated by a giant red dying sun. As far as the eye could see ruins extended. A great river had once flowed through Charn, but now only a wide ditch of grey dust remained. In Charn, Digory Kirke★ awoke Jadis and all her evil by striking a forbidden bell. Through him she was drawn first into our world and then into Narnia.★

Chervy the Stag In *The Horse and His Boy*,★ he informs Corin★ of the Calormene★ attack on Anvard.★

Chesterton, Gilbert Keith (1874–1936) A celebrated convert to Christianity who influenced C.S. Lewis' thinking. He wrote, like Lewis, in defence of both Christian faith and fantasy. An essayist, critic, novelist, and poet, his best known writings include *The Everlasting Man, Orthodoxy,* the *Father Brown Stories, The Man who was Thursday, The Napoleon of Notting Hill,* and biographies of Robert Browning and others. Typical of his astuteness as a critic is his comment on George MacDonald★ in his *The Victorian Age in Literature*: '. . . a Scot of genius as genuine as Carlyle's; he could write fairy-tales that made all experience a fairy-tale. He could give the real sense that every one had the end of an elfin thread that must at last lead them into Paradise. It was a sort of optimist Calvinism.'

Chief Voice In *The Voyage of the 'Dawn Treader'*,★ the leader of the Dufflepuds★ who tells brave Lucy Pevensie★ their history. All the other Dufflepuds repeat what he says with approval.

Chlamash   In *The Horse and His Boy*,★ a Tarkaan or Lord of Rabadash's.★

***Christian Reflections* (1967)**   Published after C.S. Lewis' death, this collection of essays represents the breadth of his popular theology. One essay, 'Christianity and Literature',★ had previously appeared in *Rehabilitations and Other Essays.*★

The contents are as follows.

Christianity and Literature.★ An early attempt by C.S. Lewis to relate his faith to literature.

Christianity and Culture. In this, the value or otherwise of culture is considered, against those who try to make culture into a religion. Lewis is considering high culture, not culture as distinct from nature (where culture includes all human formative activity, including society and politics as well as the sciences and humanities). He affirms, however, the value of all human employments, when offered to God. 'The work of a charwoman and the work of a poet become spiritual in the same way and on the same condition.'

Religion: Reality or Substitute? Lewis considers the question of whether faith is a substitute for some real well-being we have failed to achieve on earth.

On Ethics. As in *The Abolition of Man*,★ C.S. Lewis argues for the objectivity of moral values. Mankind cannot create a new system of values, only obey or disobey values that all human beings acknowledge. 'Those who urge us to adopt new moralities are only offering us the mutilated or expurgated text of a book which we already possess in the original manuscript.' A so-called new morality would deprive us of our full humanity.

De Futilitate. Lewis examines the modern sense that life is futile and meaningless.

The Poison of Subjectivism. Similar in theme to *The Abolition of Man.*★

The Funeral of a Great Myth. An attack on popular ideas of evolution and progress, as distinct from evolution as a biological theory of change.

On Church Music. C.S. Lewis asks if church music has any particular religious relevance.

Historicism.★ A key essay on the belief that people can, by the use of their natural powers, discover an inner meaning and pattern in the historical process, a view Lewis repudiates.

The Psalms. Contains ideas filled out in *Reflections on the Psalms,*★ including reflections on the theme of judgement.

The Language of Religion. Religious language has been a central debate in philosophy of religion. C.S. Lewis' conclusion is that there is no specifically religious language. In the process, he rejects the notion that poetic language is merely an expression, or a stimulant, of emotion. Rather, he argues that poetic language is a real medium of information, though with necessary limitations. Religious language is not a special language, but ranges between ordinary and poetic talk.

Petitionary Prayer: A Problem Without an Answer. Prayer is a theme that constantly preoccupied C.S. Lewis, and he returns to it in *Letters to Malcolm: Chiefly on Prayer.*★

Modern Theology and Biblical Criticism. This is a paper Lewis read at a Cambridge theological college in 1959, giving his criticisms of modern, liberal theology (*see* THEOLOGY, C.S. LEWIS AND).

The Seeing Eye. In this magazine article, Lewis' thoughts were sparked off by a Russian astronaut's report that he had not found God in outer space. This report revealed much about modern misconceptions of reality. 'Looking for God—or Heaven—by exploring space,' wrote C.S. Lewis, 'is like reading or seeing all Shakespeare's plays in the hope that you will find Shakespeare as one of the characters or Stratford as one of the places.

Shakespeare is in one sense present at every moment in every play.'

'Christianity and Literature' (1939) An essay which first appeared in *Rehabilitations and Other Essays.* ★ It represents C.S. Lewis' early thinking on the subject. For his fully developed views on the place of literature in human life, see his book, *An Experiment in Criticism*★ (1961).

C.S. Lewis begins his essay by pointing out that Christian literature as such has no literary qualities peculiar to itself—it depends on the basic qualities of structure, suspense, variety, diction, and the like. By these norms a work is good or poor literature. Furthermore, the poorness of poor Christian writing, for example, a bad hymn, will consist to some degree in confused or erroneous thought and unworthy sentiment.

It is not so much these structural norms about which he is concerned. Rather, he disagrees violently with the circle of ideas used in modern literary criticism. This conflict is more of attitudes than of clearly defined concepts. He asks what the key words of modern criticism are. They are words such as creative (as opposed to derivative), spontaneity (as opposed to convention), and freedom (as opposed to rules). Great authors are innovators, pioneers, explorers. Bad authors bunch in schools and follow models.

In contrast, while the New Testament says nothing explicitly about literature, it does reveal quite a different emphasis. For Lewis, this emphasis is tellingly suggested in the apostle Paul's passage about the woman being the glory of a man, as a man is the glory of God. The idea is that man is derived from God in Adam, and woman derived from man in Eve. Man imitates God, and woman imitates man. There is a hierarchy here of imitation.

Lewis says that in pointing out this scheme of imitation

he is not building a theological system. 'As a layman and a comparatively reclaimed apostate' he has no intention of doing this. He does feel, however, that he can suggest that the stages of this hierarchy (Father over Son in the Trinity, angels over human beings, a husband over his wife) are connected by imitation, reflection, and assimilation. This is why we are commanded to imitate, or put on, Christ—that is, to model ourselves upon him. Thus, we are told in Galatians 4:19, Christ is to be formed or portrayed inside each believer. Furthermore, Christ on earth seemed to speak of copying or modelling himself upon what he sees the Father doing.

In the New Testament, the art of life is the art of imitation. The mentality this generates, Lewis argues, rules out the dominant values of modern criticism, such as originality. '"Originality", in the New Testament,' he writes, 'is quite plainly the prerogative of God.' Lewis points out: 'Our whole destiny seems to lie in the opposite direction, in being as little as possible ourselves, in acquiring a fragrance that is not our own but borrowed, in becoming clear mirrors filled with the image of a face that is not ours ... the highest good of a creature must be creaturely—that is, derivative or reflective—good.'

C.S. Lewis couches this idea of reflection or imitation in terms of a literary theory. 'Applying this principle to literature, in its greatest generality, we should get as the basis of all critical theory the maxim that an author should never conceive himself as bringing into existence beauty or wisdom which did not exist before, but simply and solely as trying to embody in terms of his own art some reflection of eternal Beauty and Wisdom. ... It would be opposed to the theory of genius as, perhaps, generally understood; and above all it would be opposed to the idea that literature is self-expression.'

See also LITERARY CRITIC, C.S. LEWIS AS A;

MEANING AND IMAGINATION; *THE PERSONAL HERESY*.

Christmas, Father   In *The Lion, the Witch and the Wardrobe*,★ this familiar figure appears in Narnia★ as the White Witch's curse of perpetual winter begins to break with Aslan's reappearance. Her boast had been that it would be ever winter but never Christmas. Father Christmas is a portent of change. Also, he gives magical presents to three of the four Pevensie★ children who will become Kings and Queens of Narnia.

Chronological snobbery   C.S. Lewis believed that one of the strongest myths of our day is that of progress. Change is considered to have a value in itself. We are increasingly cut off from our past (and hence a proper perspective on the strengths and weaknesses of our own age). He expressed this concern with the myth of progress in his inaugural lecture at Cambridge University, *De Descriptione Temporum.*★ From his friend Owen Barfield he gained the term 'chronological snobbery' to characterise this attitude. He explains this snobbery in *Surprised by Joy*:★

> Barfield . . . made short work of what I have called my 'chronological snobbery,' the uncritical acceptance of the intellectual climate common to our age and the assumption that whatever has gone out of date is on that account discredited. You must find out why it went out of date; was it ever refuted (and if so by whom, where and how conclusively) or did it merely die away as fashions do? If the latter, this tells us nothing about its truth or falsehood. From seeing this one passes to the realization that our age is also 'a period,' and certainly has, like all periods, its own characteristic illusions. They are likeliest to lurk in those widespread assumptions which are so ingrained in the age that no one dares to attack or feels it necessary to defend them.

City Ruinous In *The Silver Chair*,★ a ruined city close by Harfang★ in the northern wastelands. According to the Green Witch,★ a King who once dwelt there had the following words inscribed on the ruins:

> Though under Earth and throneless now I be,
> Yet, while I lived, all Earth was under me.

The Green Witch's Underland★ lay under it.
See also NARNIA: Geography.

Clipsie In *The Voyage of the 'Dawn Treader'*,★ the little daughter of the Chief Voice,★ the leader of the Dufflepuds.★ She spoke the spell that made the Dufflepuds invisible.

Clodsley Shovel In *Prince Caspian*,★ a loyal Old Narnian mole met by Caspian.★

Cloudbirth In *The Silver Chair*,★ a centaur and renowned healer who tends the burnt foot of Puddleglum.★

Coalblack In *The Silver Chair*,★ the horse of Prince Rilian.★

Coghill, Nevill (1899–1980) Nevill Coghill was Professor of English Literature at Oxford from 1957 to 1966. After serving in World War I, he read English at Exeter College, Oxford, and in 1924 was elected a Fellow there. He was a friend of C.S. Lewis' from undergraduate days, and like him hailed from Ireland. His Christianity influenced Lewis as a young man. He was admired for his theatrical productions, and for his translation of Chaucer's *Canterbury Tales* into modern English couplets.

Colin In *The Horse and His Boy*,★ he fights, together with his brother Cole, for King Lune★ against the troublesome Calormenes.★

Cor A twin son of King Lune★ of Archenland, who was lost in Calormen,★ to the south, for many years. There he had the name Shasta. The famous Narnian tale of how he returned to Archenland, learned his true identity, and gained his Calormene wife, Aravis, ★ is retold in *The Horse and His Boy*. ★ To them was born Ram the Great, the most notable of all the Kings of Archenland. Cor's identical twin was named Corin. ★

Coriakin In *The Voyage of the 'Dawn Treader'*, ★ a magician who, like Ramandu, ★ is a retired star of the sky. As a punishment, Aslan★ gave him the task of governing the Dufflepuds. ★

Corin In *The Horse and His Boy*, ★ the younger twin brother of Cor, ★ who was lost for years in Calormen. ★ He would have been heir to the Archenland★ throne had Cor not been restored, but was quite content not to become King. He was nicknamed Thunder-fist because he was a great boxer.

Cornelius, Doctor In *Prince Caspian*, ★ a half-dwarf who is the tutor of Caspian, ★ later King Caspian X. He is loyal to the 'Old Narnia', and teaches the young Prince the true history of Narnia. ★

Cullen, Mary Cook-housekeeper at the Lewis' Belfast home, Little Lea, between 1917 and 1930. She was nicknamed by the Lewis brothers 'The Witch of Endor'.

Cure Hardy In *That Hideous Strength*, ★ a picturesque village with sixteenth-century almshouses and a Norman church. The steam train on the branch line from Edgestow★ passed through here on its way to the terminus at St Anne's. Its existence was jeopardised by a N.I.C.E. ★ plan to divert the River Wynd into a reservoir in the narrow valley in which the village lay. This was to supply water to Edgestow when it was expanded into a major centre of population. The plan was another example of the Institute's disregard for 'outdated' values such as beauty.

D

Daaran In *Till We Have Faces*,★ a nephew of Queen Orual★ of Glome★ and Prince of Phars.★

Dancing Lawn In *Prince Caspian*,★ the setting of the Great Council of Caspian★ and his Narnian friends.

Dark Island In *The Voyage of the 'Dawn Treader'*,★ an island which appeared to the voyagers as a dark spot in the ocean. Here dreams come true.

The Dark Tower and Other Stories (1977)   A collection of two unfinished narratives, and three short stories, two of which appeared in *The Magazine of Fantasy and Science Fiction*. One fragment, 'The Dark Tower', was apparently written after *Out of the Silent Planet*★ and before *Perelandra*,★ and is about time rather than space travel. It owes much to David Lindsay's★ *A Voyage to Arcturus*. Lewis abandoned it as unsatisfactory. The other fragment, 'After Ten Years', was unfinished because of illness and age, and perhaps his grief over the death of Joy Davidman★ Lewis. It is a historical novel which shows the promise of his great novel, *Till We Have Faces*.★

Davidman, Helen Joy (1915–60)   C.S. Lewis' wife, and subject of his book, *A Grief Observed*, written after her death from cancer at the age of forty-five. Joy Davidman was a poet and novelist, and also published an interesting theological study of the Ten Commandments, *Smoke on the Mountain*. C.S. Lewis' attraction to the American was at first merely intellectual, that of friendship.★ She was a brilliant Jewess on the verge of divorce, with two young sons. Joy had been converted from Marxism to Christianity partly through reading C.S. Lewis.

A short time after making his acquaintance, Joy Davidman came to live in Oxford with her sons. She and Lewis became on close terms, and they married in a civil ceremony to give her British nationality so that she could stay in the country. In retrospect he wrote: 'Her mind was lithe and quick and muscular as a leopard. Passion, tenderness and pain were all equally unable to disarm it. It scented the first whiff of cant or slush; then sprang, and knocked you over before you knew what was happening.'

In the autumn of 1956 they learned that Joy had terminal cancer. It was sudden, unexpected news, and Lewis was deeply shocked. Cancer was an old acquaintance. Her two boys were close to the age the Lewis brothers were when their mother died; the parallels were uncomfortable. A bedside Christian wedding ceremony took place on 21st March 1957. Joy came home to The Kilns to die.

After prayer for healing, she had an unexpected reprieve. By July she was well enough to get out and about. They had a fortnight's holiday in Ireland. It was the beginning of the happiest few years of both their lives. Lewis confessed to his friend Nevil Coghill:★ 'I never expected to have, in my sixties, the happiness that passed me by in my twenties.'

Lewis' brother, Warnie, points out that the marriage fulfilled 'a whole dimension to his nature that had previously been starved and thwarted'. It also put paid to a bachelor's doubt that God was an invented substitute for love. 'For those few years H. and I feasted on love,' he recalled in *A Grief Observed*, 'every mode of it. If God were a substitute for love we ought to have lost all interest in Him.'

The cancer eventually returned, but the Lewises were

able to have a trip to Greece in the spring of the year of her death, a journey much desired by both of them.

Further reading

Lyle Dorsett, *And God Came In: The extraordinary story of Joy Davidman—her life and marriage to C.S. Lewis* (1983); Brian Sibley, *Shadowlands: The Story of C.S. Lewis and Joy Davidman* (1985).

Dawn Treader In *The Voyage of the 'Dawn Treader'*,★ the galleon in which the children, Eustace Scrubb★ and Jill Pole★, sail almost to Aslan's Country★ at the World's End. Shaped like a dragon, it had green sides and a purple sail. Pauline Baynes★ provided a useful cutaway illustration of the ship for the book.

De Descriptione Temporum **(1955)** This was C.S. Lewis' inaugural lecture as professor in the newly formed Chair of Medieval and Renaissance English Literature at the University of Cambridge. The lecture reveals his sympathies with an earlier age, even though he was ever concerned to communicate as a writer to a modern reader. He recognised that his assumptions and ideas were distasteful to many modern people. Lewis argued that he was, in fact, a relic of Old Western Man, a museum piece, if you like; that even if one disagreed with his ideas, one must take account of them as being from a rare (and therefore valuable) specimen of an older world.

Lewis' *De Descriptione Temporum*, which has some striking parallels with Francis Schaeffer's essay *Escape from Reason*, argues that the greatest change in the history of the West took place around the beginning of the nineteenth century, and ushered in a characteristically modern mentality. Christians and ancient pagans have more in common with each other than either has with the modern world. The change can be observed in the areas of politics, the arts, religion, and the birth of machines. The machine has, in fact, been absorbed into the inner life of modern people as an archetype. Just as older machines are replaced by new and better ones, so too (believes the modern) are ideas, beliefs and values. This notion that newer is better, the myth of progress, owes much to the 'myth of universal evolutionism' which actually predated Darwin.

The theme of this lecture complements his book, *The Abolition of Man*,★ and, like that book, is illustrated by his science fiction story, *That Hideous Strength*.★

Deathwater Island   In *The Voyage of the 'Dawn Treader'*,★ to the east of Burnt Island,★ and not more than twenty acres in size. The voyagers discovered that it was rocky and rugged with a tall central peak. Its only flora was perfumed heather and coarse grass. Only seagulls appeared to live there.

Two streams were found, one of which flowed from a small mountain lake guarded by cliffs. To the horror of the visitors, anything dipped into the lake turned to solid gold. This explained the naked gold statue lying in its waters. It was the transformed body of Restimar, one of the missing seven Lords. As a result of this grisly discovery Reepicheep★ gave the island its name.

See also NARNIA: Geography.

Denniston, Arthur and Camilla   In *That Hideous Strength*,★ a young Christian couple who join the company of Elwin Ransom★ at St Anne's. They provide an important contrast with the marriage of Mark and Jane Studdock.★ Arthur is a brilliant sociologist, and Fellow of Northumberland College at the University of Edgestow.★ According to one of the 'progressive element' at Bracton College★ he 'seems to have gone quite off the rails ... with his Distributivism and what not'. He was the chief rival for Mark Studdock's job when he had applied to Bracton several years earlier—but was not the 'right sort of man' for the progressive element. Mark and he had originally been friends as undergraduates but had grown apart because of Mark's desire for success and the lure for him of the 'inner ring'.★ Like C.S. Lewis, Arthur and Camilla liked weather of all descriptions. Jane was surprised to discover this when she was invited on a picnic with them on a foggy autumn day. Arthur explained: 'That's why Camilla and I got married. . . . We both like Weather. Not this or that kind of weather, but just Weather. It's a useful taste if one lives in England.'

Destrier In *Prince Caspian*,★ the horse of Caspian.★

Devine, Dick (Lord Feverstone) In *Out of the Silent Planet*,★ Professor Weston's★ fellow conspirator in a plan to kidnap a human sacrifice for the rulers of Malacandra.★ The two lived at The Rise, a country house near Sterk,★ where a rocket-ship had been built in Weston's laboratory. By coincidence, Devine had been at school at Wedenshaw with Ransom,★ his victim (where Ransom had disliked him as much as anyone he could remember, a dislike which was mutual). He was also at Cambridge at the same time as Ransom. Ransom had been puzzled at the appointment of this flashy and over-confident man to a Fellowship at Leicester, and further puzzled by his ever increasing wealth. Devine eventually became 'something in the city' and later an MP. He funded Weston's experiments with space-travel, and had plans for an ocean-going yacht, expensive women, and a big place on the Riviera with ill-gotten wealth from Malacandra's mineral resources. Behind his wasted life there were genuine abilities, revealed when he saved the spacecraft returning from Mars by his persistence at the controls during its perilous flight.

More emerges about him when he reappears in *That*

Hideous Strength★ after the war as Lord Feverstone, MP, now a Fellow of Bracton College★ and deeply implicated in the evil plots of the N.I.C.E.★ Though apparently likeable with his infectious laugh, his ruthlessness is revealed in his verbally brutal treatment of elderly Canon Jewel in the committee meeting which determined the fate of ancient Bragdon Wood.★ Politically, he was totalitarian to the heart, taking, he said, Clausewitz's view that total war is most humane in the long run (redefining 'humane' in the process). He graphically represents Lewis' theme of the abolition of mankind and human values. To Jane Studdock★ he was 'that man with the loud, unnatural laugh and a mouth like a shark, and no manners'. There was something shifty about him. Mark Studdock★ noticed that he never looked a person in the face.

As the stranglehold of the N.I.C.E. tightened, Devine was appointed Emergency Governor at Edgestow.★ He enjoyed the spectacle of the massacre at the great banquet at Belbury.★ After slipping away to Edgestow he was fittingly engulfed in its destruction.

Digory Kirke *See* KIRKE, DIGORY.

Dimble, Dr Cecil In *That Hideous Strength*,★ a Fellow in Literature of Northumberland College, in the University of Edgestow;★ a Christian, like C.S. Lewis, who did not suffer fools gladly. An elderly man, he had lived in Edgestow for twenty-five years, and was a close friend of Elwin Ransom.★ He had been Jane Studdock's★ tutor during her last years as an undergraduate. In his house there was a constant danger of the conversation taking a literary turn, in which King Arthur★ and the matter of Britain might come up, as he had a deep knowledge of Arthurian legend. He was prone to speculate aloud, letting his thoughts take him wherever their logic led. Cecil Dimble was scrupulously polite, even with those he disliked, such as Mark Studdock.★ Even then, his conscience had troubled him for years about lack of charity towards Jane's husband. He suffered from a habitual self-distrust.

When the N.I.C.E.★ requisitioned their cottage, the Dimbles joined Ransom's community at The Manor at St Anne's. His shrewd mind was a great help to Ransom in interpreting the enemy's moves, and he was also practical, able to search for Merlin★ despite knowing better than almost anyone the dangers involved. His fluent knowledge of Old Solar,★ the Great Tongue, was especially valuable in communicating with the magician.

According to N.I.C.E. intelligence, Dimble posed no threat—they saw him as purely academic in a worthless discipline, and impractical, unknown to anyone except a few scholars in his own subject, a nonentity. In this respect Cecil Dimble parallels the humble hobbit, Frodo Baggins, in J.R.R. Tolkien's★ *The Lord of the Rings*, confounding the wisdom of wicked powers by having a strategic role in the battle of good against evil.

Dimble, 'Mother' Margaret ('Margery') In *That Hideous Strength*,★ the wife of Cecil Dimble,★ a humorous, easy-natured and childless woman who mothered generations of women students. In appearance she was grey-haired and double-chinned. She was able to like her husband's pupils of both sexes in the University of Edgestow.★ Their homely house consequently 'was a kind of noisy *salon* all the term'. Lewis draws her character with affection, an archetypal mother figure with affinities with the young Green Lady★ of Perelandra,★ essentially 'grave, formidable and august . . . a kind of priestess or sybil'. She helped Jane Studdock★ and introduced her to the community at St Anne's.

The Discarded Image: An Introduction to Medieval and Renaissance Literature (1964) C.S. Lewis' study of medieval allegory, one result of which was *The Allegory of*

Love,★ suggested to him the writing of an allegory himself, *The Pilgrim's Regress*.★ It also led him to think hard and deeply about the truth-status of the main medieval picture of reality. This also meant considering the position of various world models in our thinking about truth, knowledge and reality.

The Discarded Image arose out of a series of lectures C.S. Lewis gave many years earlier on the medieval world image which provided a background to literature up to the seventeenth century. The lectures did much the same as Basil Willey's books did for the background to the seventeenth-, eighteenth- and nineteenth-century literature.

C.S. Lewis came to the conclusion that a world model is not meant to represent reality itself (though obviously people have identified such models with reality). If it did represent reality, some element from the real world could be substituted for the model; the model did not really matter. (In a parallel way, in imaginative literature, nothing can be substituted for a good image or allegory— the image is, in some sense, necessary for there to be meaning.★) Like John Milton before him, C.S. Lewis saw that if the medieval world model did not literally portray reality, if it was fictional, then it could still be used imaginatively. Milton employed it in his *Paradise Lost*, even though he was well aware of the scientific revolution in thought created by Galileo and Copernicus. In the twentieth century, Lewis of course employed the medieval world model in his science fiction trilogy and *The Chronicles of Narnia*. Lewis helps his readers (of all ages) to feel the imaginative power of this model. It has an integrated picture of the heavens, the earth, and mankind itself, with the human being as a miniature world, a microcosmos.

C.S. Lewis concludes *The Discarded Image* by hoping

that no one thinks he is recommending a return to the medieval model. He has only sought a proper regard of world models, respecting each and making an idol of none. Each age inevitably has its own 'taste in universes'. Thinking of chronological snobbery,★ Lewis added: 'We can no longer dismiss the change in Models as a simple progress from error to truth. No Model is a catalogue of ultimate realities, and none is a mere fantasy. Each is a serious attempt to get in all the phenomena known at a given period, and each succeeds in getting in a great many. But also, no less surely, each reflects the prevalent psychology of an age almost as much as it reflects the state of that age's knowledge.'

Our world model will eventually change, like others before it. Lewis suggested that the change was more likely to come from a change in the mental temper of a future age than from some dramatic discovery about the physical universe. This change in mentality will shape questions asked of nature,★ and thus what is considered evidence in support of a world model.

> The new Model will not be set up without evidence, but the evidence will turn up when the inner need for it becomes sufficiently great. It will be true evidence. But nature gives most of her evidence in answer to the questions we ask her. Here, as in the courts, the character of the evidence depends on the shape of the examination, and a good cross-examiner can do wonders. He will not indeed elicit falsehoods from an honest witness. But, in relation to the total truth in the witness's mind, the structure of the examination is like a stencil. It determines how much of that total truth will appear and what pattern it will suggest.

See also LITERARY CRITIC, C.S. LEWIS AS A; NATURE.

Divine Love   See *THE FOUR LOVES*.

Doorn   In *The Voyage of the 'Dawn Treader'*,★ the chief among the Lone Islands, a group of islands some 400 leagues to the east of Narnia.★ These islands had been under Narnian rule since the tenth King of Narnia, Gale, freed the islanders from a dragon.★ The town of Narrow-haven is Doorn's major settlement. Caspian★ and the other voyagers were displeased to discover Narrowhaven to be a centre of a slave trade to Calormen.★ After skilfully deposing the Governor, despite inferior forces, Caspian gave Lord Bern★ the post.

Dragon   In *The Voyage of the 'Dawn Treader'*,★ an old and dying dragon is discovered by Eustace Scrubb★ on Dragon Island.★ (It later turns out to be one of the lost Narnian Lords—Octesian★—for whom the party of voyagers is searching, transformed into the hideous shape.) Upon his death, the unpleasant Eustace himself becomes a dragon, and only Aslan★ is able to restore him to his boy nature.

Dragon Island   Discovered and named by Caspian★ of Narnia★ in *The Voyage of the 'Dawn Treader'*,★ it lies to the east of the Lone Islands.★ It is named after a sad dragon★ who lived there, which was the transformed shape of the missing Narnian Lord, Octesian.★ The mountainous island had deep bays rather like Norwegian fjords, ending in steep valleys that often had waterfalls. Cedars and other trees covered what little level land there was. Beside the ill-fated dragon, a few wild goats lived there.

   See also NARNIA: Geography.

Drinian   In *The Voyage of the 'Dawn Treader'*,★ Caspian's★ loyal Captain of the ship.

Dufflepuds   Encountered on the Island of Voices★ in *The Voyage of the 'Dawn Treader'*,★ these monopods (one-footed creatures) had been made invisible by a spell. Lucy Pevensie★ is persuaded to find the spell in the magician's book to make them visible again. They have a humorous way of talking about the obvious. The name is a contraction of their original title, 'duffers', and the new name of 'monopods' given them by the voyagers.

Dumnus In *Prince Caspian*,★ a faun.

Dymer **(1926; new edition 1950)** An anti-totalitarian poem that has some similarities with *Spirits in Bondage*,★ and written while Lewis was still an unbeliever in Christianity. It is included in *Narrative Poems*.★

The hero, Dymer, escapes from a perfect but inhuman city into the soothing countryside. Various adventures overtake him. In contrast to Dymer's idealism,★ a revolutionary group rebel against the perfect city in anarchy, claiming Dymer's name. Fresh in Lewis' mind when he wrote were the bloody events of the Russian Revolution and of his native Ulster. He regarded popular political causes as 'daemonic'.

In *Dymer* the young C.S. Lewis attacks Christianity bitterly, regarding it as a tempting illusion that must be overcome and destroyed in one's life. Christianity is lumped together with all forms of supernaturalism, including spiritism.

Old Theomagia, Demonology,
Cabbala, Chemic Magic, Book of the Dead,
Damning Hermetic rolls that none may see
Save the already damned—such grubs are bred
From minds that lose the Spirit and seek instead
For spirits in the dust of dead men's error,
Buying the joys of dream with dreamland terror.

By the time Lewis wrote *Dymer*, he seems to have rejected atheism and crude materialism in favour of idealism, hence the reference to losing 'the Spirit'. Teaching philosophy for a year at Magdalen in 1924–25 helped him to see the flaws in idealism as well, which he was later to reject for theism and Christianity.

Dyson, H.V.D. 'Hugo' (1896–1975) A friend of C.S. Lewis' from undergraduate days, Hugo Dyson was seriously wounded at Passchendaele before reading English at Exeter College, Oxford. After lecturing in English at Reading University he was, in 1945, elected Fellow and Tutor in English Literature at Merton College, Oxford. He retired in 1963.

E

Earthmen In *The Silver Chair*,★ gnome creatures who live in the Green Witch's★ realm of Underland—called by them the Shallow Lands. They originally came from Bism,★ deep below the earth's surface. At the time of their slavery to the Witch they all looked sad. Physically, they differed greatly from each other—some had tails, others had round faces, long pointed or trunk-like or blobbed noses, beards, or horns on their foreheads.

Eastern Ocean In *The Chronicles of Narnia*,★ a great ocean washing the shores of all the countries on the east.

See also NARNIA: Geography.

Edgestow In *That Hideous Strength*,★ a small Midland university town more beautiful, in C.S. Lewis' opinion, than either Oxford or Cambridge. Before the arrival of the N.I.C.E.,★ 'no maker of cars or sausages or marmalade had yet come to industrialize the country town'. The university itself was tiny, having only four colleges, including Bracton,★ and had a fine Norman church. Mark and Jane Studdock★ lived in a flat on a sandy hillside suburb over the central and academic part of Edgestow. The Dimbles★ also lived there. Their typically English country cottage was requisitioned by the N.I.C.E., along with Bracton College property south of the River Wynd, including Bragdon Wood.★ The Birmingham road lay to the east, Worcester in the other direction. Stratford to the east, and Oxford, were not a great distance away. Edgestow lay at the heart of ancient Logres, and Merlin★

had once worked in what was now Bragdon Wood. The N.I.C.E. engineered a great riot in the town, allowing their Institutional Police to take control. At this time, and later, very many of its citizens fled as refugees, saving themselves from its destruction which purged the evil that the N.I.C.E. had brought. The scene of destruction was like an event from a novel by Charles Williams,★ and like the judgement on Gwyntystorm in *The Princess and Curdie*, by George MacDonald.★

Edmund, King *See* PEVENSIE, PETER, SUSAN, EDMUND AND LUCY.

Education C.S. Lewis makes many references to education in his fiction. Experiment House,★ for instance, in the story of *The Voyage of the 'Dawn Treader'*,★ embodies his dislike of modern educational methods. Mark Studdock,★ in *That Hideous Strength*,★ is characteristic of many of today's intelligensia—actually uneducated by classical standards. Judged only by his satire, however, Lewis would seem intensely prejudiced. This is misleading. His powerful essay, *The Abolition of Man*,★ revealed anti-human values being unwittingly embodied in some typical recent school textbooks.

Lewis nowhere more clearly put forward his vision of education than in his early essay, 'Our English Syllabus', in *Rehabilitations and Other Essays*.★ He confesses: 'Human life means to me the life of beings for whom the leisured activities of thought, art, literature, conversation are the end, and the preservation and propagation of life merely the means. That is why education seems to me so important: it actualizes that potentiality for leisure, if you like for amateurishness, which is man's prerogative. You have noticed, I hope, that man is the only amateur animal; all the others are professionals. ... The lion cannot stop hunting, nor the beaver making dams, nor the bee making honey. When God made the beasts dumb He saved the world from infinite boredom, for if they could speak they would all of them, all day, talk nothing but shop.'

Eldila   In C.S. Lewis' science fiction trilogy, angel-like beings who serve the Old One through Maleldil the Young.★ Dr Elwin Ransom★ first comes across them on Malacandra★ in *Out of the Silent Planet.*★ They are barely discernable to human eyes, though their voices are audible. Ransom learns from a sorn★ that the eldila were placed on Malacandra from its creation to rule it. The overall ruler of the eldila on a planet is called the Oyarsa, and has some similarity to classical gods associated with Mars, Venus, Mercury, and other planets. The Oyarsa also steer their planets through Deep Heaven. Earth (or Thulcandra, the Silent Planet) is atypical in having a Dark Oyarsa who has turned away from Maleldil. Earth is consequently in quarantine from the rest of the universe.

Emeth the Calormene   *Emeth* is Hebrew for 'truth', and Emeth in *The Last Battle*★ symbolises what is best in human knowledge unenlightened by Christ. He is a Calormene★ who attains to the New Narnia★ because he is able to acknowledge Aslan★ when the moment of truth arises. Orual★ is a somewhat similar figure in *Till We Have Faces.*★

Emperor-over-sea   In *The Chronicles of Narnia,*★ a meta-phorical term for the father of Aslan,★ representing God★ the Father, of the biblical Trinity.

English Literature in the Sixteenth Century (Excluding Drama) (1954)   Volume 3 of *The Oxford History of English Literature*. The book is based upon embryonic lectures given at Cambridge University in 1944. As well as providing a thorough history of the period, the book is notable for its introduction, 'New Learning and New Ignorance', which adds to the themes laid out in *The Discarded Image*★ and his inaugural lecture to the Chair of Medieval and Renaissance Literature at Cambridge, *De*

Descriptione Temporum.★ He points out, for example, a transformation in the concept of magic that happened with the influence of a new empiricism. This new empiricism is what eventually led to the rise of modern science.

Lewis' introduction is of great interest to theologians, philosophers, and historians of ideas, as well as literary students. He points out that in this period, 'a Protestant may be Thomistic, a humanist may be a Papist, a scientist may be a magician, a sceptic may be an astrologer'. He regards the idea of historical periods as a mischievous conception but a methodological necessity, and points out the grave dangers of historicism.★

Writing this volume allowed him to expound one of his favourite authors, Edmund Spenser, though space severely restricted him. Where he quotes from neo–Latin authors he translates into sixteenth-century English, not simply 'for the fun of it' but to guard against false impressions created by reading modern attitudes into the past.

C.S. Lewis concludes that the period 'illustrates well enough the usual complex, unpatterned historical process; in which, while men often throw away irreplaceable wealth, they not infrequently escape what seemed inevitable dangers, not knowing that they have done either nor how they did it.'

The book's contents are as follows.

Introduction: New Learning and New Ignorance.

Book I. Late Medieval. The Close of the Middle Ages in Scotland. The Close of the Middle Ages in England.

Book II. 'Drab.' Religious Controversy and Translation. Drab Age Verse. Drab and Transitional Prose.

Book III. 'Golden.' Sidney and Spenser. Prose in the 'Golden' Period. Verse in the 'Golden' Period.

Epilogue: New Tendencies.

See also LITERARY CRITIC, C.S. LEWIS AS A.

Erimon In *Prince Caspian*,★ a Lord of Caspian★ IX, executed by the usurping Uncle Miraz★ on a trumped-up charge of treason.

Erotic love *See THE FOUR LOVES.*

***Essays Presented to Charles Williams* (1947)** *See* THE INKLINGS.

Essur In the novel, *Till We Have Faces*,★ a kingdom lying to the west of Phars,★ and separated from it by a high mountain range. Great forests and rushing rivers, and its richness in game, distinguish the country. It is also notable for a hot spring close to its capital. In recent times, the worship of Istra★ had been introduced. The legends of Istra follow closely the events in the life of Princess Psyche★ of Glome.★ Apuleius' account of the myth of Cupid and Psyche is virtually identical to that of the Istra legends.

Ettinsmoor In *The Silver Chair*,★ a desolate region of moorland north of Narnia★ and the Shribble River. Beyond Ettinsmoor lies the region of giants. Years before the events recounted in the story, Caspian★ X had fought the giants and forced them to pay tribute.

See also NARNIA: Geography.

Experiment House In *The Silver Chair*,★ the experimental school attended by Eustace Scrubb★ and Jill Pole.★ It is partly a satire on modern educational methods (see EDUCATION★) and partly based on grim memories of C.S. Lewis' own school experiences.

***An Experiment in Criticism* (1961)** Though literary criticism, this book should be read by all who take reading seriously. As C.S. Lewis' mature reflections on fiction, story, and myth,★ it helps us to understand what he was trying to do in his own fiction and poetry. He is also concerned with the function of the imagination.★

C.S. Lewis argues that literature exists for the enjoyment of readers, and books therefore should be judged by the kind of reading that they evoke. Instead of judging whether a book is good or bad, it is better to reverse the process and consider good and bad readers. When you have an idea of what a good reader is, you then can judge a book by the way in which it is read. A good book cannot be read in the same way as a bad one.

Good reading has something in common with love, moral action, and the growth of knowledge. Like all these it involves a surrender, in this case by the reader to the work being read. A good reader is concerned less with altering his or her opinion than in entering fully into the opinions and worlds of others.

'The good reader,' argues C.S. Lewis, 'reads every work seriously in the sense that he reads it whole-heartedly, makes himself as receptive as he can.' Shelley had said, 'What is love? Ask him who lives, what is life? Ask him who adores, what is God?' C.S. Lewis adds, Ask him who is a reader, what is literature?

Lewis presents the evidence of a good reader, himself, in *An Experiment in Criticism*. He concludes talking about the specific good or value of literature in terms of its content or meaning.★ (He had previously discussed literary qualities, including narrative ones.) This value or good is that 'it admits us to experiences other than our own. . . . Those of us who have been true readers all our life seldom fully realize the enormous extension of our being which we owe to authors. . . . The man who is contented to be only himself, and therefore less a self, is in prison. My own eyes are not enough for me, I will see through those of others. Reality, even seen through the eyes of many, is not enough. I will see what others have invented. Even the eyes of all humanity are not enough. I regret that the brutes cannot write books. . . . In reading great literature I become a thousand men and yet remain myself. Like the night sky in the Greek poem, I see with a myriad eyes, but it is still I who see. Here, as in worship, in love, in moral action, and in knowing, I transcend myself; and am never more myself than when I do.'

See also LITERARY CRITIC, C.S. LEWIS AS A.

F

Farrer, Austin (1904–68) A distinguished theologian and friend of C.S. Lewis'. He was Chaplain and Fellow of Trinity College, and Warden of Keble College, Oxford. ★

Further reading

P. Curtis, *A Hawk Among Sparrows: A Biography of Austin Farrer* (1985).

Farrer, Katherine (1911–72) Wife of Austin Farrer★ and friend of C.S. Lewis, and particularly of Joy Davidman★ Lewis.

Farsight In *The Last Battle*,★ the talking eagle who reports the downfall of Narnia to King Tirian.★

Father Time In *The Silver Chair*,★ the children discover a sleeping giant in Underland. He had a snowy beard that covered him to his waist. They are told that he is old Father Time, once a King in Overland. He has sunk into the Deep Realm and there dreams of the happenings in the upper world. He will not wake until the end of the world. Father Time appears again in *The Last Battle*,★ having been given a new name, and helps to end the Old Narnia★ by blowing his horn.

Felimath *See* LONE ISLANDS.

Felinda In *The Magician's Nephew*,★ a dead world like Charn.★

Fenris Ulf In *The Lion, the Witch and the Wardrobe*,★ the vicious talking wolf who is Captain of the Secret Police of the White Witch, Jadis.★

Fledge *See* STRAWBERRY.

The Four Loves **(1960)** The four loves distinguished by C.S. Lewis are affection, friendship, eros, and charity (divine love). This anatomy of love was written during the period of his short but happy marriage to Joy Davidman.★ He shows how each love is able to merge into another, or even become another. It is vital, however, not to lose sight of the real differences that give each love its valid character.

He argues that 'we must join neither the idolaters nor the "debunkers" of human love. . . . Our loves do not make their claim to divinity until the claim becomes plausible. It does not become plausible until there is in them a real resemblance to God, to Love Himself.'

Affection is the humblest and most widespread of the four loves. Most of whatever tangible and consistent happiness we find in our lives can be explained by affection. It is not a particularly appreciative love. This very lack of discrimination gives it the potential to broaden the mind, and to create a feeling for other people of all shapes and sizes. Lewis approved of a comment made by someone: 'Dogs and cats should always be brought up together. It broadens their minds so.' Affection seeps through the whole texture of our lives. It is the medium of the operation of the other loves.

C.S. Lewis constantly explored the virtues and dangers of affection in his fiction. In *The Great Divorce*,★ for example, the ghost of a mother still desires to possess her son after death. In the novel, *Till We have Faces*,★ the deep affection Orual★ feels for her sister Psyche★ turns into a destructive jealousy that she cannot distinguish from love.

Friendship is the least instinctive, biological, and

necessary of our loves. Today it is hardly considered a love, and C.S. Lewis is virtually unique among contemporary Christian thinkers in devoting so much of his attention to this theme. Lewis points out that the ancients put the highest value upon this love, as in the friendship between David and Jonathan. The ideal climate for friendship is when a few people are absorbed in some common, and not necessary, interest. Lovers are usually imagined face to face; friends are best imagined side by side, their eyes ahead on their common interest. Friendship, as the least biological of the loves, refutes sexual or homosexual explanations for its existence. It is also sharply different from membership of an inner ring.★

Friendship was deeply important to C.S. Lewis throughout his life. Arthur Greeves★ was a lifelong friend, as was Owen Barfield.★ Friendship formed the basis of the association of The Inklings,★ core figures in which included J.R.R. Tolkien★ and Charles Williams.★ His brother, Warnie (W.H. Lewis★), was also his friend from childhood, and in Joy Davidman★ he found a friend as well as a wife. He had other female friendships, too, including Sister Penelope★ and Jane McNeill.★

Friendship, reckoned C.S. Lewis, made good people better and bad people worse. Sharing a disinterested point of view was not itself good.

Eros is the kind of love that lovers are within or 'in'—the state of being in love. It is different from mere physical, sexual desire in that eros primarily wants the beloved, not sex as an end in itself. In eros love, a person is taken out of him- or herself, and thus enlarged as a person. Eros would value the beloved above happiness and pleasure, and would wish to retain the beloved even if the result was unhappiness. Lewis characteristically felt that were we not human beings, we should find eros hard to imagine. As it is, we find it difficult to explain.

Lewis' friend Charles Williams explored eros, and in his thought, fiction, and poetry, developed a theology of romantic love. This deeply influenced Lewis, and eros is an important theme in *That Hideous Strength*★ (in the marriage of Jane and Mark Studdock★) and in *Till We Have Faces*★ (in Psyche's★ love for the god of the mountain, the West-wind★). It was to have been a theme of the unfinished novel, *After Ten Years*.

Charity, or divine love, the fourth love, transcends all earthly loves in being a gift-love. All human loves are by nature (even unfallen nature) need-loves. As created beings we, by necessity, have to turn to God for our fulfilment and meaning. This pattern is repeated throughout creation, in our dependence on other people and upon nature.★ Our human loves are potential rivals to the love of God, and can only take their proper place if our first allegiance is to him. All God's love for us and for his creation is gift-love, as he has no need of the universe and its inhabitants for his existence and personal fulfilment.

As with several other of his books of popular theology, Lewis concludes by looking to heaven★ as the ultimate context of human life. It is the divine likeness in all our human loves (affection, friendship, and eros) that is their heavenly, and thus permanent, element. It is only what is heaven-like that can enter heaven; all else, when shaken, will fall. Thus any love for someone or something that is allowed to be a proper love has a heavenly element and is, in fact, also a love for God. Our own loves, like our moral choices, judge us. When those that enter heaven see God, they will find that they know him already.

See also THE ALLEGORY OF LOVE.

The Fox   The Greek slave in *Till We Have Faces*★ engaged by King Trom★ to teach his daughters. 'The Fox' is one of his nicknames (others include 'word-weaver' and 'Greekling'). His real name is Lysias, and he has sons and a daughter in far-off Greece. The Fox is short, thick-set, and very bright-eyed, always full of great intellectual curiosity. His nickname derives from the fact that when he arrived in Glome, whatever of his hair and beard was not grey was reddish. The Fox became Queen Orual's closest advisor, and taught her to think like a Greek, as well as to read and write the language. She never, however, allowed this to make her lose touch with the common people of Glome,★ and their worship of Ungit.★

The Fox followed the philosophy of the Stoics, and particularly Zeno and other Greek philosophers of the third century BC. He dismissed the stories of the gods as 'only lies of poets. ... Not in accordance with nature'. The world, The Fox believed, can be understood by the principles of right reason. He opposed the supernatural-ism★ that filled the very air of Glome.

Fox, Adam (1883–1977)   A member of The Inklings,★ Fellow of Magdalen College, Oxford,★ and Dean of Divinity there from 1929. In 1938 he was elected Professor of Poetry at Oxford. He became a Canon of Westminster Abbey in 1942. Among his publications were *Plato for Pleasure* (1945), *Meet the Greek Testament* (1952) and *Dean Inge* (1960).

Frank the Cabby   In *The Magician's Nephew*,★ an Edwardian London cabby. The character perhaps owes something to Diamond's father in *At the Back of the North Wind*, by George MacDonald.★ Frank is accidentally drawn into Narnia★ as it is being created, and, with his cockney wife Helen, is the first to rule there. His second son was the first King of Archenland.★ All humans in Narnia or its surrounding countries descended either from Frank and Helen or from the Telmarines★ who stumbled into its world. Aslan commanded that Narnia be ruled by sons and daughters of Adam.

See also NARNIA: History.

Friendship   *See THE FOUR LOVES*.

G

Gale In *The Chronicles of Narnia*,★ the ninth King of Narnia★ in descent from King Frank.★ He delivered the population of the Lone Islands★ of the Eastern Ocean★ from a dragon. In gratitude they gave the islands over to Narnian sovereignty.

See also NARNIA: History.

Galma In *The Voyage of the 'Dawn Treader'*,★ an island off the coast of Narnia★ and about a day's sailing north-east of Cair Paravel.★ King Caspian★ X of Narnia stopped here on his great journey across the Eastern Ocean.★ Galma's governing Duke marked the occasion by a great tournament.

Ginger the Cat An evil and clever cat who joins forces with the perverse Shift,★ a talking ape, in *The Last Battle*.★ After meeting Aslan★ face to face he loses the ability to speak.

Girbius In *Prince Caspian*,★ a faun.

Glasswater Creek Mentioned in *Prince Caspian*,★ a creek that leads to the hill of the Stone Table.★

Glenstorm A centaur in *Prince Caspian*★ who lives in a mountain glen. He is a particularly noble creature with glossy chestnut flanks and a golden-red beard, as befits a prophet and stargazer.

Glimfeather A talking owl in *The Silver Chair*★ who is as big as a dwarf. In the service of the now elderly King Caspian★ X, he takes under his wing Jill Pole★ and Eustace Scrubb.★ Glimfeather aids them in their endeavour to find lost Prince Rilian★ by carrying them one by one to a Parliament of Owls and then, with another owl, to Marshwiggle★ country to the north of Narnia.★

Glome   Glome was a kingdom bordering on Phars★ and Caphad,★ described in the novel, *Till We Have Faces.*★ The capital, also called Glome, was situated well back and west of the River Shennit, and a day's journey north-west of the border town of Ringal. The royal palace stood on a hillside above the city. The older part of the building was made of wood and the rest of painted brick. On the second floor was a small five-sided room sometimes used as a prison.

Near the city lay stretches of mud, reeds, and plenty of wildfowl on each side of the River Shennit, which tended to flood during heavy rain.

About a mile beyond a ford which served the city was the temple of Ungit,★ deity of Glome, whom the far-off Greeks called Aphrodite. Four great stones, twice the height of a man, were erected there in an egg-shaped ring. Within the ring, and in the brick-and-thatched temple, stood a shapeless stone, representing Ungit. She was considered to be the mother and sometimes wife of the West-wind,★ god of the mountain, who dwelt on the Grey Mountains. The foothills of these lay further north-east of the city, past the temple. Here Psyche★ (or Istra) was left as a sacrifice to the god. Psyche was the half-sister of Orual,★ who became Queen of Glome.

The country's cattle and its silver mines played a leading role in its economy.

See also SUB-CREATION; ESSUR.

Glozelle   In *Prince Caspian,*★ one of the Lords of the usurper Miraz★ who plans the tyrant's defeat by getting him to accept Peter Pevensie's★ challenge to a duel.

Glubose   In *The Screwtape Letters,*★ the tempter assigned to the crabbed mother of the patient looked after by the inexperienced Wormwood.★ Wormwood's uncle, Screwtape,★ urges him to liaise with Glubose to induce all the characteristics the patient dislikes in his mother.

Gnomes   In *The Silver Chair*,★ the inhabitants of Underland★ and Bism.★ They are short, fat, white-faced, goblin-like creatures, but with no malice towards 'overlanders', as they call those who live above the world's crust.

God

Men are reluctant to pass over the notion of an abstract and negative deity to the living God. . . . An 'impersonal God'—well and good. A subjective God of beauty, truth and goodness, inside our own heads—better still. A formless life-force surging through us, a vast power we can tap—best of all. But God Himself, alive, pulling at the other end of the cord, perhaps approaching at an infinite speed, the hunter, king, husband—that is quite another matter. There comes a moment when the children who have been playing burglars hush suddenly: was that a *real* footstep in the hall? There comes a moment when people who have been dabbling in religion ('Man's search for God'!) suddenly draw back. Suppose we really found Him? We never meant it to come to *that*! Worse still, supposing He had found us? (*Miracles*, Chapter 11).

Throughout his life C.S. Lewis loved particular things, distinctiveness in people and places, books and conversations. This was an affinity he shared with his mentor, George MacDonald.★ In Lewis' book, *Miracles*,★ which is key for understanding his view of God, many connections are made between the deep reality of particular things and the underlying factuality—the utter concreteness—of God.

Lewis pointed out that it is one thing to speak about

beauty, truth, or goodness, and about God as a great force of some kind. People will listen in a friendly manner. But it is quite another matter if you talk about a God who commands, acts, and who has definite ideas and a pointed character.

Many non-Christians, Lewis points out, say that God is beyond personality, and mean by that God is impersonal, less than a person. If you want that kind of God there are many religions to choose from. Christians, on the other hand, find God beyond personality because he is *more* than a person. Only Judeo-Christianity has this kind of God.

Lewis felt that people often hide from the idea of a definite, personal God by calling it crude or primitive. In fact, they reject the idea very often because the thought of a God who does things and makes demands is distasteful. Lewis became convinced that far from being impersonal, God is far more personal than we can imagine, and are ourselves.

We realise God's concreteness and reality best not by merely thinking about him but by obeying and worshipping him. Lewis accepts St Paul's appeal to 'put on Christ'. At first, this has to be rather like pretending to be Christ as a child might pretend to be a nurse or fireman; but by this conscious effort we eventually begin to enter into the life of Christ. The prime purpose of life is to 'lose' ourselves and to enter the divine life. Of course it is the easy way out (for there is no cost) to think of God as a formless life-force surging through us, as Lewis was tempted to do when he contemplated the possibility that God existed after all.

For Lewis, God is therefore fact, rather than the result of a rational argument. To this fact of God we bring to bear views of life and the world that we already hold. We interpret this divine fact, or even explain him away. Unlike modern theologians such as Paul Tillich or Don

Cupitt, Lewis is not afraid to call God a fact that is given to us, a definitive thing. Rather than being an abstract concept or a human symbol, God is overwhelmingly concrete and real. Lewis felt that if we fully understood *what* God is we should see that there is no question *whether* he is. He is the centre of all existence. In Lewis' vivid phrase, he is the 'fountain' of facthood. To some people he is discoverable everywhere, to some nowhere—depending on whether we are blind or see.

We often make a basic mistake when trying to imagine God as unchangeable, invisible, infinite and eternal. We are prone to miss his overwhelming life, energy, joy and concreteness, to fall into the folly of conceiving him as less definite than ourselves. This is why the central statement we can make about God is that he is.

Lewis' view of God as the utterly concrete thing, the basic fact, was part and parcel of the supernaturalism that marks all his writings. In an age of increasing secularisation, where the supernatural becomes more and more implausible, Lewis stands out in holding to the reality of the unseen world. He, like Francis Schaeffer, has refreshed and renewed the reality of God for many people in the late twentieth century.

Soon after his conversion to theism, Lewis wrote about his progress, and later gave a fuller account in *Surprised by Joy*.★ He claimed that he was an 'empirical theist'. He meant that he had come to theism as a result of uncomfortable facts, not merely by reasoning in a theological or philosophical manner (though he did plenty of that). Lewis always stressed the danger that our theoretical reasoning —which has to be abstract—can easily draw us from the particularity of the world. God is present to us first of all in given things, facts which resist being grasped fully in abstractions. Often, Lewis felt, picture language and stories came closer to grasping the concreteness of reality.

The pre-Christian Lewis felt the concreteness of God first of all through stories and myths—but his reason demanded that God's existence must be perceived in literal facts and events. This prepared him for finding God through the literal facts of Christ's incarnation, life, death and resurrection. These events were not merely a story, though they were like many good stories that God had been pleased to give to the human race. Such 'good stories', felt Lewis, were real though unfocused shafts of divine light and truth. He fashioned one such 'good story' himself, *Till We Have Faces*,★ based upon an ancient myth.

C.S. Lewis believed that God has done three basic things to reveal himself to mankind. The first was to install within people a conscience. The second was to send what Lewis dubbed 'good dreams'. By these he meant 'those queer stories scattered all through the heathen religions about a god who died and comes to life again and, by his death, has somehow given new life to men'. The third was to give the Scriptures to the Jewish people, climaxed in the incarnation of Christ and the writings of the New Testament. These three acts of God were closely related in Lewis' mind. For example, he believed that the Genesis creation story might possibly have been derived from earlier pagan myths, although he believed that the biblical retelling was the one chosen by God, the 'vehicle of the earliest sacred truth'. The creation account was not less true than history as we know it, but more so. Its symbols portray the essence, the meaning, of the historical event. We have a three-dimensional rather than a two-dimensional picture of creation.

God as revealer is tied up for Lewis with our innate sense of the fittingness of things. We are *meant* to be moral, rational creatures, but rationality is hard work—a lifetime's training of our thinking, emotions, imagination, and behaviour. We have a sense of order that needs cultivating with loving care. The greatest objective fact we have to attend to is God himself. Like life, literature, those we love, our needy neighbour, and other aspects of reality, he as the source of reality makes right and proper demands upon our attention. These aspects of reality cannot, however, be his rivals, no matter the strength of their demands.

It was vital for C.S. Lewis that belief in God does not undermine our whole system of thinking which leads us to regard certain things as true—unlike naturalism.★ He states that a system which has no place for thought cannot itself be true. Such a system undermines the validity of the very process of thinking by which it comes to the conclusion that it is true.

Like George MacDonald, Lewis saw God essentially as 'the glad creator' and hence regarded the incarnation as the central miracle, springing from God's involvement with his creation. Christian faith, beginning as it does with concrete historical events, endorses and delights in the reality and 'thereness' of the universe.

> Christian teaching by saying that God made the world and called it good teaches that Nature or environment cannot be simply irrelevant to spiritual beatitude in general, however far in one particular Nature, during the days of her bondage, they may have drawn apart. By teaching the resurrection of the body it teaches that Heaven is not merely a state of the spirit but a state of the body as well: and therefore a state of Nature as a whole. . . . God . . . is the glad creator. He has become Himself incarnate (*Miracles*, Chapter 16).

For many readers of C.S. Lewis, he is most memorable for the fresh images of God and Christ that he created, enabling people in our modern world to see again the meaning of God's reality. These images include Aslan,★ the Emperor-over-sea,★ Maleldil the Old, the Landlord, and even the pagan insights of the character of the West-wind,★ the god of the mountain in *Till We Have Faces*. Lewis' delight in God's creation was at the heart of his fantasy writing (*see* MEANING AND IMAGINATION), and his theology of romance.★

See also THEOLOGY, C.S. LEWIS AND; MYTH; NATURE; JOY.

God in the Dock   See *UNDECEPTIONS*.

God of the Grey Mountains   In *Till We Have Faces*,★ a god, in the mythology of the land of Glome,★ who dwells in the Grey Mountains. He is also referred to as the Shadow-brute and the West-wind. As son of the goddess Ungit,★ he is a debased image of Cupid, who appears in the classical myth of Cupid and Psyche.★ The people of Glome sacrifice Princess Psyche to the god in appeasement for various calamities, and he takes her as his bride, placing her in his palace. He turns out to be a god of beauty rather than a hideous monster.

See also PSYCHE'S PALACE.

Golg   A gnome★ in *The Silver Chair*,★ originally from Bism★ but met by Puddleglum★ and the others in Underland.★

The Great Divorce (1945)   Like *The Screwtape Letters*,★ this story was first serialised in a religious periodical, and also concerns the relation of heaven★ and hell. C.S. Lewis casts his story in the form of a dream, with himself as narrator, and does not wish his reader to think that information is being presented about the actual state after death. This of course does not mean that Lewis denies an actual heaven and hell. He is, in fact, concerned in this story to show their plausibility and reality.

The story opens in hell, with C.S. Lewis standing in a bus queue on a pavement in a long, shabby street. He had wandered for hours in similar, mean streets. Hell is an endless conurbation of perpetual twilight, where people move further and further away from each other. A new building just has to be thought to be made, but lacks sufficient reality to keep out the rain that constantly falls.

Anyone in hell who wishes can take a bus trip to heaven, or at least its outlands. Lewis takes such a trip with a varied collection of ghosts. Upon arrival in heaven the passengers find it painfully solid, hard and bright in comparison to hell. Solid people who have travelled vast distances to meet the ghosts try to persuade them to stay, pointing out that they will gradually adjust to heaven and become more solid as they forsake particular follies that hold them back from heaven. Much of the story is taken up with encounters between solid people and ghosts, who were friends, relations, or spouses on earth. Lewis himself meets his master, George MacDonald,* who explains many mysteries of salvation and damnation to him. Lewis particularly questions him about his apparent universalism, the belief that all people will be saved. For Lewis, universalism is ruled out by the reality of human will. Hell is, in fact, chosen by the damned. Lewis' portrayal of the damned adds to Sartre's brilliant comment, 'Hell is other people,' the reality that hell is also oneself.

C.S. Lewis handles the question of salvation and damnation very sensitively. Out of all the bus passengers, only one accepts the invitation to stay in heaven, after allowing a red lizard of lust perched on his shoulder to be destroyed by a colossal angel. Lewis' portrait of an apostate bishop strikes home painfully, exposing theological liberalism. He returns to hell to read a paper to its Theological Society.

In both *The Screwtape Letters* and *The Great Divorce*, Lewis highlights practical matters of the Christian life such as family problems, selfishness, disagreement, greed, and the persistence of bad habits. Fantasy proves a powerful medium for examining such matters, remembered long after a sermon is forgotten.

Great River In *Prince Caspian*,★ the river leading to Aslan's How★ for which the children search. It runs its course from Lantern Waste★ in the west, across Narnia,★ into the Eastern Ocean.★

See also NARNIA: Geography.

Green Lady *See PERELANDRA.*

Green Witch In *The Silver Chair*,★ the witch who tries to dominate Narnia★ during the reign of King Caspian★ X. She appears to the travellers Jill Pole,★ Eustace Scrubb★ and Puddleglum★ as a tall, beautiful young woman wearing a green kirtle. The witch enchanted and dominated Caspian's son, Rilian,★ in her Shallow Lands.★ Eventually she reveals her true nature as she transforms into a green serpent.

See also WHITE WITCH.

Greeves, Arthur *See THEY STAND TOGETHER.*

A *Grief Observed* (1961) Originally published under a pseudonym, N.W. Clerk (*see* NAT WHILK), this slim book sets out C.S. Lewis' pilgrimage through bereavement after losing his wife, Joy Davidman.★ *A Grief Observed* complements his study, *The Problem of Pain*.★ He wrote it in four exercise books as a kind of journal of grief. Whereas *The Problem of Pain* explores suffering generally and theoretically, the journal observes it specifically and personally (or existentially). Like the earlier book, *A Grief Observed* affirms the presence of God in the deepest human darkness, even when he for long seems absent.

Biographically, *A Grief Observed* reveals the quality of relationship between Lewis and Joy Davidman. He remembers: 'She was my daughter and my mother, my pupil and my teacher, my subject and my sovereign; and always, holding all these in solution, my trusty comrade, friend, shipmate, fellow-soldier.'

Griffle   In *The Last Battle*,★ the chief of a band of dwarves who believe that only they themselves are worth believing in and fighting for. This is after being disillusioned by Shift★ and his trickery.

Gumpas   In *The Voyage of the 'Dawn Treader'*,★ the slave-trading and bureaucratic Governor of the Lone Islands,★ whom Caspian replaces with the worthy Lord Bern.★

H

Hag   In *Prince Caspian*,★ an accomplice of the surly dwarf, Nikabrik.★ She had a nose and a chin that stuck out like nutcrackers, and dirty grey hair.

Handramit   The fertile lowlands in the great artificial chasms of Malacandra in *Out of the Silent Planet.*★

Harandra   The harsh outer surface or highland of Malacandra in *Out of the Silent Planet.*★ The seroni (or sorns★) like to live here.

Hardcastle, Major 'Fairy'   In *That Hideous Strength*,★ the psychopathic controller of the Institutional Police of the N.I.C.E.★ She is a lesbian who enjoys torturing Jane Studdock.★

Harfang   The stronghold of wicked giants north of Ettinsmoor★ in *The Silver Chair*.★ The children, and even Puddleglum,★ were persuaded they were friendly by the Green Witch.★ Marshwiggles★ and man are considered delicacies for a feast.

Harfang stands on a small hill overlooking the ruins of the giant City Ruinous.★ Among the crumbling ruined stone, pillars as tall as factory chimneys can be seen in places. Large sections of pavement can be seen from Harfang to bear the words 'UNDER ME', all that remains of a verse about Underland.★

Harwood, Alfred Cecil (1898–1975)   A lifelong friend of C.S. Lewis' who first met Owen Barfield★ when Barfield was a scholar at Christ Church, Oxford.★ Both were introduced to Jack Lewis in 1919 through a mutual acquaintance, Leo Baker. Harwood was, like Barfield, an anthroposophist. In 1931, Warren Lewis★ described him in his diary as a 'pleasant, spectacled, young looking man, with a sense of humour of a whimsical kind, to whom I took at sight . . . we found ourselves seeing everything with much the same eye.'

Havard, Dr R.E. 'Humphrey' (1901–85) The son of an Anglican clergyman, 'Humphrey' Havard was received into the Roman Catholic Church when aged thirty. He studied medicine after reading chemistry and became a doctor. In 1934 he took over a medical practice in Oxford with surgeries in Headington and St Giles (near The Eagle and Child public house). He was C.S. Lewis' doctor, and a member of The Inklings.★ He appears briefly as a character in *Perelandra*.★

Heaven Heaven, for C.S. Lewis, is a literal place, though, in our present, fallen situation, it will not be discovered by searching through the universe in space rockets. It is a new nature★ that God has planned, the ultimate context of a fully human life, bodies and all. The theme of heaven's reality runs through Lewis' writings, particularly his fiction, and is closely linked with his characteristic theme of joy★ or *sehnsucht*.

Before his conversion to Christianity, as an atheist, Lewis was uninterested in immortality, and only became convinced about life after death a year into his Christian life. He desired God himself, and the desire for heaven was a spin-off from this. As heaven is part of creation, it is not worthy of our ultimate aim. Lewis, however, felt that it was no more mercenary to desire heaven than to wish to marry the person one loves.

In this present life, the situation is like being on the wrong side of a shut door, with heaven on the other side. Morning was one of Lewis' favourite images of heaven. We respond to the freshness and purity of morning, but that does not make us fresh and pure.

C.S. Lewis isolated five promises about heaven for the believer. One is that we shall be with Christ. Another is that we shall be like him. We shall share his glory, the right to honour and admiration. We shall in some sense be fed, feasted, and entertained. Finally, there will be work to do: we shall be office bearers of responsibility in the universe.

Heaven is founded upon the paradox that the more we abandon ourselves to Christ, the more fully ourselves we become. Thus, while redemption by Christ improves people in this present life, the consummation of human maturity is unimaginable. In heaven, both the individuality and society of persons will be fulfilled, both diversity and harmony. Heaven is varied; hell monotonous. Heaven is brimful of meaning;★ hell is the absence of meaning. Heaven is reality itself, hell a ghost or shadow.

C.S. Lewis believed that heaven is probably unimaginable, even though we have the biblical images to take us as far as they can. Parable, allegory, and fiction is the closest that we can come to speaking of heaven. This is why he explored heaven so much through fantasy, as in *The Great Divorce*,★ *The Voyage of the 'Dawn Treader'*,★ *The Last Battle*,★ and *Perelandra*.★ In his prose, he particularly speaks of heaven in *The Problem of Pain*,★ *Letters to Malcolm*,★ and in the sermon, 'The Weight of Glory'.

In *The Last Battle*, the children see the land of Narnia★ die for ever and freeze over in blackness. They are filled with regret. Later, as they walked in a fresh morning light in Aslan's Country★ they wondered why everything seemed strangely familiar. At last they realised that this was again Narnia, but now different—larger and more vivid, more like the real thing. It was different in the way that a real thing differs from its shadow, or waking life from a dream.

Lewis' point can be illustrated from the situation that faced Mary in the Gospels. She at first did not recognise her risen Master, but mistook him for the most real of persons, a gardener. When he said her name, she saw that it was of course him. Yet he was also different. His physical presence was a bit of heaven.

We miss the wonder of such a historical event, our perceptions dulled by familiarity or by carelessness towards the past, but when we see this kind of situation cast into fiction, as Lewis does so consummately well, we glimpse its meaning afresh.

Hermit of Southern March In *The Horse and His Boy*,★ he looks after the wounded Aravis★ and the talking horses while Cor★ continues his journey to warn King Lune★ of the Calormene★ danger. A tall, robed figure with a beard that reaches his knees, the hermit is 109 years of age and has a pool with the properties of a crystal ball.

Historicism *See* HISTORY.

History In much of his literary criticism, C.S. Lewis was a literary historian. In an important essay, 'Historicism' (1950), first published in book form in *Christian Reflections*,★ he expressed his attitude to the study of history. This essay contains both an affirmation and a denial concerning the meaning★ of history.

On the one hand, C.S. Lewis believes absolutely that human history is 'a story written by the finger of God'. On the other hand, he firmly rejects all claims to know the inner meaning and patterns of history by means of mere rational observation of events. Writing history is of course worthwhile, but grand philosophies of history (historicisms) are doomed to futility. Such grand schemes have been worked out by thinkers such as Hegel, Marx, and even Augustine. He comments: 'If by one miracle, the total content of time were spread out before me, and if, by another, I were able to hold all that infinity of events in my mind and if, by a third, God were pleased to comment on it so I could understand it, then, to be sure, I could do what the Historicist says he is doing. I could read the meaning, discern the pattern.'

C.S. Lewis wants instead to emphasise trust in God and an openness to ordinary human reality—the 'primary history' in which God reveals himself in the moment by moment experience of life to each one who seeks him. That this view of history does not lead to scepticism about the value of culture is clear from another key essay, 'Learning in War-Time',★ where he points out the abiding value of scholarship.

See also LITERARY CRITIC, C.S. LEWIS AS A.

Hnohra In *Out of the Silent Planet,*★ the hross★ who teaches Dr Elwin Ransom★ the language and cultures of the beings on Malacandra.★

The Horse and His Boy (1954) Set in the period of Narnia's★ Golden Age, most of the story unfolds in the cruel southern land of Calormen.★ Cor,★ a lost son of King Lune★ of the friendly country of Archenland,★ north of Calormen, has been brought up by a poor fisherman. He has the name Shasta, and knows nothing of his true origin, but has a strange longing to travel to the northern lands.

The story also concerns a high-born Calormene girl, Aravis,★ who runs away from home to flee an unpleasant marriage. Both children independently encounter Narnian talking horses, in captivity in Calormen, who tell them about the freedom of Narnia's pleasant land, and who escape with the children. They meet up on the road.

When passing through Calormen's capital, Tashbaan,★ Aravis uncovers a treacherous plot to conquer Archenland and Narnia, led by the spiteful Prince Rabadash,★ foiled in his suit of Queen Susan★ of Narnia. With great courage, and some failures, the children are able to warn the two northern countries of their danger. The Calormene plot fails, Cor is restored to his father, the two horses, Bree★

and Hwin,★ return to their talking companions in Narnia, and Cor and Aravis marry, to become King and Queen of Archenland after Lune's death.

Several of the characters familiar to readers of *The Lion, the Witch and the Wardrobe*★ appear in this book, including most of the Pevensie★ children and the faun, Mr Tumnus.★ Both the sceptical horse Bree and the disdainful Aravis have to encounter Aslan.★

In this tale perhaps more than any other C.S. Lewis embodies his love of 'Northernness', which he shared with his friends J.R.R. Tolkien★ and Arthur Greeves,★ and which is an important element in Tolkien's Middle-earth. The book also reveals some of the extent to which the geography of the world of which Narnia is a part is drawn from the late medieval picture of reality that Lewis loved so deeply, as portrayed in his brilliant study, *The Discarded Image.*★

House of Correction for Incompetent Tempters   In *The Screwtape Letters,*★ one of the many departments of hell. Tempters are initially trained at the Tempters' Training College, run by Dr Slubgob.

Hrossa   In *Out of the Silent Planet,*★ intelligent inhabitants of the planet Malacandra who outwardly look like gleaming black animals, a little like otters or seals, yet are walking land creatures. From the hrossa Elwin Ransom★ learns the language of Old Solar.★ They are practical, food-gathering beings, with a penchant for poetry.

See also TALKING ANIMALS; PLANETS.

Hwin   The talking Narnian★ mare who plays an important part in the tale known as *The Horse and His Boy.*★ She helps Aravis★ escape an unpleasant marriage. There are many delightful contrasts between her character and that of Bree,★ the other talking horse involved in this famous Narnian tale.

Hyaline Splendour   In *The Horse and His Boy*,★ the ship of King Edmund★ and Queen Lucy.★

Hyoi   In *Out of the Silent Planet*,★ the hross★ whom Dr Elwin Ransom★ first encounters on Malacandra. Much to Ransom's distress, Hyoi is later shot by one of the earth men.

See also TALKING ANIMALS; PLANETS.

I

Idealism, C.S. Lewis and In the early years of this century, and in England (particularly in Oxford★), idealism predominated in philosophy. Idealism was linked in many minds with Christianity, or with spiritual views which opposed naturalism★ and a rapidly spreading secularisation. Idealism in England was especially associated with T.H. Green (1836–82), F.H. Bradley (1846–1924), and J.M.E. McTaggart (1866–1925).

There is both a broad and narrow sense of idealism. The broad sense is the view that the basis of the universe is ultimately spiritual. The narrow (and more useful) sense covers theories in which it is held that physical objects can have no existence apart from a mind which is conscious of them. For idealists in this sense who believe in God, the divine mind and the human mind have fundamental similarities.

As a young atheist in Oxford, C.S. Lewis was at first staunchly opposed to idealism. He was an out and out realist. He believed, for instance, that the similarity of human languages was due to the similarity of human throats.

His brilliant friend Owen Barfield,★ with whom he had a formative 'Great War', persuaded Lewis eventually to accept some tenets of idealism. C.S. Lewis did not stay long here, however, but moved from idealism to theism, and eventually to Christian belief.

After his conversion to Christ, C.S. Lewis' position,

philosophically, was a modified realism. Significantly, he was influenced by the great realist metaphysician, the Australian Samuel Alexander (1859–1938). Lewis rejected the grand impersonality of idealist systems, and even the goal of a total system of thought. He preferred the individuality of places and people, seasons and times, moods and tones of feeling. God★ himself was the most concrete of existences. Christ's incarnation had a joyous logic to it, as did the revelation of God to mankind in the human (yet authoritative) writings of the Bible.★

For all his realism, C.S. Lewis drew imaginative nourishment from idealist systems such as the thought of Plato★ or the medieval model of the universe (*see THE DISCARDED IMAGE*). As a thinker, C.S. Lewis rejected attempts at a natural theology, stressing the importance of presuppositions over where we get to in our knowing. He illustrated this vividly in the case of the miraculous in his book, *Miracles.*★ Having decided never to rule out the possibility of the miraculous in advance, Lewis' thinking was boldly supernaturalist, yet unflinchingly realistic in tone. His realism is so marked that in places he appears sceptical of the validity of theoretical thinking in view of its inevitable abstraction from concrete things, events and persons. C.S. Lewis' combination of realism and supernaturalist vision is his hallmark, a combination that is irresistible to numerous readers.

C.S. Lewis' thinking has been described in terms of sacramental theology,★ for example by Leanne Payne in her study, *The Real Presence.* Such an attempt, however, fails to do justice to the basic realistic tenor of C.S. Lewis' thinking in *Miracles,*★ *The Problem of Pain,*★ *Mere Christianity,*★ and other popular theological writings.

Oxford idealism was dramatically swept away by logical positivism, already weakened by the realism of G.E. Moore (1873–1958) and Bertrand Russell (1872–

1970). On the Continent, idealism was disintegrated by secular and religious existentialism. Theologically, existentialism made a deep impression on the thought of Rudolf Bultmann (1884–1976), whose view on myth* in the Gospels was far from that of C.S. Lewis.

C.S. Lewis himself seemed to search for an alternative to the old idealism that was more than his pre-Christian materialism, and which certainly stood in contrast to the new theology of existentialism or the old liberal theology of rationalism. Many forms of realism are compatible with theism, and he found his own. Some of his more creative ideas are summed up in his seminal sermon on what he called 'transposition'.* His view of reality was fundamentally tied up with a highly original view of meaning* which he gradually articulated, and in which meaning is associated with, and perhaps identified with, reality. Thinking about meaning strengthened his pre-occupation with myth, and with the relationship between myth and fact or reality.

See also NATURALISM AND SUPER-NATURALISM.

Ilgamuth   In *The Horse and His Boy*,* one of the Lords of Rabadash,* slain by Darrin of Archenland.*

Ilkeen   In *The Horse and His Boy*,* the location in Calor-men* of the beautiful palace of Ahoshta Tarkaan.*

Imagination   *See* MEANING AND IMAGINATION.

The Inklings   These were a group of mainly male friends, all people of talent, who met together at least once a week to talk about ideas, to read to each other for pleasure and criticism pieces they were writing, and to enjoy a good evening of 'the cut and parry of prolonged, fierce, masculine argument'. 'The Inklings' embodied C.S. Lewis' ideals of life and pleasure. In fact, he was the life and soul of the party. Their important years were the 1940s, especially the war years when Charles Williams* was resident in Oxford.*

The group was no mutual admiration society or 'inner ring'.★ They mainly felt deeply the truth of the poet Blake's aphorism: 'Opposition is true friendship.' Lewis himself was 'hungry for rational opposition'. His friend Professor John Lawlor thinks that to attack Lewis in this way was probably the first step towards friendship★ with him. J.R.R. Tolkien★ remembered how much Lewis felt at home in this kind of company. 'C.S.L. had a passion for hearing things read aloud, a power of memory for things received in that way, and also a facility in extempore criticism, none of which were shared (especially not the last) in anything like the same degree by his friends.'

Though the two most celebrated members of the group—Tolkien and Lewis—are sometimes considered out of touch with the real world, the fact is that their values have captured an audience of numerous millions. If they are unconnected with real modern life, why have so many of their contemporaries and more recent readers responded to them? The Inklings undoubtedly represent an important part of twentieth-century cultural history, in which literature still has a high place, however unpalatable this fact may be to some of their critics.

Other members of the informal group included Lewis' brother (Major W.H. 'Warnie' Lewis★), Owen Barfield★ (author of a key book in Lewis' thinking, *Poetic Diction*), and Charles Williams. The latter wrote poetry, novels, plays, literary criticism, and off-beat theology. He powerfully influenced Lewis, though Tolkien was not so taken with him.

When Charles Williams died suddenly in May 1945, Lewis was shocked. In appreciation, some of The Inklings and Dorothy L. Sayers★ contributed to the lively, *Essays Presented to Charles Williams*. One of the contributions was Tolkien's famous essay 'On Fairy Stories' (later republished in his *Tree and Leaf*). Another was a dazzling piece about language and metaphor by Owen Barfield. Dorothy Sayers put in a piece about Dante's *The Divine Comedy*, which she later translated. Lewis himself contributed an essay about his personal love of stories as such. One feels, reading this book, the intellectual excitement that doubtless ran throughout the meetings of The Inklings.

C.S. Lewis describes a typical meeting in a letter to an absent member—his brother—in 1939. The 'new Hobbit' is a reference to the first volume of *The Lord of the Rings*. 'On Thursday we had a meeting of the Inklings ... we dined at the Eastgate. I have never in my life seen Dyson so exuberant—"A roaring cataract of nonsense". The bill of fare afterwards consisted of a section of the new Hobbit book from Tolkien, a nativity play from Charles Williams (unusually intelligible for him, and approved by all), and a chapter out of a book on the Problem of Pain from me.'

From Humphrey Carpenter's authoritative study, *The Inklings* (1978), it turns out that The Inklings had a modest and unassuming Boswell, Warnie Lewis, to whose memory, appropriately, he dedicated his book. Warnie Lewis, more than anyone at the time, seemed aware of the uniqueness and identity of The Inklings, valuing the group at least because of his affection for his brother.

Other members not so far mentioned, and chronicled by Humphrey Carpenter, were J.A.W. Bennett, Lord David Cecil, Nevill Coghill,★ Commander Jim Dundas-Grant, Hugo Dyson,★ Adam Fox,★ Colin Hardie, Dr 'Humphrey' Havard,★ Gervase Mathew,★ R.B. McCallum,★ C.E. ('Tom') Stevens,★ Christopher Tolkien, John Wain★ and Charles Wrenn.

One of the favourite haunts of The Inklings was The Eagle and Child public house in St Giles (known more familiarly as The Bird and Baby). It has since been renovated, but a plaque is now placed there in memory, which reads:

C.S. LEWIS

his brother, W.H. Lewis, J.R.R. Tolkien, Charles Williams and other friends met every Tuesday morning, between the years 1939–1962 in the back room of this their favourite pub. These men, popularly known as the 'Inklings', met here to drink Beer and to discuss, among other things, the books they were writing.

W.H. Lewis was sceptical of the idea of The Inklings representing a school of literature or theology. He is probably right to be so in view of the diversity of its members at one time or another. However, Lewis hankered for others who shared his core beliefs, and some of the main Inklings like Williams, Tolkien and even Barfield did, though Barfield never became an orthodox Christian. Even though he was baptised into the Anglican Church he remained committed to anthroposophism.

Speaking in America, Owen Barfield remembered the way Lewis affected all the groups he was part of, including The Inklings. The first way was unconsciously and unobtrusively by the sheer force and weight of his personality, and, as Barfield put it, 'a rather loud voice when he was in high spirits'. He would set the tone and decide the topic of conversation. Barfield recalled that on one occasion, when the topic was not of interest to Lewis (it could have been politics or economics) he merely turned aside from the conversation, picked up a book, and proceeded to read it instead of talking.

The second way Lewis affected a group was that irrespective of the subject that was brought up, he always turned it round to the point where it was a moral issue or problem. If anyone did not think that a moral issue was involved, Lewis reminded him that there *ought* to be.

Thinking specifically of The Inklings, Barfield wondered if something was not happening to 'The Romantic Impulse' during its life. He could discern four important strands, each mainly identified with Lewis, Tolkien, Williams, or himself: (1) the yearning for the infinite and unattainable—Lewis' *sehnsucht* or joy;★ (2) in Barfield's own words, 'The conviction of the dignity of man and his part in the future history of the world conceived as a kind of progress towards increasing immanence of the divine in the human' (Barfield's own position); (3) the idealisation of love between the sexes, as in Charles Williams' thought and writings; and (4) the opposite of tragedy, the happy ending, Tolkien's idea of the *eucatastrophe*.

As literary artists, Lewis, Tolkien and Williams certainly seemed to try to redeem the romantic tradition which had been distorted by the Romantic Movement and its predecessors in the eighteenth century. This early and later romanticism had reacted against the dominant form of humanism which had made a god out of reason. It reacted with irrationalism, and a nurturing of natural instincts and feeling. It sought the origin of mankind in nature,★ and rejected traditional philosophy and hierarchical social structure, both of which thought of, and pictured, mankind's origins as being in God. Tolkien, Lewis and Williams attempted to redeem the romantic tradition by enriching, strengthening, and purifying it with orthodox Christianity and with reason, following in the footsteps of John Bunyan and his *Pilgrim's Progress*, nearly 300 years earlier (*see* THEOLOGY OF ROMANCE; ROMANTICISM).

In their attempt, they rehabilitate an understanding that has almost been lost by modern people. Lewis, Tolkien, and Williams, following Owen Barfield's *Poetic Diction*, saw that there is a rightness or correctness in the imagination itself. Furthermore, without the enrichment of proper imagining, thought is impoverished, and eventually becomes meaningless. Paradoxically, therefore, through fantasy or the play of imagination, thought makes true contact with reality.

C.S. Lewis was fond of giving, as an example of the rightness of imagination, the traditional equations of light with truth and of darkness with error. Fairy tales make use of these stock, archetypal, 'natural', or proper equations. In Bunyan's *Pilgrim's Progress*, doubt is pictured as the strong Doubting Castle, and despair as its owner, Giant Despair. To think of doubt and despair as a castle and a giant is satisfying and 'natural'; in some sense, true and real. The turning of a majority of modern artists and writers to a subjective view of the imagination has helped to create a crisis in meaning.*

The three men attempted, in their fiction and poetry, to provide true or objective images that had a place in the contemporary world. Although a novel, a play, or a poem is not meant primarily to put over Christian or even moral truths, or to be 'about life'—imagination has a different function from theoretical thinking—images embodied in such works of literature can enrich and liberate our thinking by enriching and defining our concepts, and can enhance our experience of the world by enlarging our perception of, and sensitivity to, existence.

Further reading

Humphrey Carpenter, *The Inklings: C.S. Lewis, J.R.R. Tolkien, Charles Williams and their friends* (1978); John Wain, *Sprightly Running: Part of an Autobiography* (1962).

'The Inner Ring' An essay which first appeared in print in *Transposition and Other Addresses.*★ Its theme is illustrated in C.S. Lewis' science fiction story, *That Hideous Strength.*★ Lewis saw the lure of the inner ring as a perversion of friendship,★ which 'causes perhaps half of all the happiness in the world, and no Inner Ringer can ever have it'. Unlike friendship, the desire to be on the inside of a group leads to a perpetual anxiety, even if achieved, whereas real friendship is 'snug and safe' because it is free of this desire. Lewis believed that in most associations of business and profession there were inner rings as well as the official hierarchies. 'You are never formally and explicitly admitted by anyone. You discover gradually, in almost indefinable ways, that it exists and that you are outside it; and then later, perhaps, that you are inside it.' Inner rings provide a climate in which evil becomes easier. Until a person conquers the fear of being an outsider, an outsider they will remain.

In *That Hideous Strength*, the lure of the inner ring of Belbury★ on Mark Studdock★ dramatically illustrates its danger.

Intelligence Department In *The Screwtape Letters*,★ part of the bureaucracy of hell. Although hell dislikes knowledge, which it regards as hateful and mawkish, a certain amount is necessary to have effective power on earth to upset the Enemy's plans. Devils assigned to human patients pass information back to the department. Screwtape★ laments the inability of the department to penetrate the purposes of the Enemy.

Island of the Star *See* RAMANDU'S ISLAND.

Island of Voices In *The Voyage of the 'Dawn Treader'*,★ the low-lying island to the west of Deathwater Island★ in the Eastern Ocean.★ It has lawns and parks that are noticeably well kept. The only important building is a stone house, approached through an avenue of trees belonging to the island's Governor, Coriakin.★

When the voyagers landed on the island they at first thought it uninhabited. This mistake is understandable because the main inhabitants, the Dufflepuds,★ had been made invisible. Their voices, however, could still be heard, hence the origin of the island's name.

Istra   In *Till We Have Faces*,★ Psyche's★ name in her native Glome.★ Psyche is the Greek form of her name, preferred by Psyche herself, Orual,★ and The Fox.★

J

Jadis *See* WHITE WITCH.

Jewel the Unicorn In *The Last Battle*,★ Jewel, a talking
beast, is the dearest friend of Tirian,★ last King of
Narnia.★ They saved each other's lives in war. Jewel's
feelings as he enters the New Narnia, remade by Aslan,★
illustrate C.S. Lewis' constant and special theme of joy.★

Joy C.S. Lewis' autobiography up to his conversion at
the age of thirty-three is recorded in *Surprised by Joy*,★ and
somewhat in his long allegory, *The Pilgrim's Regress*.★
These tell us that his lengthy, varied, and reluctant
pilgrimage to truth was greatly influenced by a certain
distinct tone of feeling which he discovered in early
childhood, and which stayed with him on and off
throughout his adolescence and early manhood.

This longing for beauty or joy he learned from gazing
at the Castlereagh Hills of Belfast from his nursery
windows. Later, reading of northern myths and sagas
intensified this dissatisfaction. Towards the end of his life,
Lewis personified the imaginative longing in a character in
Till We Have Faces.★ This character is based upon the
Psyche★ of an ancient Roman writing. Because myths and
otherworldly tales can often define this longing for
beauty, Lewis defended and wrote this unrespectable type
of literature throughout his distinguished career.

There is a relationship between love and zest for life and
the desire for beauty that constantly fascinated Lewis. The
stories of George MacDonald,★ which shaped Lewis'

imagination, are dominated by a joyful quality of holiness or goodness in life—but it was no platonic★ spirituality. MacDonald's stories (including his novels) concern the homely and ordinary, transformed by a new light. Lewis captured this exactly when he wrote: 'The quality which had enchanted me in his imaginative works turned out to be the quality of the real universe, the divine, magical, terrifying and ecstatic reality in which we all live.'

C.S. Lewis' own imaginative creations, such as *The Chronicles of Narnia*,★ sprang from this love of life. He seems to have been very preoccupied with joy, as he called it, throughout the 1940s and early 1950s. The last chapter of *The Problem of Pain*★ (1940) speaks of it; a sermon, 'The Weight of Glory' (1941), tries to define the desire; *The Voyage of the 'Dawn Treader'*★ (1952) is about the Narnian mouse Reepicheep's quest for Aslan's Country★ at the World's End; *Surprised by Joy* (1955) traces the twin threads of Lewis' thinking and his longing for beauty up to his conversion; and in *Till We Have Faces* (1956) the Princess Psyche has a love of this beauty that is stronger than death. In *Transposition and Other Addresses*★ (1949) Lewis wrote: 'We do not want merely to see beauty. . . . We want something else which can hardly be put into words—to be united with the beauty we see, to pass into it, to receive it into ourselves, to bathe in it, to become part of it. That is why we have peopled air and earth and water with gods and goddesses and nymphs and elves.'

Such joy, thought Lewis, inspired the writer to create fantasy. The creation of another world is an attempt to reconcile human beings and the world, to embody the fulfilment of our imaginative longing. Imaginative worlds, wonderlands, are 'regions of the spirit'. Such worlds of the numinous may be found in some science fiction, some poetry, some fairy stories, some novels, some myths, even in a phrase or sentence. Lewis claimed in *Of Other*

Worlds: 'To construct plausible and moving "other worlds" you must draw on the only real "other world" we know, that of the spirit.'

In a doctorial thesis, *Romantic Religion in the Works of Owen Barfield, C.S. Lewis, Charles Williams, and J.R.R. Tolkien,* Robert J. Reilly sees Lewis as an advocate of 'romantic religion', or 'the attempt to reach religious truths by means and techniques traditionally called romantic, and . . . to defend and justify these techniques and attitudes of romanticism by holding that they have religious sanction.'

Another PhD dissertation specifically concerns the theme of joy in C.S. Lewis' work, Corbin Carnell's *The Dialectic of Desire*. He argues that Lewis illuminates a state of mind which has been a recurrent theme in literature. This is the compulsive quest 'which brings with it both fleeting joy and the sad realization that one is yet separated from what is desired'. Joy, for C.S. Lewis, is the key both to the nature of human beings and to their Creator.

C.S. Lewis saw this unquenchable longing as a sure sign that no part of the created world, and thus no aspect of human experience, is capable of fulfilling fallen mankind. We are dominated by a homelessness, and yet by a keen sense of what home means.

In *Surprised by Joy*, Lewis reported his sensations of joy, some of which were responses to natural beauty and others of which were literary or artistic responses, in the belief that other people would recognise similar experiences of their own. Even some who cannot through Lewis' autobiographical account, however, respond to this experience when reading his fiction. He claimed that distant hills, seen from his nursery window, taught him longing, and made him for good or ill a votary of the 'Blue Flower' before he was six years old. The Blue Flower is the symbol of *sehnsucht*, or inconsolable longing, in

German literature and Scandinavian ballads, dating back
to the Middle Ages.

For C.S. Lewis, joy was a foretaste of ultimate reality,
heaven* itself, or, the same thing, our world as it was
meant to be, unspoilt by the fall of mankind, and one day
to be remade. 'Joy,' wrote C.S. Lewis, 'is the serious
business of Heaven.'

In attempting to imagine heaven, Lewis discovered that
joy is 'the secret signature of each soul'. He speculated that
the desire for heaven is part of our essential (and unful-
filled) humanity:

> There are times when I think we do not desire heaven;
> but more often I find myself wondering whether, in our
> heart of hearts, we have ever desired anything else. . . .
> Are not all lifelong friendships born at the moment
> when at last you meet another human being who has
> some inkling (but faint and uncertain even in the best) of
> that something which you were born desiring, and
> which, beneath the flux of other desires and in all the
> momentary silences between the louder passions, night
> and day, year by year, from childhood to old age, you
> are looking for, watching for, listening for? You have
> never *had* it. All the things that have ever deeply
> possessed your soul have been but hints of it—tantaliz-
> ing glimpses, promises never quite fulfilled, echoes that
> died away just as they caught your ear. But if it should
> really become manifest—if there ever came an echo that
> did not die away but swelled into the sound itself—you
> would know it. Beyond all possibility of doubt you
> would say 'Here at last is the thing I was made for.' We
> cannot tell each other about it. It is the secret signature
> of each soul, the incommunicable and unappeasable
> want, the thing we desired before we met our wives or
> made our friends or chose our work, and which we

shall still desire on our deathbeds, when the mind no longer knows wife or friend or work. While we are, this is. If we lose this, we lose all. (*The Problem of Pain,* Chapter 10).

C.S. Lewis' portrayal of joy can be seen as providing valuable data of a key human experience, data which has philosophical and religious importance. It was also central to his apologetics for the Christian faith.

See also HEAVEN.

K

Ketterley, Andrew *See* ANDREW, UNCLE.

Ketterley, Letty In *The Magician's Nephew,*★ the aunt of Digory Kirke★ who is caring for his dying mother, and sister of Uncle Andrew.★ She is unimpressed by Jadis★ the Witch, who hurls her across the room.

Kidrash In *The Horse and His Boy,*★ the father of Aravis★ who tries to marry her off to the ugly and aged new Grand Vizier, Ahoshta.★ It is claimed in Calormen★ that he is a descendant of the god Tash.★

Kirke, Digory Digory appears as a boy in *The Magician's Nephew,*★ then as a grown-up in *The Lion, the Witch and the Wardrobe*★ and *The Last Battle.*★ As a boy, he and his dying mother lodge with his Uncle Andrew★ in Edwardian London. With his neighbour, Polly Plummer,★ he travels to other worlds by means of magical rings, and is present at the creation of Narnia★ by Aslan,★ the talking lion. By the beginning of World War II he is an elderly Professor who owns a country house of historical interest. The Pevensie★ children arrive as evacuees, and stumble across a way into Narnia through his wardrobe built of wood that grew from a magical Narnian apple. Later, he becomes poor and is forced to sell the house and tutor students, including Peter Pevensie. Digory's surname might be an affectionate tribute to Lewis' own tutor, W.T. Kirkpatrick. C.S. Lewis uses the name 'Kirk' again in *The Pilgrim's Regress*★ for Mother Kirk, representing the church.

L

Lantern Waste   In *The Magician's Nephew*,★ the children enter an empty world and see Narnia★ created by Aslan. An Edwardian London lamppost grows here from a piece of lamppost brought by the White Witch.★ In later years children again enter Narnia near here through a wardrobe, in the story, *The Lion, the Witch and the Wardrobe*.★ Lantern Waste is west of Beaversdam.

See also NARNIA: Geography; NARNIA: History.

Lasaraleen   In *The Horse and His Boy*,★ an old friend of Aravis,★ who helps her to escape from the great Calormene★ city of Tashbaan.

***The Last Battle* (1956)**   Based upon biblical prophecies of the end of the world, this story tells the end of *one* world, the world of which Narnia★ is a part, how all worlds are linked, and how the great talking lion Aslan★ is the key to this link. Thus *The Chronicles of Narnia*★ draw to their conclusion, and the consistency of their otherworldliness is established. It won the high-ranking Carnegie Medal for the best children's book of its year. As in all the stories, children from our world are in Narnia to help or to rule. In this case, Eustace Scrubb★ and Jill Pole★ come. One of the strangest features of the story, a twist reminiscent of Charles Williams, ★ is that all the principal characters from our world are already dead as a result of a train accident. There are some similarities with Lewis' *The Great Divorce*,★ in that events after death are imagined, and a vision of heaven★ is presented.

The Last Battle tells of the passing of Narnia and the beginning of the new Narnia. It recounts the attempt of Shift★ the Talking Ape to delude the creatures of Narnia that Aslan★ has returned. Shift drapes Puzzle, a simple donkey, in a lion skin found floating in the river. He then persuades the talking animals that Puzzle is Aslan returned, and that he, Shift, is his spokesperson. Worse, he forms an alliance with Narnia's traditional enemy, Calormen.★

Young King Tirian,★ the last of the Narnian rulers, and seventh in descent from Rilian,★ hears of evil things happening—talking trees cut down, Narnian animals enslaved—and cannot believe that Aslan has returned and that this is his will. With his loyal unicorn, Jewel,★ he resists the Calormenes and is captured. Like several before him in previous ages, he calls for help from our world. Eustace and Jill are sent in answer to his prayer. The true Aslan also returns.

In our world, Professor Digory Kirke★ and Polly Plummer,★ the very first visitors to Narnia (as recounted in *The Magician's Nephew★*), had called together all those who had been in Narnia. There is a train crash which kills all those who answer the call, both those in an arriving train and those awaiting it at the station. All go into Narnia, though only Eustace and Jill are active participants in the final battle against evil, helping Tirian, Jewel and the loyal Narnians.

The visitors see Aslan's judgement of all the inhabitants of Narnia and its other countries, and then are called 'further up and further in' to a new Narnia. They discover that it is now permanently linked to their own, familiar world of England, also transfigured. They would never again have to part from Aslan, though now they see him in a new form.

'Learning in War-time'   An important essay that first

appeared in book form in the collection, *Transposition and Other Addresses.*★ C.S. Lewis argued that nothing—not even war—can rightfully occupy the whole of our lives, except God himself. A person is not defined by any of his or her temporal functions. War might require dying for, but it should never be lived for. Since the fall of mankind, war is a permanent human state. All aspects of our lives are to be given to God, including our scholarship. This gives all parts of our life their proper place and allows them to be good in an ultimate sense.

Lefay, Mrs In *The Magician's Nephew,*★ the faerie godmother of Uncle Andrew.★ She passed on to him a box of dust from Atlantis★ to destroy, but which he kept. She is perhaps named after Morgan Le Fay of Arthurian legend.

Letters of C.S. Lewis C.S. Lewis' letters are eventually expected to be published as the *Collected Letters* in as many as six volumes. Many of his letters, however, have already been published. *Letters of C.S. Lewis* (1966), edited, with a memoir, by his brother, W.H. Lewis,★ grew out of an unpublished biography. *Letters to An American Lady* (1967), edited by Clyde S. Kilby, is a collection of letters to a lady Lewis never met, Mary Willis Shelburne. The largest collection so far, *They Stand Together: The Letters of C.S. Lewis to Arthur Greeves (1914–1963),*★ edited by Walter Hooper, is made up of letters to one of Lewis' closest Ulster friends, Arthur Greeves. *Letters to Children* (1985), edited by Lyle W. Dorsett and Marjorie Lamp Mead, contains a foreword by Douglas Gresham, one of the sons of Joy Davidman★ Lewis. In 1989, *Letters: C.S. Lewis and Don Giovanni Calabria*, was published, edited and translated by Martin Moynihan.

A revised and enlarged edition of the *Letters* edited by W.H. Lewis was brought out in 1988, edited by Walter Hooper, and containing some changes to Warnie Lewis' sometimes rather free editing. This is therefore not strictly a replacement for the 1966 volume, which is worth obtaining if possible.

Letters to Malcolm: Chiefly on Prayer (1964)   Malcolm is an imaginary friend of C.S. Lewis' to whom he writes twenty-two letters on the theme of prayer, and much else, including heaven★ and the resurrection of the body. In the book, Lewis writes as having known Malcolm from undergraduate days.

Some have felt that Lewis' theological writings lack an experiential depth (or a shyness of spiritual experience). This last book concerns one of the most experiential subjects of the Christian life, and Lewis handles it with great power. From the moment of his conversion to theism, Lewis was a thorough-going supernaturalist, and thus the question of petitionary prayer made in time to a God outside of space-time was a central one to him. He saw it as God's prerogative to change actual events in the light of the prayers of his people.

The letter format allowed C.S. Lewis to explore and speculate on prayer in a manner impossible in a more didactic book. Prayer, for Lewis, was necessary for our understanding of our relation to our Father Creator.

Now the moment of prayer is for me—or involves for me as its condition—the awareness, the reawakened awareness, that this 'real world' and 'real self' are very far from being rock-bottom realities. I cannot, in the flesh, leave the stage, either to go behind the scenes or to take my seat in the pit; but I can remember that my apparent self—this clown or hero or super—under his grease-paint is a real person with an off-stage life. The dramatic person could not tread the stage unless he concealed a real person: unless the real and unknown I existed, I would not even make mistakes about the imagined me. And in prayer this real I struggles to

105

speak, for once, from his real being, and to address, for once, not the other actors, but—what shall I call Him? The Author, for He invented us all? The Producer, for He controls all? Or the Audience, for He watches, and will judge, the performance?

Lewis, Albert (1863–1929)   The father of C.S. Lewis and a Belfast Corporation County solicitor, from 1889 to 1928. When his wife, Flora Lewis,★ died of cancer, Albert Lewis was unable to cope with his grief, and sent the nine-year-old C.S. Lewis off to England to boarding school at 'Belsen'.★ Relations between Mr Lewis and his two sons were often strained.

Lewis, C.S.   Known to his friends as 'Jack' (he did not like 'Clive Staples'), C.S. Lewis was born in the outskirts of Belfast on 29th November 1898, and died in his Oxford home, The Kilns, almost sixty-five years later on 22nd November 1963. He was equally a scholar and a story-teller. The story of his early life, his conversion from atheism to Christianity, and his awareness of joy★ and longing for a fulfilment outside of his own self, is told in his autobiography, *Surprised by Joy,*★ and his allegory, *The Pilgrim's Regress.*★

His published letters, especially *Letters of C.S. Lewis,*★ *They Stand Together,*★ and *Brothers and Friends: The Diaries of Major Warren Hamilton Lewis,*★ give vivid insights into his life. Jack Lewis was devoted to his brother W.H. 'Warnie' Lewis. The two brothers were brought together by their common interest in creating imaginary worlds as boys, particularly Boxen,★ and also by the death of their mother of cancer. Mrs Flora Lewis died when Jack was nine. Their father never got over the loss and relations between father and sons became more and more strained as time went on. Mr Albert Lewis★ had no talent for happiness, and withdrew into the safe monotony of routine. The richest heritage he gave to Jack Lewis was, literally, a houseful of old books which the gifted boy explored unimpeded.

In the year of his mother's ghastly death, Jack was sent off to Hertfordshire to join his brother at a school dubbed 'Belsen'.★ This title seems no great exaggeration. The brutal headmaster was several years later certified insane. In 1910 Jack was moved first to Campbell College, Belfast, the next year to 'Chartres' (Cherbourg House) in Malvern, and later to Malvern College ('Wyvern'), Worcestershire. He was never happy, however, until he was finally sent to a private tutor in Bookham called W.T. Kirkpatrick. His brother Warnie wrote, in his introduction to *Letters of C.S. Lewis:* 'The fact is he should never have been sent to a public school at all. Already, at 14, his intelligence was such that he would have fitted in better among undergraduates than schoolboys; and by his temperament he was bound to be a misfit, a heretic, an object of suspicion within the collective-minded and standardising public school system.' Characteristically, Jack wrote his first article for a school magazine, entitled, 'Are Athletes Better Than Scholars?'

His private tutorage under the Irishman W.T. Kirkpatrick was one of the happiest periods of his life. Not only did he rapidly mature and grow under the stringent rationality of this teacher, but he discovered the beauty of the English countryside and fantasy writers such as William Morris. Full of the discovery of George MacDonald's★ *Phantastes*, Jack wrote about its power to Arthur Greeves,★ his lifelong Ulster friend, in 1915: 'Of course it is hopeless for me to try to describe it, but when you have followed the hero Anodos along the little stream of the faery wood, have heard about the terrible ash tree . . . and heard the episode of Cosmo, I know you will agree with me.' In *Surprised by Joy,* Jack describes the effect as baptising his imagination.

The Great War had broken out, and its shadow loomed over Jack's peace. Warnie was already on active duty. Jack was not old enough to enlist until 1917. He spent his nineteenth birthday on the front line. In spring 1918, Jack was wounded in action and was eventually discharged after a spell in hospital. During all this time he had been writing poetry and preparing a book of poems, *Spirits in Bondage*,* for publication. At the front he lost a billet-mate called 'Paddy' Moore. Before his death, Jack had promised him that should anything happen to him, he would take care of Paddy's widowed mother and sister. Jack in fact looked after Mrs Janie Moore* until her death in 1951. Her troublesome personality and opposition to his later Christian beliefs was a thorn in the flesh both to him and later Warnie, who joined The Kilns household in 1931.

By 1923 Jack had confirmed his brilliance by gaining a Triple First at Oxford* University. He won a temporary lectureship in philosophy at University College. Then Magdalen College appointed him as a Fellow, lecturing and tutoring in English. He was an Oxford Don until 1954, when Cambridge University invited him to the new Chair of Medieval and Renaissance Literature, where he described himself as an 'Old Western Man' in his in-augural lecture. C.S. Lewis' pupils included such figures as the critic Kenneth Tynan,* George Sayer,* the poet John Betjeman, Harry Blamires, and novelist and poet John Wain.*

In the early Oxford days, Professor J.R.R. Tolkien* became one of Jack's lifelong friends. They would criticise one another's poetry, drift into theology and philosophy, pun or talk university politics. Tolkien helped to force Jack to reconsider the claims of Christianity. He was first 'cornered' by theism* and then biblical Christianity. The movement of Jack's thinking at this time is vividly captured in his book *Miracles*.★ He later confessed: 'I never had the experience of looking for God. It was the other way round: He was the hunter (or so it seemed to me) and I was the deer. He stalked me like a redskin, took unerring aim, and fired. And I am very thankful that that is how the first (conscious) meeting occurred. It forearms one against subsequent fears that the whole thing was only wish fulfilment. Something one didn't wish for can hardly be that.'

In 1952 Jack met an American lady, Helen Joy Davidman,★ with whom he had corresponded for some time. She was a poet and novelist who had been converted from atheism and Marxism to Christianity, partly through reading Jack's books. When she was free to remarry, and was dying of cancer, Jack married her. She came home to The Kilns to die in spring 1957, but had a miraculous stay of execution. In fact she lived until 1960, and was able to have a final holiday in Greece with Jack. The happiness that had come to him so late in life, and subsequent bitter bereavement, is recorded in his *A Grief Observed*.★

Jack never got over the loss, and this was combined with constant worry about his gentle brother's alcoholism. The last book he saw to press, *Letters to Malcolm: Chiefly on Prayer*,★ affirmed his hope in heaven.★

As well as *The Chronicles of Narnia*★ for children, Jack wrote a classic science fiction trilogy, a novel (*Till We Have Faces*★), other fiction, literary criticism, cultural criticism, ethics, theology and poetry. He was the centre of an informal circle of Christian writers in Oxford, The Inklings,★ which included J.R.R. Tolkien, Charles Williams,★ and was influenced by George MacDonald.

See also LITERARY CRITIC, C.S. LEWIS AS A; THEOLOGY, LEWIS AND.

Further reading

C.S. Lewis, *The Pilgrim's Regress* (1933, 1943); *Surprised by Joy: The Shape of My Early Life* (1955); *Letters of C.S. Lewis* (1966); *They Stand Together: The Letters of C.S. Lewis to Arthur Greeves* (ed Walter Hooper, 1979); W.H. Lewis, *Brothers and Friends: The Diaries of Major Warren Hamilton Lewis* (ed Clyde S. Kilby and Marjorie L. Meade, 1982); Humphrey Carpenter, *The Inklings: C.S. Lewis, J.R.R. Tolkien, Charles Williams and their friends* (1978); Roger Lancelyn Green and Walter Hooper, *C.S. Lewis: A Biography* (1974); Lyle W. Dorsett, *And God Came In: The extraordinary story of Joy Davidman—her life and marriage to C.S. Lewis* (1983); Brian Sibley, *Shadowlands: The Story of C.S. Lewis and Joy Davidman* (1985); William Griffin, *C.S. Lewis: The authentic voice* (1988); George Sayer, *Jack: C.S. Lewis and his times* (1988); Douglas Gresham, *Lenten Lands: My childhood with Joy Davidman and C.S. Lewis* (1989).

Lewis, Flora Hamilton (1862–1908)　C.S. Lewis' mother was the daughter of the church rector at St Mark's, Dundela, Belfast, the Lewis family church. Today, a stained-glass window in memory of C.S. Lewis' parents can be seen in the church, put there by the Lewis brothers. Flora gained a first class honours degree in logic and a second class honours in mathematics, at Queen's University, Belfast. Lewis recalled that neither of his parents 'had the least taste for that kind of literature to which my allegiance was given the moment I could choose books for myself. Neither had ever listened for the horns of elfland. There was no copy of Keats or Shelley in the house, and the copy of Coleridge was never (to my knowledge) opened. If I am a romantic,' he concludes, 'my parents bear no responsibility for it.'

The grim, uncushionable blow of his mother's death

from cancer took away all that was stable in the nine-year-old C.S. Lewis' life. His father, unable to cope with his grief, immediately sent him off to a boarding school which Lewis dubbed, feelingly, 'Belsen', in *Surprised by Joy*.★ A dying mother appears in the Narnia★ tale, *The Magician's Nephew*,★ but her story has a happy ending.

Lewis, Helen Joy Davidman   *See* DAVIDMAN, JOY.

Lewis, Warren Hamilton 'Warnie' (1895–1973)   *See BROTHERS AND FRIENDS; LEWIS, C.S.*

Lilygloves   In *Prince Caspian*,★ a chief mole, a talking animal,★ who helped to plant an orchard at Cair Paravel.★ At the time of the events recorded in this book, the orchard has run wild for centuries.

Lindsay, David (1878–1945)   His *A Voyage to Arcturus* (1920) is today recognised as one of the masterpieces of science fiction, though its first edition sold under 600 copies, making it difficult for Lindsay to sell subsequent work. C.S. Lewis, hearing of it, found great difficulty in obtaining a copy. When he did, it greatly influenced his own science fiction trilogy, particularly *Out of the Silent Planet*,★ and his unfinished, *The Dark Tower*.

Writing in 1944 of *Out of the Silent Planet*, Lewis responded to an enquiry about influences on his work: 'The real father of my planet book is David Lindsay's *Voyage to Arcturus*, which you also will revel in if you don't yet know it. I had grown up on [H.G.] Well's stories of that kind: It was Lindsay who first gave me the idea that the "scientifiction" appeal could be combined with the "supernatural" appeal. ... His own spiritual outlook is detestable, almost diabolist I think, and his style is crude: but he showed me what a bang you could get from mixing these two elements.'

Lindsay's 'Tormance', in far-off Arcturus, perhaps gets its name from a contraction of 'torment' and 'romance'.

In an essay 'On Stories', which appeared in *Essays*

Presented to Charles Williams,★ Lewis wrote that David Lindsay's 'Tormance is a region of the spirit. He is the first writer to discover what "other planets" are really good for in fiction. No merely physical strangeness or merely spacial distance will realize that idea of otherness which is what we are always trying to grasp in a story about voyaging through space: you must go into another dimension. To construct plausible and moving "other worlds" you must draw on the only real "other world" we know, that of the spirit.'

David Lindsay's other tales of fantasy were *The Haunted Woman* (1922), *Sphinx* (1923) and *Devil's Tor* (1932). He also wrote a historical novel, *The Adventures of M. de Mailly* (1926). In 1970 a memorial volume appeared, *The Strange Genius of David Lindsay* (1970), including articles by Colin Wilson and E.H. Visiak (who finds parallels between *A Voyage to Arcturus* and Milton's *Paradise Lost*).

The Lion, the Witch and the Wardrobe (1950)   This is the first tale of Narnia★ that C.S. Lewis wrote. Its inspiration owed something to evacuee children who lodged in Lewis' Oxford★ home, The Kilns, and began with a picture that he saw in his head of 'a faun carrying an umbrella and parcels in a snowy wood'. Four children, Peter, Edmund, Susan and Lucy Pevensie,★ are evacuated from wartime London to stay with Professor Digory Kirke★ (who, as a boy, had visited Narnia, as recounted in *The Magician's Nephew*★).

In one room of his vast house is a bulky wardrobe, made out of a tree which grew from a Narnian seed. Through this wardrobe the children enter a snowy wood in Narnia's Lantern Waste.★ Three of them join forces with the talking animals★ who are loyal to Aslan,★ the great talking lion, creator of Narnia. Edmund, however, turns traitor and goes over to the White Witch,★ who has Narnia in her spell, so that it is always winter and never

Christmas. Aslan pays the terrible cost of Edmund's treachery by sacrificing his own life to break the witch's magic. Narnia is freed, Aslan returns to life, the witch is destroyed, and the creatures that she had turned to stone are unpetrified by the lion.

See also NARNIA: History.

Literary critic, C.S. Lewis as a C.S. Lewis was an outstanding literary critic, being invited to the newly created Chair of Medieval and Renaissance Literature at Cambridge University in 1954 as a result of his study of these periods. Prior to that he was for almost thirty years Fellow and Tutor in English at Magdalen College, Oxford. His main works of literary criticism are *The Allegory of Love: A Study in Medieval Tradition*★ (1936), *Rehabilitations and Other Essays*★ (1939), (with E.M.W. Tillyard) *The Personal Heresy: A Controversy*★ (1939), *A Preface to 'Paradise Lost'*★ (1942), (with Charles Williams) *Arthurian Torso*★ (1948), *English Literature in the Sixteenth Century (Excluding Drama)*★ (1954), *Reflections on the Psalms*★ (1958), *Studies in Words*★ (1960), *An Experiment in Criticism*★ (1961), *The Discarded Image: An Introduction to Medieval and Renaissance Literature*★ (1964), *Studies in Medieval and Renaissance Literature* (1966), (edited by Alistair Fowler) *Spenser's Images of Life*★ (1967) and *Selected Literary Essays* (1969).

Literature is more than mere written language. R. Wellek and A. Warren's definition in *Theory of Literature* is useful: 'The term "literature" seems best if we limit it to the art of literature, that is, to imaginative literature. . . . We recognize "fictionality," "invention," or "imagination" as the distinguishing trait of literature.'

What is C.S. Lewis' place in twentieth-century literary criticism? Generally, recent literary theories have had one of three dominant emphases: they have been author-centred, text-centred, or reader-centred. It is worth

113

making a simple thumbnail sketch of these positions to see C.S. Lewis' contribution to criticism and continuing value as a critic more clearly.

Traditionally, criticism has been concerned with what is extrinsic to the literary text, its origin, authorship, original setting, and the like. It has needed to know about the activities and thinking of the author. This has been described by recent critics as the 'intentional fallacy', and part of it by C.S. Lewis as 'the personal heresy'. Traditional criticism interpreted the meaning of a piece of literature by concentrating on the author and his or her social and cultural world. Questions of origin and authority are central, standing in the stream of Western metaphysics.

In the 1940s and 1950s the so-called 'New Criticism' shifted from an extrinsic to an intrinsic regard for the text. It moved away from authorial intent to an emphasis on the autonomy of the literary work. The New Criticism was rooted in the thought of T.S. Eliot, I.A. Richards, and William Empson. As a trend, it included several American scholars and F.R. Leavis in Britain.

The trend takes its name from John Crowe Ransom's *The New Criticism* (1942). It sees the text as self-sufficient, with the author's intention and background unimportant. The literary text is typically perceived as an artifact or 'verbal icon'. A parallel in the modern novel is John Fowles' (and others') rejection of an all-knowing narrator. The New Criticism requires a close reading of the text, and has been deeply influential in English Studies.

Another text-centred movement is structuralism. Structuralism is actually rooted in linguistics, but has affected many disciplines, as described by Jean Piaget in his book, *Structuralism* (1971). It is a general theory about human culture. It sees all aspects of culture characterised by signs, the meaning of which lie in their interrelatedness. Metaphor is key to all human thought from the time of the cave man to our present Information Age, being based upon our human ability to recognise similarity in difference. Literature is particularly important to structuralism because its 'material' is language itself. Instead of appreciating the originality and genius of an author, the concern of structuralist criticism is with the writer's actual transformations of deep structures or pre-existing meanings.

In contrast, reader-centred theories emphasise the reader's role in creating the meaning of the literary text. Softer views within this camp are interested in the objective interaction between the reader and the text, rather on the analogy of an orchestra performing a musical score. Just as the music lives as it is performed, the text is realised as it is read. There are therefore good and bad readers, ideal readers, competent readers. Feminist or Marxist criticism (or other ideologies) can fall into a reader-centred approach, as can psycho-analytical criticism. This approach has drawn attention to the 'pre-understanding' or world-view of the reader in coming to the text.

An important recent movement in literary criticism is Deconstruction. This is part of a wider trend seeking the dismantling of all Western metaphysics, including Christian theism. As in the thought of Don Cupitt, 'God' is a symbol of human aspirations and has no objective reference—there is no thing or person called God which exists. Deconstruction questions the basis of author-, text- and reader-centred approaches. It rejects any univocal, unambiguous view of meaning.* Jacques Derrida is a central force behind Deconstruction at present. He links the 'myth' of authorial presence in a text with authority. Concepts of authority need to be abandoned. Literary meaning is an 'endless labyrinth'. He exalts writing over speech, seeing earlier literary critics as speech centred and thus 'logocentred'.

Deconstruction is part of what is being called 'post-structuralism'. Such an abandonment of Western metaphysics, particularly theism, can be found in the movement, expressed for example by Roland Barthes in his essay, 'The Death of the Author': 'Literature (it would be better from now on to say *writing*), by refusing to assign a "secret", an ultimate meaning, to the text (and to the world as text), liberates what may be called an anti-theological activity, an activity that is truly revolutionary since to refuse to fix meaning is, in the end, to refuse God and his hypostases—reason, science, law.' Not only is God dead, as prophesied by the philosopher Nietzsche, but also the author and the critic.

In the kind of movements sketched above, literary criticism has become an important part of the shaping of contemporary culture. Can C.S. Lewis' own work in this area still contribute to this momentous debate?

Though Lewis died over a quarter of a century ago, his literary criticism has much to contribute today. He still offers a sturdy defence of a literary criticism based upon theism, and what he would call 'Old Western values'. He would see much contemporary criticism as helping the cause of those working for the abolition of mankind, in dismantling transcendent, objective values. More re-markable, he also avoids, in my view, the extremes of reader-, author- or text-centredness, while appreciating the importance of all these three dimensions of literary meaning.

The critic David Lodge sums up Lewis' position as a historical approach to literature. For him, C.S. Lewis' literary criticism 'shows a remarkable range of interest and expertise, but Lewis was probably best known and admired for his work on medieval literature, especially his masterly book on the literature of Courtly Love, *The Allegory of Love: a study in medieval tradition. . . .* C.S. Lewis in many ways represented the "Oxford" tradition of literary criticism at its best: relaxed, knowledgeable, enthusiastic, conservative. Certainly he stood for principles and practice antithetical to those of the *Scrutiny* group at Cambridge. . . . It is clear that he regarded the study of literature as primarily a historical one, and its justification as the conservation of the past. *De Descriptione Temporum* expresses eloquently, learnedly and wittily this conception of the subject and Lewis' doubts about its viability in the future.'

De Descriptione Temporum★ was C.S. Lewis' inaugural lecture at Cambridge. However, Lewis is not simply a literary historian. His historical work had a double purpose: to shed light on the *textual* meaning (eg its iconography) rather than the author's personality, society, or other extrinsic features, and to value a historically distant text as a remarkable window into a previous cultural world. That world was the fruit of corporate human imagination and power, containing values that we need to take into account. We need perspectives on the narrow limitations of our own world model of today.

As regards the reader, in his seminal *An Experiment in Criticism*★ he attacks the evaluative criticism of F.R. Leavis and others. He rejects their 'good' and 'bad' literature in favour of 'good' and 'bad' readers. Good readers attend to and receive the text rather than using it for some end. Literary texts are intended to have readers. Some texts may be too poor to merit the attention of readers. But where a good reader finds nourishment in a text, one can be sure that meaning is captured there: presence, transcendence, authority, power, insight, and understanding.

Much of C.S. Lewis' critical work was on Spenser, Chaucer, the Arthurian tales, Milton, and Dante, as well as on myth,★ allegory,★ world models, meaning,★ story, metaphor, linguistics and fairy stories. He also wrote key essays on John Bunyan, Jane Austin, Shelley, and William Morris, many of them collected in *Selected Literary Essays*. It is noteworthy that his literary criticism was a living inspiration, resulting in, rather than hindering, fictional writing such as his science fiction trilogy, *The Chronicles of Narnia*,★ and *Till We Have Faces*.★ The marriage was fruitful, and that means something. He was himself an author, a critic, and a good reader.

See also THEOLOGY, C.S. LEWIS AND.

Further reading

Tremper, Longman, *Literary Approaches to Biblical Interpretation* (1987); Peter Barry, (ed) *Issues in Contemporary Critical Theory* (1987); David Lodge, (ed) *20th Century Literary Criticism: A reader* (1972).

Lone Islands   A group of islands comprising Felimath,★ Doorn★ and Avra,★ and visited by the travellers in *The Voyage of the 'Dawn Treader'*.★ Ancient King Gale of Narnia★ had once rid these islands of a dragon and, in gratitude, was given them to be part of Narnia. They lie 400 leagues to the east of that land in the Eastern Ocean.
  See also NARNIA: Geography; NARNIA: History.

Love   *See THE FOUR LOVES.*

Lucy, Queen   *See* PEVENSIE, PETER, SUSAN, EDMUND AND LUCY.

Lune, King   The jolly father of Cor (or Shasta★) and Corin,★ and King of Archenland★ during the Golden Age of Narnia★. He ruled from the strategic castle at Anvard.★ Lune features in the famous Narnian tale, *The Horse and His Boy*.★

M

McCallum, Ronald B. (1898–1973) A member of The Inklings★ and Fellow of Pembroke College, Oxford,★ until 1955, when he was elected Master of Pembroke.

MacDonald, George The Scottish writer George Mac-Donald (1824–1905) was born in Huntly in rural Aberdeenshire, the son of a weaver. C.S. Lewis regarded his own debt to him as inestimable. Like C.S. Lewis, he lost his mother in boyhood, a fact that touched his thought and writings. His views on the imagination anticipated those of Lewis and J.R.R. Tolkien,★ and inspired G.K. Chesterton. He was a close friend of Charles Dodgson (Lewis Carroll) and John Ruskin, the art critic. His insights into the unconscious mind predated the rise of modern psychology. Like Lewis and Tolkien, he was a scholar as well as a story-teller. George MacDonald made a brief and memorable appearance in C.S. Lewis' *The Great Divorce,★* for Lewis regarded him as his 'master'.

MacDonald's sense that all imaginative meaning originates with the Christian Creator became the foundation of C.S. Lewis' thinking and imagining. Two key essays, 'The Imagination: its functions and its culture' (1867) and 'The Fantastic Imagination' (1882), remarkably foreshadow Tolkien's famous essay 'On Fairy Stories' (1947). Tolkien's views on imagination persuaded C.S. Lewis of the truth of Christianity on a windy night in 1931. Many years before, Lewis had stumbled across a copy of

MacDonald's *Phantastes* (1858), resulting in what he described as a baptism of his imagination.

George MacDonald wrote nearly thirty novels, several books of sermons, a number of abiding fantasies for adults and children, short stories, and poetry. His childhood is beautifully captured in his semi-autobiographical *Ranald Bannerman's Boyhood* (1871). He never lost sight of his humble childhood and adolescence, living in a cottage so small that he slept in the attic. He was a happy boy, riding, climbing, swimming and fishing, and reading while lying on the back of his beloved horse. We catch many glimpses of the countryside he knew and loved in his writings.

George MacDonald entered Aberdeen University in 1840, and had a scientific training. For a few years he worked as a tutor in London. Then he entered Highbury Theological College and married. He was called to a church in Arundel, where he fell into disfavour with the deacons, who reduced his small salary to persuade him to leave. Some of the poorer members, however, rallied around with offerings they could ill afford. Then he moved to Manchester for some years, preaching to a small congregation and giving lectures. The rapidly growing family was always on the brink of poverty. Fortunately, the poet Byron's widow, recognising MacDonald's literary gifts, started to provide financial help. The family moved down to London, living in a house then called The Retreat, near the Thames at Hammersmith, later owned by William Morris.

Many famous writers and artists came to visit the MacDonalds, as well as people who shared a concern for London's desperate and crowded poor. One friend was Charles Dodgson, who let the MacDonald children hear his story, *Alice in Wonderland*. As a result of their enthusiasm he decided to publish it. One of MacDonald's sons, Greville, remembered calling a cab for the poet Tennyson.

For a time George MacDonald was Professor of Literature at Bedford College, London. Because of continued ill health the family eventually moved to Italy, where MacDonald and his wife were to remain for the rest of their lives. There were, however, frequent stays in Britain during the warmer months, and a long and successful visit to the United States on a lecture tour. One of his last books, *Lilith* (1895) is among his greatest, a fantasy with the same power to move and to change a person's imaginative life as *Phantastes*.

In her book, *The Stars and the Stillness*, Kathy Triggs points out the paradox of a leading nineteenth-century writer being virtually forgotten today, and hazards some reasons for this. We live in a post-Christian world where MacDonald's values are alien. Television and other claims on our time deprive us of the leisure to tackle his lengthy novels. Yet, she points out, we lose out on so much if we neglect to read him. His theological insights are still needed today. He was the master of ageless symbolism in his imaginative work; a fact that so captured C.S. Lewis, bringing him face to face with the quality of holiness, though he did not acknowledge it for many years.

Further reading

Greville MacDonald, *George MacDonald and his wife* (1924); C.S. Lewis, *George MacDonald: an anthology* (1946); R.N. Hein, *The Harmony Within: The Spiritual Vision of George MacDonald* (1982); Kathy Triggs, *The Stars and the Stillness: A Portrait of George MacDonald* (1986); William Raeper, *George MacDonald* (1987).

Macgowan, John (1726–80) A Baptist minister and author of *Infernal Dialogues*, a forerunner of C.S. Lewis'

The Screwtape Letters,★ though Lewis never read it. There are striking similarities of aim, and in the relationship of the devils—one devil is the uncle of another. John Macgowan wrote several other popular works including *Death: A Vision,* and a life of the biblical character Ruth.

McNeill, Jane Agnes (1889–1959) A close family friend and neighbour of C.S. Lewis' in his childhood. She was the daughter of the headmaster of Campbell College, briefly attended by Lewis. Both Lewis brothers dedicated books to her, C.S. Lewis' choice being *That Hideous Strength.*★ Was it coincidence that a leading character is called Jane?

Macready, Mrs In *The Lion, the Witch and the Wardrobe,*★ Professor Digory Kirke's★ formidable housekeeper in his large country house.

***The Magician's Nephew* (1955)** This tale tells of the creation of Narnia★ by Aslan.★ It also tells us about the Edwardian childhood of Professor Digory Kirke,★ who owned the big country house with the wardrobe in *The Lion, the Witch and the Wardrobe,*★ and about how the London gas lamppost came to be in Narnia at all. Also, it speaks of the origin of the White Witch,★ and explains the arrival of evil in Narnia—showing the evil as older than that world.

Digory and his dying mother were staying with his Uncle Andrew★ and Aunt Letty in London, his father being in India. He made friends with Polly Plummer,★ his neighbour, and the two were tricked into an experiment with magic rings by the uncle, a mad scientist.

At first they found themselves in the dying world of Charn,★ blighted by Jadis, the White Witch, whom Digory awakes from a spell, despite warnings from Polly. They are unable to leave her behind as they return to London with the aid of the rings. There Jadis wreaks havoc, until the children are able to whisk her back to The

Wood Between the Worlds, but not before she had wrenched off a handle from a lamppost, intending to use it to punish those who opposed her. The trio, along with Frank,★ a London cabby, and his horse, and Uncle Andrew, end up in an empty world of Nothing, in time to hear Aslan's creation song. At the words and music of the lion's song mountains, trees, animals and other creatures come into being to make Narnia and the world of which it is a part. The sequence is reminiscent of passages from J.R.R. Tolkien's★ *The Silmarillion*, with which Lewis was familiar in unfinished form.

Aslan gives Digory the opportunity of undoing the evil he had brought into Narnia. His task is to find a magic apple, the seed of which would produce a tree to protect the young world from Jadis for many a year. Polly joins him on the adventure, which requires journeying into the mountains of the Western Wild to find a delightful valley. In a garden there, on a hilltop, grew an apple tree with the magic apples. To help them, the cabby's horse, Strawberry, renamed Fledge★ by Aslan, is transformed into a flying and talking horse to carry them.

Upon the children's return, Aslan allows Digory to bring back an apple from the tree which immediately sprang up from the apple's seed, to restore his dying mother. C.S. Lewis' own mother, Flora Hamilton Lewis,★ died when he was a boy in Edwardian Belfast.

In the fecundity of new growth associated with Narnia's creation, the metal pole brought by the witch grows into a lamppost in Lantern Waste,★ and, back in the twentieth century, a great apple tree grows from the core of the magic apple eaten by Mrs Kirke. Later, after the great tree fell, Digory had it made into a large wardrobe, the very same wardrobe that features in *The Lion, the Witch and the Wardrobe*.

Malacandra The name for Mars in Old Solar.★ *See OUT OF THE SILENT PLANET*; THE PLANETS.

Maleldil the Young   In *Out of the Silent Planet*,★ the name by which God's Son was known in Old Solar,★ he who had become incarnate as a rational creature on the Silent Planet, Earth.

Mars   *See OUT OF THE SILENT PLANET.*

Marshwiggle   In *The Silver Chair*,★ long and frog-like creatures who are occupied with most of the watery and fishy work in Narnia. The most famous marshwiggle is Puddleglum.★

Master Bowman   In *The Voyage of the 'Dawn Treader'*,★ the sailor in the company who shot the dreadful sea serpent.

Materialism   *See*   NATURALISM   AND   SUPER-NATURALISM.

Mathew, Gervase (1905–76)   One of The Inklings,★ and a contributor to *Essays Presented to Charles Williams*.★ Educated at Balliol College, Oxford, he joined the Catholic order of Dominicans in 1928 and was ordained a priest in 1934. He lectured in modern history, theology and English at Oxford, and wrote books on Byzantium and medieval England.

Mavramorn   In *The Voyage of the 'Dawn Treader'*,★ one of the seven Lords for whom the voyagers searched. They found him sleeping under a spell on Ramandu's Island.★

Meaning   *See* MEANING AND IMAGINATION.

Meaning and Imagination   The question of meaning (both of reality itself and of language) is central in the twentieth century. It is a key theme running throughout the writings of C.S. Lewis. For him, meaning was intimately tied up both with the role of the imagination, and with the fact that the entire universe is a dependent creation of God. He saw reason as the organ of truth, and imagination as the organ of meaning. Reason and imagination each had their own integrity, an integrity he attempted to respect in his fiction and theoretical writings.

He was also concerned with their interrelationship, both within a mature person and in their complementary roles in the pursuit of knowledge. He particularly stressed the dependence of even the most abstract of thinking upon imagination.

C.S. Lewis, like his friend J.R.R. Tolkien,★ believed that in some real sense the products of imagination in the arts could be true. Myth★ could become fact. In writing fantasies like *The Chronicles of Narnia*★ and *The Hobbit* they felt that they were discovering inevitable realities that were not the product of theories of the conscious mind (even though rational control is not relinquished in the making of good fantasy). It was this attitude which prompted both men to create consistent secondary worlds, or sub-creations,★ like Middle-Earth and Perelandra.★

Fiction, for C.S. Lewis, was the making of meaning. It reflects the greater creativity of God when he originated and put together his universe and ourselves. Meaning is at the core of real things and events. Natural objects are not mere facts. Human beings are not merely personalities. Objects, events and people are *real* insofar as they are in relationship to other objects, events, and persons, and ultimately in relationship to God. With persons, this relationship is more than that of an object to God its Creator; it involves personal characteristics like choice. The complex web of relationships that is the hallmark of reality confers objects, events and people with meaning. In themselves, they do not mean; they refer elsewhere to their meaning.

The heart of Lewis' Christian view of meaning is captured by a Dutch Christian philosopher: 'Meaning is the mode of being of all that is created. This universal character of referring and expressing, which is proper to our entire created cosmos, stamps created reality as meaning, in accordance with its dependent non-self-sufficient nature. Meaning is the being of all that has been created and the nature even of our selfhood. It has a religious root and a divine origin' (Herman Dooyeweerd). A similar view seems to have been held by the brilliant thinker, Michael Polanyi, at least in equating meaning and being as a consequence of a theistic view of the universe.

C.S. Lewis has sometimes been accused of crude rationalism; the belief that reason alone is enough to convince us that A is true and B is false. Lewis, however, saw reason itself in the light of the primacy of meaning (that is, in the light of the reference of all things, events, and people to God). In *Miracles*,★ he points out that when we analyse our thinking as an actual event, two levels are evident. One level is the physical facts about the actual state of our brain at the time—the natural state of that particular bit of the universe. Our thinking, as an event, is obeying the laws of physics and chemistry, and mechanistic principles. The other level is the *meaning* to which these physical facts point, providing the character of the event that enables it to be called thinking. We always think *about* something; our thoughts *refer to* or *mean* something other than themselves as events.

As a literary critic,★ C.S. Lewis also saw literary works in the light of the primacy of meaning. A good literary work takes us into meanings not normally or often perceived by us (or even its author). These meanings give the work its character, even though the actual literary arrangement of the work, with all the skill that that involves, is a necessary condition for receiving the meanings.

It is on the relationship between concept and meaning, and thought and imagination, that C.S. Lewis makes his most distinctive contribution to our understanding. He has set an agenda that could be fruitful in literary criticism, philosophy, linguistics, and theology. He argues that good imagining is as vital as good thinking, and either is impoverished without the other.

C.S. Lewis set out some key ideas, which owed much to his friend Owen Barfield,★ in an essay in *Rehabilitations*:★

> It must not be supposed that I am in any sense putting forward the imagination as the organ of truth. We are not talking of truth, but of meaning: meaning which is the antecedent condition both of truth and falsehood, whose antithesis is not error but nonsense. . . . For me, reason is the natural organ of truth; but imagination is the organ of meaning. Imagination, producing new metaphors or revivifying old, is not the cause of truth, but its condition. It is, I confess, undeniable that such a view indirectly implies a kind of truth or rightness in the imagination itself . . . the truth we [win] by metaphor [can] not be greater than the truth of the metaphor itself; and . . . all our truth, or all but a few fragments, is won by metaphor. And thence, I confess, it does follow that if our thinking is ever true, then the metaphors by which we think must have been good metaphors. It does follow that if those original equations, between good and light, or evil and dark, between breath and soul and all the others, were from the beginning arbitrary and fanciful—if there is not, in fact, a kind of psycho-physical parallelism (or more) in the universe— then all our thinking is nonsensical. But we cannot, without contradiction, believe it to be nonsensical. And so, admittedly, the view I have taken has metaphysical implications. But so has every view.

There are a number of suggestive ideas here, many of which Lewis developed and refined in later years, leading to his definitive statement about literature, *An Experiment in Criticism*.★ Some of the basic ideas are as follows. (1) There is a distinction between reason and imagination as regards roles—reason is to do with theoretical truths, imagination is to do with meanings. (2) There are standards of correctness, or norms, for the imagination, held tacitly and universally by human beings. (3) Meaning is a condition of the framing of truth; poor meanings make for poor thoughts. (4) The framing of truths in propositions necessitates the employment of metaphors supplied by the imagination. Language and thought necessarily relies upon metaphor.

One of the most controversial and difficult points here is that meaning is somehow a condition of thought in a manner obviously different from how the physical brain is. A footnote in Barfield's *Poetic Diction* sheds light on this, if 'poet' is read as 'the imagination': 'Logical judgments, by their nature, can only *render more explicit* some one part of a truth *already implicit in their terms*. But the poet makes the terms themselves. He does not make judgments, therefore; he only makes them possible—and only he makes them possible.' Imagination is the maker of meaning, the definer of terms in a proposition, and as such is a condition of truth.

The place of metaphor in thinking was central to C.S. Lewis' beliefs. In *Miracles*, he points out that to speak of anything beyond the perceptions of our five senses, metaphorical expression is required; this is as true in the fields of psychology, economics, philosophy, and politics as it is in the fields of religion and poetry. To speak of supersensibles, he argues, is inevitably to talk '*as if they could be* seen or touched or heard (e.g. must talk of "complexes" and "repressions" *as if* desires could really be tied up in bundles or shoved back; of "growth" and "development" *as if* institutions could really grow like trees or unfold like flowers; of energy being "released" *as if* it were an animal let out of a cage).'

Meldilorn   In *Out of the Silent Planet*,★ the habitation of the ruling Oyarsa, the great eldila.★ Meldilorn is an island on a sapphire lake set within a border of purple forest. It lies in the Marsian handramit,★ or lowland. On the island is a broad avenue of monoliths, and magnificent trees.

Mere Christianity (1952)   One of the most well known of C.S. Lewis' books, *Mere Christianity* is a revised and enlarged edition of three previous books of talks given on BBC radio, *Broadcast Talks* (called *The Case for Christianity* in the USA) (1942), *Christian Behaviour* (1943) and *Beyond Personality* (1944). It is straightforward and lucid, and its contents are captured in its part-titles: 'Right and wrong as a clue to the meaning of the universe', 'What Christians believe', 'Christian behaviour', and 'Beyond personality: or first steps in the doctrine of the Trinity'.

C.S. Lewis was invited to give popular talks on BBC radio early in 1941, when war had made people generally more thoughtful about ultimate issues. Lewis had to weigh up two dislikes—the radio, and travelling to London—but his sense of duty won. He regarded England as post-Christian, and felt that many people had the attitude that they had rejected Christianity, whereas they had never had it. His feelings about the first set of talks were recorded in a letter. The broadcasts were pre-evangelism 'rather than evangelism, an attempt to convince people that there is a moral law, that we disobey it, and that the existence of a Lawgiver is at least very probable and also (*unless* you add the Christian doctrine of the Atonement) that this imparts despair rather than comfort.'

Some years after the BBC talks, C.S. Lewis recorded a series for radio which was the basis for his book, *The Four Loves*.★ It was broadcast only in the United States. These are now the only recordings of Lewis' voice available (from Word publishers).

Merlin   In *That Hideous Strength*,★ the magician from the

129

time of King Arthur who returns to help save Logres, the true Britain. *See* ATLANTIS.

Miracles: A Preliminary Study (1947; revised new edition 1960) This book, which reveals more than any other C.S. Lewis' view of God* and nature,* was intended for people for whom the question of miracles is real. It is not couched in the specialist language of theology or philosophy, though it has an enormous amount to contribute to both theology and philosophy of religion. The book was substantially revised and improved after Chapter 3 in the first edition, 'The Self-Contradiction of the Naturalist', was criticised by philosopher Elizabeth Anscombe at the Oxford University Socratic Club.* The substance of her critique, and Lewis' response, is found in the essay, 'Religion without Dogma?', in *Undeceptions.**

The first part of the book, consisting of the first seven chapters, describes two basic attitudes of thought about life, the universe, and everything. The first, which Lewis felt was now habitual in the modern person, he called naturalism.* This materialistic view sees the natural universe as all that is; nature is 'the whole show'. Nothing else exists. Any reality beyond what can be perceived by the five senses lacks plausibility. The possibility of miracles is ruled out in advance; seeking evidence for a miracle is as silly as looking for Santa Claus. The second, and opposite, view is supernaturalism, the theistic view that the universe is a dependent creation of God. Time, space, and geometry are all God's creation, and only exist now because he chose to make them out of nothing.

For C.S. Lewis, the naturalist sees nature as a pond of infinite depths made up of nothing but water. The supernaturalist sees nature as a pond with a bottom— mud, earth, rock, and finally the planet itself.

The central point is that if naturalism is true, miracles

are impossible. If supernaturalism is true, miracles are possible, and, indeed, to be expected.

Lewis points out two insurmountable difficulties with naturalism. It undermines the validity of thought itself, therefore even the claims of naturalism to be true. It also reduces the 'oughtness' of things to 'isness'. If moral obligation turns out only to be caused naturally, then it is no longer an obligation. We can only then be forced or manipulated into behaving as some other people (the Nazis, for example) wish us to.

For C.S. Lewis, both conscience and reason provide an analogy for the way a miracle imposes itself upon the natural order. Both conscience and reason are testimonies to the reality of the supernatural world.

After this preparation, C.S. Lewis proceeds to his main theme, the biblical miracles, particularly the incarnation of Christ. He is greatly concerned with demolishing modern chronological snobbery. ★ This is the tendency to treat the past as more primitive than the present, and as therefore superseded. There are two characteristic ways that this attitude bars itself from the New Testament miracles. One is to see the people of that time as gullible in accepting as miracles events that today would have a natural explanation. The other is to see their imagery as mythological and therefore in need of de- or re-mythologising in modern terms. The idea of God coming down to earth from up there in heaven is an example.

C.S. Lewis' treatment of both modern fallacies is brilliant and helpful. Of particular interest is his treatment of the function of imagery and metaphor in language. He presents some seminal ideas on the relationship between imagination and thinking, meaning★ and truth. Such ideas were at the very foundation of his own thinking, scholarship and fictional work.

See also THEOLOGY, C.S. LEWIS AND.

Miraz, King   In *Prince Caspian*,★ the Prince's wicked uncle who had stolen the throne from King Caspian★ IX. He was aided and abetted by Queen Prunaprismia, and came to a bad end.

Monopods   *See* DUFFLEPUDS.

Moonwood   In *The Last Battle*,★ a hare with such exceptional hearing that it was said that he could sit by Cauldron Pool under the waterfall and hear what was whispered at Cair Paravel.★

Moore, Mrs Janie (1872–1951)   The lady adopted by C.S. Lewis almost as a mother in fulfilment of a promise made to her son, a billet-mate of Lewis' during the Great War. Mrs Moore, along with her surviving child Maureen, shared Lewis' household from soon after the war. With typical generosity, Lewis focused on her virtues, praising her hospitality. His brother, 'Warnie', was less charitable; he could not understand how Lewis put up with her. As far as Warnie was concerned, 'Minto', as she was dubbed, was Jack Lewis' thorn in the flesh. He sketched out her life and character for posterity in a journal entry a few days after her death in *Brothers and Friends: The Diaries of Major Warren Hamilton Lewis*★ (entry 17th January 1951).

Mount Pire   In *The Horse and His Boy*★, a mountain in Archenland★ created when Fair Olvin fought the two-headed giant, Pire, and turned him into stone. Shasta★ uses the twin-peaked mountain as a landmark for finding Archenland.

Muil   In *The Voyage of the 'Dawn Treader'*,★ the westernmost of the Seven Isles.★ It is separated from the Isle of Brenn★ by a choppy strait.

Mullugutherum   In *The Silver Chair*,★ the Warden of the Marches of Underland.★ He was chief of the earthmen★ in the Underworld realm, the Shallow Lands,★ of the Green Witch.★

Myth   C.S. Lewis, like his friend J.R.R. Tolkien,★ placed the highest value on the making of myth—or mythopoeia —in imaginative fiction and poetry. Some stories are outright myths—as is the story of Cupid and Psyche* retold by Lewis in *Till We Have Faces.* ★ Other stories have what Lewis called a 'mythical quality'. Examples he gave were the plots of *Dr Jekyll and Mr Hyde*, H.G. Wells' *The Door in the Wall*, Kafka's *The Castle,* and the conceptions of Gormenghast in Mervyn Peake's *Titus Groan* and of the Ents and Lothlorien in Tolkien's *The Lord of the Rings*. Both Lewis and Tolkien aspired to myth-making in their fictional creations. They had a theology of myth (*see* THEOLOGY OF ROMANCE).

Recognising that the term 'myth', like 'romanticism',★ has many loose meanings (including 'untrue'), C.S. Lewis tried to pin down its meaning in his *An Experiment in Criticism.* ★ A story that achieves myth has a number of characteristics. (1) It is independent of the form of words used to tell the story. (2) Narrative features, such as suspense or surprise, play little part in the distinctive pleasure of myth. (3) Our empathy with the characters of the story is at a minimum; we do not imaginatively transport ourselves into their lives. (4) Myth is always fantasy, dealing with the impossible and preternatural. (5) Myth is never comic; though the experience may be joyful or sad it is always grave. (6) The experience, in fact, is awe-inspiring, containing a numinous quality.

In defining myth in terms of its effect upon us, Lewis was clear that one person's myth may only be a story to another. A story may give enjoyment to a person without being perceived as myth, even though it is myth.

C.S. Lewis regarded the nineteenth-century writer George MacDonald★ as one of the greatest masters of myth-making, especially in *Phantastes* (which, Lewis says, 'baptised' his imagination long before he became a Christian believer) and *Lilith*.

Myth has had a central place in modern anthropology, and also in contemporary theology. At the time of his conversion, C.S. Lewis wrestled with the anthropology of James G. Frazer (1854–1941), as represented in the widely influential *The Golden Bough: A Study in Magic and Religion* (abridged edition 1922). Later in his life, C.S. Lewis made known his disquiet with key ideas of myth propounded in contemporary theology, ideas associated, for example, with Rudolf Bultmann (1884–1976). Lewis saw serious errors in Frazer's view of myth, and in the understanding of myth in the work of leading biblical critics.

Sir James Frazer explored magic and religions throughout the world in the hope of tracing an important part of the evolution of human thought. As a result, *The Golden Bough* (originally in thirteen volumes) is truly encyclopedic. In seeking a unified development, Frazer denied the value of asking whether religions were true or false. Christianity had no uniqueness, a theme that is increasingly heard in contemporary theology, through John Hick and others. Frazer helped to lay the foundation for the relativism that is so familiar today.

Though at first they seemed devastating to Christian belief, C.S. Lewis came to the conclusion that similarities between biblical teaching and ancient myths can argue for the truth of Christianity as well as against it. Describing his recent conversion to Christianity to Arthur Greeves in a letter of 18th October 1931, Lewis explains:

Now the story of Christ is simply a true myth: a myth working on us in the same way as the others, but with this tremendous difference that *it really happened*: and one must be content to accept it in the same way, remembering that it is God's myth where the others are men's myths: i.e. the Pagan stories are God expressing

Himself through the minds of poets, using such images as He found there, while Christianity is God expressing Himself through what we call 'real things'. Therefore it is *true*, not in the sense of being a 'description' of God (that no finite mind could take in) but in the sense of being the way in which God chooses to (or can) appear to our faculties. The 'doctrines' we get *out of* the true myth are of course *less* true: they are translations into our *concepts* and *ideas* of that wh[ich] God has already expressed in a language more adequate, namely the actual incarnation, crucifixion, and resurrection. . . .

James Frazer had documented many myths of dying and rising gods throughout the world. As C.S. Lewis grew as a Christian thinker, he continued to reflect on such myths. He argued that 'We must not be nervous about "parallels" and "pagan Christs": they *ought* to be there—it would be a stumbling block if they weren't.' He explored such 'parallel' themes in his powerful 'myth retold', *Till We Have Faces*.

At the heart of Christianity, C.S. Lewis believed, is a myth that is also a fact—making the claims of Christianity unique. But by becoming fact, Lewis points out, it did not cease to be myth, or lose the quality of myth. Lewis praised John Milton for retaining the tangible quality of myth in most of *Paradise Lost*, his great epic which is one of the most powerful of credal affirmations in Christian literature. Lewis strove to follow Milton's example in his own fiction.

Rudolf Bultmann is widely considered to be the most significant and influential New Testament scholar of this century. Bultmann's key belief was that 'faith must not aspire to an objective basis in dogma or in history on pain of losing its character as faith'. Bultmann saw the Gospel records as myths, and myths as attempts to portray happenings in the world as having supernatural causes. In the case of Christ's virgin birth, the event could only have occurred with divine intervention into the world of cause and effect. The modern person, Bultmann believes, cannot accept the idea of supernatural causes of events in the world we see. We must strip the Gospels of myths, and get to the core of what Christ's followers believed in the first century. They were 'objectifying' their beliefs in myths appropriate to their day.

C.S. Lewis' counter to this kind of thinking is found in his apologetical study, *Miracles*.★ There he argues that a supernaturalist view is not outmoded, but is essential for proper human thinking and intellectual discovery at any time or place. He also addressed modern biblical critics directly on one occasion (*see* THEOLOGY, C.S. LEWIS AND). Lewis objected to biblical critics who saw the Gospels as legend or romance rather than a factual, historical record. As a literary critic, and avid reader of myth, Lewis felt that they had little idea of what myth actually is. In several instances, he found them poor readers of the texts they had pored over, perhaps for years.

Like Bultmann, however, C.S. Lewis did recognise the difficulties modern people have in reading the Gospels. Bultmann's procedure was to 'demythologise'. Lewis, who wanted as an orthodox 'mere Christian' to retain the Gospels as the greatest story but true, chose rather to *remythologise* central Christian beliefs. He attempted stories that would put over Christian meanings in a modern way, particularly in his Narnia★ stories for children (of all ages) and his science fiction trilogy. Even his historical novel, *Till We Have Faces*, is fresh and contemporary as a work of art.

N

Nain In *Prince Caspian,*★ King of Archenland★ in the dark time of Miraz★ of Narnia.★

Narnia *See* NARNIA: History.

Narnia, The Chronicles of Seven tales for children by C.S. Lewis which cover almost half of this century and over two and a half millennia of Narnian years from its creation to its final days. In chronological order the titles are *The Magician's Nephew,*★ *The Lion, the Witch and the Wardrobe,*★ *The Horse and His Boy,*★ *Prince Caspian.*★ *The Voyage of the 'Dawn Treader',*★ *The Silver Chair*★ and *The Last Battle.*★ In reading order, it is preferable to enjoy *The Lion, the Witch and the Wardrobe* first.

Narnia: Geography In *The Chronicles of Narnia,*★ a small country south of which lies Archenland★ and Calormen.★ It is a land inhabited by both talking and dumb beasts and trees, the chief of all its creatures being also its creator, Aslan,★ a talking lion. To the far west lies the land of Telmar,★ and nearer the Western Wild—a mountainous region covered with dark forests or with snow and ice. From this region rushes a river which becomes a waterfall under which is Caldron Pool.★ From this flows the River of Narnia which runs all the way to the Eastern Ocean.★ Lantern Waste★ lies to the east of the wilderness.

Narnia's capital is Cair Paravel,★ the seat of human Kings and Queens, located at the mouth of the River of Narnia. The marshwiggles★ (found only in Narnia) live to the north of Cair Paravel. More northerly lies the River

Shribble, and then the forlorn moorland of Ettinsmoor.★ Further north still is a mountainous region and Harfang,★ a stronghold of giants. Near Harfang are the ruins of a once great city, under which lie a number of subterranean lands, including the kingdom of the Green Witch,★ destroyed in the time of Prince Rilian,★ son of Caspian,★ the tenth Telmarine★ King.

To Narnia's east lies the vast Eastern Ocean,★ in which are many islands, and finally the Silver Sea and the World's End, where is Aslan's Country.★

Narnia is also the name of a small Italian town mentioned by Livy.

See also NARNIA: History.

Narnia: History Because the time of earth is different from that of Narnia, the children who are drawn into Narnia on a number of occasions find themselves at various points in its history. Thus, although *The Chronicles of Narnia*★ cover only about fifty years of our history (from the beginning to the mid twentieth century) we get a picture of the entire history of Narnia from its creation to its unmaking and the new creation of all worlds, including Narnia and England.

Narnia's creation is recounted in *The Magician's Nephew.*★ Digory Kirke★ and Polly Plummer,★ after entering the old and dying world of Charn★ through a pool in the Wood Between the Worlds,★ find their way by accident into a land of Nothing. Here, gradually, Narnia is created before their eyes by the song of Aslan.★ Unfortunately Digory brings evil into that perfect world in the form of Jadis,★ destroyer of Charn,★ whom he had previously awakened in that world.

Jadis goes off to the fringes of Narnia, but reappears in later ages as the White Witch★ who puts a spell over Narnia of winter that never comes to Christmas. The arrival of the four Pevensie★ children through the ward-

robe (told in *The Lion, the Witch and the Wardrobe**)
coincides with the return of Aslan and the beginning of the
end of her curse. Aslan's death on behalf of Edmund
Pevensey, and his return to life by a deeper law than the
one by which she operates her magic, leads to her defeat
and death. Narnia's Golden Age follows.

With the return of the children to their world, Narnia
slowly falls into disorder. The Telmarines,* led by
Caspian* I, occupy the land and silence the talking beasts
and trees. 'Old Narnia' only survives under cover as
Aslan's remnant keep faith alive that he will return. Prince
Caspian* (his story is told in the book of that name),
brought up by his wicked Uncle Miraz* and Aunt
Prunaprismia,* who have deposed his father Caspian IX,
learns of the myth of Old Narnia and longs for it to be
true. He escapes a plot to kill him and joins forces with the
old Narnians. In the nick of time, help comes from the
four Pevensie children drawn back into Narnia.

He becomes Caspian X after adventures at sea recounted in *The Voyage of the 'Dawn Treader'.** His son,
Prince Rilian,* is kidnapped and held in servitude in an
underworld for ten years by a witch of the line of Jadis.
She plots to take over Narnia using him as a puppet
King. As told in the chronicle of *The Silver Chair,** he is
rescued by a cousin of the Pevensie children, Eustace
Scrubb* and his school friend Jill Pole,* who are brought
into Narnia for this task.

After many ages, the last King of Narnia, Tirian,* and
indeed Narnia itself, are threatened by a devilish plot
which uses a counterfeit Aslan and links up with the
Calormene* forces (who are a constant threat to Narnia's
security). This is Narnia's darkest hour. As recounted in
*The Last Battle,** Tirian prays for help from the sons and
daughters of Adam, and Aslan brings Eustace and Jill to
his aid. Aslan himself finally intervenes and dissolves the

whole world. This turns out to be a beginning rather than an end as the New Narnia is revealed.

See also NARNIA: Geography.

Further reading

Walter Hooper, *Past Watchful Dragons* (1980); Martha C. Sammons, *A Guide Through Narnia* (1979).

Narrative Poems (1969) C.S. Lewis wrote both lyrical and narrative verse, and originally hoped to make his name as a poet. This volume contains four stories, including *Dymer,*★ *Launcelot, The Nameless Isle,* and *The Queen of Drum*—about the escape of a Queen from a dictator into Fairy Land.

See also POEMS.

Narrowhaven In *The Voyage of the 'Dawn Treader'*,★ a town on the Island of Doorn★ ruled by Gumpas.★

See also LONE ISLANDS.

Nat Whilk Anglo-Saxon for 'I know not whom', used by C.S. Lewis as a pseudonym, usually in the form of the initials 'N.W.'. In the first edition of *A Grief Observed*★ he called himself 'N.W. Clerk'. *Clerk* is Middle English for 'scholar'. Playing on his pseudonym, Lewis quotes the medieval authority Natvilcius in *Perelandra*★ regarding eldila.★

Naturalism *See* NATURALISM AND SUPERNATURALISM.

Naturalism and Supernaturalism Naturalism is C.S. Lewis' name, in his book *Miracles: A Preliminary Study,*★ for the view that nature★ is 'the whole show', with nothing outside nature existing. He contrasts naturalism with its opposite, supernaturalism. This is the theistic view that nature is contingent. It has been created by God, but God did not have to create it. He could have created other natures, or not created at all. God is complete irrespective of whether or not he created a real nature outside of himself.

Two things need to be said about Lewis' formulation of nature and supernature. One is that he is representing an orthodox Judeo-Christian position, a position that many believe was an essential presupposition for the rise of modern science. The other is that Lewis' view can be formulated in other terms, and, no doubt, in more sophisticated and precise philosophical language. C.S. Lewis was deliberately popularising. In the process, his thinking (especially as embodied in *Miracles*) is more timeless than a fully fledged philosophical study of its day. He was careful to call *Miracles* a 'preliminary study'. Nevertheless, after his encounter with philosopher Elizabeth Anscombe, at a meeting of the Oxford University Socratic Club,* he greatly improved his case for the later paperback edition of *Miracles*.

C.S. Lewis' fundamental distinction between nature and supernature has, surprisingly, been criticised by some evangelicals who seem to take a position difficult to separate from deism. Two key elements of this criticism are as follows. One is a dislike of Lewis' metaphors of 'interruption of' and 'interference with' nature by the supernatural. The critics point out that God's creation in every aspect, natural and spiritual, reveals the mark of his personal hand. The other is a rejection of Lewis' analysis of the causation of thinking, in its link to the brain as a mechanism. Lewis' opponents are happy for the brain as a mechanism to have a complete causal story in terms of the laws of physics and chemistry. Thought and human consciousness has a complementary story, perceived by the dimension of faith and ourselves as responsible observers. Thus Lewis' central argument of the self-contradiction of naturalism is undermined.

This criticism, however, ignores the underlying force of Lewis' attack on naturalism, and also is un-selfcritical, by failing to realise the popular character of Lewis' study and apologetic. A number of Christian thinkers have worked on the question of causality on various hierarchical levels, such as the physical and chemical, the biological, and the historical. They have also wrestled with the logical relationship between causal levels—a necessity for any complementarian approach. This work, particularly by Michael Polanyi (who spoke several times to the Oxford University Socratic Club) and Herman Dooyeweerd, strengthens Lewis' approach, and indeed the traditional theistic position for which he stood. C.S. Lewis' own essay, *Transposition,*★ is powerfully suggestive of such an approach.

C.S. Lewis' views both of naturalism and of the self-contradiction of the naturalist are seminal for contemporary Christian apologetics. 'Naturalism' can be extended as a concept to any view which makes an aspect of the created world into a God-substitute, or idol. This aspect is therefore made transcendent, and creates an inner tension, a contradiction, in the resulting humanistic system. This internal contradiction is capable of structural analysis and exposure. A brilliant use of such 'transcendental criticism' is made by Dooyeweerd in his *A New Critique of Theoretical Thought* (1935–36).

Lewis' key metaphors, which describe the supernatural as *invading* or *interfering with* nature, do not imply a dualism in God's created world. Lewis was not a Platonist, though Plato★ was a rich source for his imagination. Lewis uses such metaphors in the context of a nature which is fallen, and hence abnormal. He believed in a real historical fall by disobedient mankind which affected the whole of nature, even though nature still reveals God himself. Unless one is an atheist or a deist, it is difficult to see why such metaphors are objectionable. Supernature, like nature, is marked by both good and evil as a result of primeval disobedience by mankind and some angels. C.S. Lewis' case would perhaps have had greater elegance if he had introduced more of the biblical concept of the cultural mandate, where mankind is commanded in Genesis to order and name the natural world. The whole human cultural process rearranges nature. Lewis could therefore have extended his analogy between supernatural acts and thinking to include culture (of which thinking is but a part). Such a broader canvas, however, might not have interested him because of his distrust of overblown systems.

Nature

'In our world,' said Eustace, 'a star is a huge ball of flaming gas.'

'Even in your world, my son,' replied the old man, 'that is not what a star is but only what it is made of' (*The Voyage of the 'Dawn Treader'*).

Like his friend Owen Barfield,★ C.S. Lewis believed that, as Ransom★ remarked to Merlin in *That Hideous Strength*,★ 'the soul has gone out of wood and water'. The world's history is one of mankind's separation from God★ on the one hand and nature on the other. This view led to Lewis' opposition to scientism (but not true science). Our separation from nature came from our wish to exalt ourselves and thus to belittle all else. Christians, Lewis believed, should recognise God's continued activity in the fecundity of natural things like trees, grass, flowers and shrubs. J.R.R. Tolkien,★ Lewis' other great friend, also held this view.

In his atheistic mid-teens, C.S. Lewis cared mainly about gods, heroes, and an ideal world of beauty. Many years later he eventually, and reluctantly, accepted a

Christian universe. He soon realised the implications of commitment to this 'real universe, the divine, magical, terrifying and ecstatic reality in which we all live'. What fixed the reality of the natural world for ever was the incarnation of God* himself as a fully human being in a fully real human body. Christ's resurrection meant that he retains this human body for ever. The environment of his resurrected body, and that of his followers in the future, could be called a new nature, though believers, Lewis included, prefer to call this environment 'heaven'.*

C.S. Lewis was once interviewed by *Time* magazine. He was asked if he found his life at Oxford, a life of writing, walking, teaching and reading, monotonous. Lewis' reply baffled them: 'I like monotony.'

It is upon the humble and common things of life that Lewis' wonderlands of the imagination are based, 'the quiet fullness of ordinary nature'. He also saw it (he learned this from George MacDonald*) as the basis of spirituality. In a letter, he wrote: 'The familiar is in itself ground for affection. And it is good, because any natural help towards our spiritual duty of loving is good and God seems to build our higher loves round our merely natural impulses —sex, maternity, kinship, old acquaintances. . . .' Conversely, as he demonstrated vividly in his *The Screwtape Letters*,* the small things are likely to play more part in the damnation of a person than great acts like murder or betrayal.

Because of the link between ordinary reality and imaginative creation, Lewis found himself as much on the defensive about fantasy as about his lifestyle. A common charge was that literary fantasy is escapism. In his book *Of Other Worlds*, Lewis says of *The Wind in the Willows* (the popular children's story by Kenneth Graham): 'The happiness which it presents to us is in fact full of the simplest and most attainable things—food, sleep, exercise, friendship, the face of nature, even (in a sense) religion.' Such fantasy is the opposite of escapism. It deepens the reality of the real world for us—the terror as well as the beauty.

In making such comments, and holding fervently to such beliefs, C.S. Lewis was in fact struggling with a most important problem for the Christian in the modern world. This is that of being contented with reality as it is given to us by God without denying that it is abnormal because of the fall of mankind at the beginning of recorded history. Such contentment is by no means synonymous with conservatism in ideas and politics—so called Cosmic Toryism. Lewis himself did not defend the status quo, carefully dissociated himself from the political Right, and even strongly believed that soon the time will come when a Christian in the Civil Service will have a problem about furthering tyranny. In the wartime, he urged RAF personnel to face the consequences of refusing to bomb civilian targets. In his satirical science fiction story, *That Hideous Strength*, the devil's party are officials! His open Christian position made him unpopular with many in the Oxford★ establishment.

For C.S. Lewis, the importance of reality lies in how it impinges upon the individual person. No one can experience the humanist's 'happiness of the greatest number'. Furthermore, what is unbearably painful to one person can be borne by another. Lewis himself clearly felt life deeply. He does not seem to be exaggerating when he once wrote in a letter, early in 1956: 'It seems to me that one can hardly say anything either bad enough or good enough about life.' In his 'myth retold', *Till We Have Faces*,★ he goes a long way towards achieving both at once.

C.S. Lewis saw Christianity as carrying the stamp of this same reality upon it. He wrote in 1953: 'Christianity is . . . hard and tender at the same time. It's the blend that does it; neither quality would be any good without the other.'

Closely linked to Lewis' zest for ordinary reality, for nature, was his attention to the details of life and experience. This power of observation added detail after detail of exuberant creation to his imaginative writings. He was very aware of nature, seasons, weather, atmosphere, and, of course, animals. In fact, he delighted to put animal characters into his books. In Narnia,★ many of the animals can speak. In *Perelandra,*★ the harmony between the new humans of Venus and its native animals beautifully evokes mankind's unfallen state. In *Out of the Silent Planet,*★ Lewis brilliantly manages to create talking animals★ that are acceptable to adult readers. The 'proper' bear in *That Hideous Strength*, called Mr Bultitude,★ was based upon an actual bear in Whipsnade Zoo. The threat to Mr Bultitude by the sinister N.I.C.E.★ illustrates Lewis' hatred of vivisection.

C. S. Lewis' letters are also full of references to animals. In a letter to an American lady he recounted: 'We were talking about cats and dogs the other day and decided that both have consciences but the dog, being an honest, humble person, always had a bad one, but the cat is a Pharisee and always has a good one. When he sits and stares you out of countenance he is thanking God that he is not as these dogs, or these humans, or even as these other cats!'

Nature, said C. S. Lewis, has the air of a good thing that has been spoiled. It is not only spoiled in and of itself, but also in the human relationship to it. One way this disfiguring comes about is in our way of seeing the natural world. Lewis vividly illustrated this in his short story, *The Shoddy Lands*. Here he takes us into the mind of a self-centred young woman who lacks a real perception of nature, and thus life. A similar impoverished view of reality in its full meaning is expressed in Lewis' disturbing picture of hell in *The Great Divorce*.★ He may have been influenced by his friend Charles Williams,★ who portrayed hell, and its inroads in our present world, as the absence of meaning.★

The natural world of God's creation imposes a fundamental limit to the human imagination. We cannot, like God, create *ex nihilo*, out of nothing. We can only rearrange elements that God has already made, and which are already brimful of his meanings. Mankind's proper mode of imaginative making is what J.R.R. Tolkien dubbed sub-creation.★

C.S. Lewis believed that evil—whether from human beings or demons—always results in the disruption or even the destruction of nature. In *The Lion, the Witch and the Wardrobe*,★ the White Witch★ kept Narnia★ in perpetual winter. In both *The Last Battle*★ and *That Hideous Strength*, places of natural beauty are despoiled for the sake of economic exploitation, expansion, and so-called progress. In 1947, C.S. Lewis wrote: 'The evil reality of lawless applied science . . . is actually reducing large tracts of Nature to disorder and sterility at this very moment.'

Because he normally wrote in a popular manner, Lewis did not always distinguish between nature as she was originally intended to be from nature as she is now. In his more specific studies, *The Problem of Pain*★ and *Miracles*,★ he goes deeper into the meaning of nature as God's creation. In *Miracles* he contrasts this Christian view with what he calls naturalism,★ the belief that nature is all that is. He could have used the term materialism, except that the term 'matter' is even more hard to pin down than 'nature'. In his book, *Studies in Words*,★ he devotes a long study to the term nature, and its family of words: *phusis* (from which the term physics is derived), and *kind*. More detail is given on the meaning of the idea of nature in other scholarly works of his, particularly *The Allegory of Love*** and *The Discarded Image.** He expounds a biblical view of nature in *Reflections on the Psalms** as well as in *Miracles.*

Ultimately, there was, for C.S. Lewis, an inevitable connection between nature and joy,* as in nature heaven itself is foreshadowed:

> The settled happiness and security which we all desire, God withholds from us by the very nature of the world: but joy, pleasure, and merriment, He has scattered broadcast. We are never safe, but we have plenty of fun, and some ecstasy. It is not hard to see why. The security we crave would teach us to rest our hearts in this world and pose an obstacle to our return to God: a few moments of happy love, a landscape, a symphony, a merry meeting with our friends, a bathe or a football match, have no such tendency. Our Father refreshes us on the journey with some pleasant inns, but will not encourage us to mistake them for home (*The Problem of Pain*, Chapter 7).

N.I.C.E.   In C.S. Lewis' science fiction tale, *That Hideous Strength*,* the N.I.C.E. is the National Institute for Co-ordinated Experiments, set up at Belbury,* near Edge-stow,* by a group of corrupt scientists seeking to remake the human race. They wish to purge it of traditional values of freedom and dignity, and represent the most satanic inner ring* in history. One N.I.C.E. member, Filostrato, reveals what he considers to be its inner purpose to Mark Studdock:* 'This Institute . . . is for something better than housing and vaccinations and faster trains and curing people of cancer. It is for the conquest of death. . . . It is to bring out of that cocoon of organic life which sheltered the babyhood of mind the New Man, the man who will not die, the artificial man, free from Nature. Nature is the ladder we have climbed up by, now we kick her away.' The appliance of science in technology is allowed to have a totalitarian rule; science is distorted into technocracy. In the process, new demons take possession. They are in fact the old demons using a new strategy. This time the domination of the whole human race appears to be within their grasp. The N.I.C.E. represents all that C.S. Lewis was attacking in his powerful essay, *The Abolition of Man*.★

Nikabrik the Dwarf   One of the Old Narnians in the tale, *Prince Caspian*,★ but highly cynical. He prefers the old, 'realistic' magic of the witches and turns against Aslan.★

Numinor   *See* ATLANTIS.

O

Octesian In *The Voyage of the 'Dawn Treader'*,★ one of the seven Telmarine★ Lords sought by the young King Caspian★ and his voyagers. He had become the dragon found dying by Edmund Pevensie★ on Dragon Island.★

Old Solar In C.S. Lewis' science fiction trilogy, the universal language of rational beings, including eldila,★ beyond the orbit of the moon and before the fall of mankind and the effects of the Tower of Babel. Earth (or Thulcandra—the Silent Planet) is unique in having a diversity of languages. Lewis invented a considerable Old Solar vocabulary in providing names and word-forms throughout the stories. The idea of inventing languages in fantasy owes much to J.R.R. Tolkien,★ Lewis' friend, who created several, including Elvish, in which he even wrote lyrics.

Orual The Queen of Glome★ in *Till We Have Faces*, and narrator of that story, in which she recounts her life. The physical ugliness of her face (but not her voice) presents a major theme of the novel, shaping many of the events. She is the half-sister of Psyche,★ and sister of Redival.★ *See TILL WE HAVE FACES.*

***Out of the Silent Planet* (1938)** The first volume of C.S. Lewis' science fiction trilogy. Dr Elwin Ransom,★ a philologist Don from Cambridge University, is kidnapped while on a walking holiday in the Midlands and taken to Malacandra★ (Mars) by Devine★ and Weston★, the latter a famous physicist and materialist (*see*

150

NATURALISM AND SUPERNATURALISM). They are under a misapprehension that the unseen ruler of Malacandra wants a human sacrifice—a fantasy created by their dark minds.

After escaping his captors, Ransom is at first terrified and disoriented by the red planet and its diversity of terrain and inhabitants—various forms of rational life related in a harmonious hierarchy. The inhabitants—sorns* (or, more properly, seroni), hrossa,* and pfifltriggi*—turn out to be civilised and amiable. Ransom, as a linguist, is soon able to pick up the rudiments of their language, Old Solar.* Because of their expectations about the mental level and sensibility of the Malacandrians, however, Weston and Devine only achieve a toehold in the language —leading at times to hilarious effects.

They cannot see the comic contrast between English and the alien language form, which is unable to disguise true meaning.* Weston addresses the Oyarsa* or ruler of Malacandra in the arrogant language of his 'scientific' religion of survival, and Ransom interprets for him. Only, in translation, the effect is not what Weston intended:

'She—' began Weston.

'I'm sorry,' interrupted Ransom, 'but I've forgotten who She is.'

'Life, of course,' snapped Weston. 'She has ruthlessly broken down all obstacles and liquidated all failures and today in her highest form—civilized man—and in me as her representative, she presses forward to that inter-planetary leap which will, perhaps, place her forever beyond the reach of death.'

'He says,' resumed Ransom, 'that these animals learned to do many difficult things, except those who could not; and those ones died and the other animals did not pity them. And he says the best animal now is the kind of man who makes the big huts and carries the heavy weights and does all the other things I told you about; and he is one of these and he says that if the others all knew what he was doing they would be pleased. He says that if he could kill you all and bring our people to live in Malacandra, then they might be able to go on living here after something had gone wrong with our world. And then if something went wrong with Malacandra they might go and kill all the *hnau* in another world. And then another—and so they would never die out.'

Who, or what, is this Oyarsa that Weston addressed? In *Out of the Silent Planet*, C.S. Lewis imaginatively recreates the medieval picture of the cosmos he later set out in his book, *The Discarded Image*.★ In Deep Heaven, the planets are guided by spiritual intelligences, or Oyarsa, who, with the exception of the one concerned with earth, are obedient to Maleldil the Young,★ their mysterious master. Our planet is the Silent Planet, Thulcandra, because it is cut off from the courtesy and order of Deep Heaven by a primeval disobedience.

C.S. Lewis was angry with the science fiction of his time, which invariably portrayed extra-terrestrial beings as evil, as the enemies of mankind. The medieval picture was exactly the reverse, and this appealed to C.S. Lewis. His reversal of the trend of SF had a profound impact which has lasted to this day.

Half humorously, Lewis complained in a letter in 1939: 'You will be both grieved and amused to hear that out of about 60 reviews only two showed any knowledge that my idea of the fall of the Bent One was anything but an invention of my own . . . any amount of theology can now be smuggled into people's minds under the cover of romance without their knowing it.'

This sort of response to *Out of the Silent Planet* was one of the things which made C.S. Lewis realise that he might have something to offer in theological and ethical writing on a broad front.

In her study, *Voyages to the Moon* (1948), Marjorie Hope Nicolson paid this tribute: '*Out of the Silent Planet* is to me the most beautiful of all cosmic voyages and in some ways the most moving. ... As C.S. Lewis, the Christian apologist, has added something to the long tradition, so C.S. Lewis, the scholar–poet, has achieved an effect in *Out of the Silent Planet* different from anything in the past. Earlier writers have created new worlds from legend, from mythology, from fairy tale. Mr Lewis has created *myth* itself, myth woven of desire and aspirations deep-seated in some, at least, of the human race. ... As I journey with him into worlds at once familiar and strange, I experience, as did Ransom, "a sensation not of following an adventure but of enacting a myth".'

Oxford   City and county town of Oxfordshire, England. It was C.S. Lewis' home from immediately after the Great War until his death in 1963.

Oxford is located at the meeting of the rivers Thames and Cherwell, about fifty miles north-west of London. Its importance as early as the tenth century is evident from its mention in the *Anglo-Saxon Chronicle* for 912.

Before World War I Oxford was known as a university city and market town. Then printing was its only major industry. Between the wars, however, the Oxford motor industry grew rapidly.

University teaching has been carried on at Oxford since the early years of the twelfth century, perhaps as a result of students migrating from Paris. The university's fame quickly grew, until by the fourteenth century it rivalled any in Europe.

University College, where C.S. Lewis was an undergraduate, is its oldest college, founded in 1249. Erasmus lectured at Oxford, and Grocyn, Colet, and More were some of its great scholars in the fifteenth and sixteenth centuries. Other Oxford scholars beside C.S. Lewis who entered wonderland were Charles Dodgson (Lewis Carroll) and J.R.R. Tolkien.★

C.S. Lewis taught philosophy for one year at University College during the absence of its tutor, then, in 1925, he was elected Fellow and Tutor in English Language and Literature at Magdalen College. He remained there until his appointment to the Chair of Medieval and Renaissance Literature at Cambridge in 1954.

During most of C.S. Lewis' life in Oxford he lived at The Kilns, on the outskirts of Oxford, at Headington. Originally this was isolated, but is now surrounded by a housing estate, where a street is named after him.

Oxford University Socratic Club (1941–72) A club set up by Miss Stella Aldwinckle to discuss questions about Christian faith raised by atheists, agnostics, and those disillusioned about religion. C.S. Lewis accepted her invitation to be its first President, a position he held until 1954, when he went to Cambridge. Its committee scoured the pages of *Who's Who* to find intelligent atheists who had the time or the zeal to come and present their creed. Leading Christian thinkers also were main speakers. C.S. Lewis himself took this position on eleven occasions. As President, Lewis usually was expected to provide a rejoinder to the speaker. Lead speakers included Charles Williams,★ D.M. MacKinnon, Austin Farrer,★ J.Z. Young, C.E.M. Joad, P.D. Medawar, H.H. Price, C.H. Waddington, A.J. Ayer, J.D. Bernal, A.G.N. Flew, J. Bronowski, Basil Mitchell, R.M. Hare, A. Rendle Short, I.T. Ramsey, Iris Murdoch, Gilbert Ryle, Michael Polanyi,

J.L. Austin, H.J. Blackham, Michael Dummett, E. Evans-Pritchard, Dorothy L. Sayers,★ and other outstanding thinkers from different academic disciplines.

Oyarsa *See* ELDILA.

P

Mr Papworth C.S. Lewis' black, curly-haired mongrel, mainly a terrier. He was also known as Tykes, Baron Papworth and Pat. He died in 1937.

Parliament of Owls In *The Silver Chair*,★ a meeting of owls. Jill Pole★ and Eustace Scrubb★ are carried to it on the back of Glimfeather.★ Lewis is probably playing with the title of Chaucer's *The Parliament of Fowls*.

Passarids In *Prince Caspian*,★ a house of Lords under Caspian★ IX. When the usurper, Miraz★ took over, they were sent to their death to fight giants to the north of Narnia.★

Pattertwig In *Prince Caspian*,★ a magnificent talking red squirrel, the size of a terrier. He is a loyal Old Narnian met by the runaway Caspian.★

Pavender A beautiful, rainbow-coloured fish found in Narnia★ which provides an excellent meal.

Peepicheek In *Prince Caspian*,★ one of Reepicheek's band of talking mice.

Penelope, Sister (b 1890) A friend of C.S. Lewis' of the Anglican Community of St Mary the Virgin at Wantage. He corresponded extensively with her. Some of this correspondence is preserved in *Letters of C.S. Lewis*.★ *Perelandra*★ is dedicated to Sister Penelope and her colleagues: 'To some ladies at Wantage.' There is a story that in one translation this dedication reads: 'To some wanton ladies.'

Perelandra (Voyage to Venus) (1943) This, the second

156

volume of Lewis' science fiction trilogy, is set on the planet Perelandra (Venus), a paradisal, oceanic world of floating islands as well as fixed lands. Dr Elwin Ransom★ is transported there to rebuff the attacks of the forces of evil incarnate in the human form of his old enemy, Weston.★ Perelandra, Ransom discovers, has its own, green-fleshed equivalent of Adam and Eve. The setting is visionary and beautifully realised. The unfallen ecology of Perelandra, which includes the communion between the Green Lady and her husband and the animal and fish life of the planet, is intended to contrast with the havoc of sin upon our world. Perelandra presents a forceful and inspiring image of perfection, where natural and spiritual are one.

While World War II rages, Ransom is taken in a casket to Perelandra by the great Oyarsa★ or unseen ruler of Malacandra★ (Mars), with whom he had become acquainted in his previous adventure in space. He is away for a whole year. On his return he recounts what happened to his friends C.S. Lewis and Dr 'Humphrey' Havard,★ an account which forms the basis of Lewis' book.

After dropping through the Venusian atmosphere, Ransom found himself in a 'delicious coolness. . . . He was riding the foamless swell of an ocean, fresh and cool after the fierce temperatures of Heaven, but warm by earthly standards—as warm as a shallow bay with sandy bottom in a sub-tropical climate. As he rushed smoothly up the great convex hillside of the next wave he got a mouthful of the water. It was hardly at all flavoured with salt; it was drinkable—like fresh water and only, by an infinitesimal degree, less insipid. Though he had not been aware of thirst till now, his drink gave him a quite astonishing pleasure. It was almost like meeting Pleasure itself for the first time.' He was in fact in paradise, brilliantly evoked by Lewis' descriptions.

One fascinating feature of Perelandra is its floating islands, which follow the contours of the sea, as hills become valleys in a constant metamorphosis. Many of the dramatic events of the story take place on the islands. In contrast are the fixed lands, upon which the newly created green humans of the planet are as yet forbidden to dwell. This command forms the basis of a re-enactment of the temptation of Eve. There are differences, however, not least as a result of the sacrifice of Maleldil the Young★ on Thulcandra (earth). Ransom plays a key part, much to his surprise, in frustrating the devilish plans of the bent Oyarsa of earth to corrupt the unspoiled world.

On one of the floating islands Ransom encounters the beautiful Green Lady and her constant animal companions, including a small dragon with scales of red gold. She was 'green like the beautifully coloured green beetle in an English garden'. She was like 'a goddess carved apparently out of green stone, yet alive'. As Ransom often found happening, what was myth★ in our world could be fact in others. When she started laughing uncontrollably at his strange appearance he realised that she was fully human.

An unwelcome visitor in a conventional spacecraft arrived in the form of Professor Weston, who lost no time in engaging the Green Lady in complex and subtle arguments, designed to wear down her resistance to the temptation to disobey the command not to live on the fixed lands. Ransom intervenes with counter-argument, but, unlike the possessed scientist, suffers the disadvantage of sleeping from sheer exhaustion. Eventually Ransom realises, to his dismay, that he must engage Weston in a physical fight to the death. Weston, given over to Satan, is now an 'Un-man'. In the bitter struggle, Ransom receives an unhealable wound to his heel.

The story climaxes in a vision of the 'Great Dance' of

the universe, in which all patterns of human and other life interweave. 'Then, at the very zenith of complexity, complexity was eaten up and faded, as a thin white cloud fades into the hard blue burning of the sky, and a simplicity beyond all comprehension, ancient and young as spring, illimitable, pellucid, drew him with cords of infinite desire into its own stillness.' As so often in C.S. Lewis' writings, the theme of joy★ is embodied.

The arguments over the nature of obedience and goodness and evil were pursued further by Lewis in his brilliant study, *The Problem of Pain,*★ published three years earlier. They relate also to Lewis' views on warfare; why he found it impossible to be a pacifist. He continued his exploration of evil in *That Hideous Strength,*★ set several years later.

Just as his sequel, *That Hideous Strength*, is paralleled by Lewis' study, *The Abolition of Man,*★ *Perelandra* is complemented by *A Preface to Paradise Lost.*★ This is his study of John Milton's great epic poem, dealing with the fall of mankind, and key themes such as hierarchy. *Perelandra* portrays the imaginative splendour of Milton's themes in a way designed to bewitch the twentieth-century reader, bypassing our prejudice against the past—what Lewis dubbed our 'chronological snobbery'.★

Peridan In *The Horse and His Boy,*★ one of the Lords and Advisors of Queen Susan★ and Kind Edmund★ in Tashbaan.★ Later, he leads a charge in battle against the army of Rabadash★ the Calormene.★

***The Personal Heresy: A Controversy* (1939)** Jointly authored with E.M.W. Tillyard, a Cambridge literary critic. C.S. Lewis contributed Chapters I, III, and V, and a concluding note, and E.M.W. Tillyard contributed Chapters II, IV, and VI, giving an opposing point of view.

C.S. Lewis argues against the view that poetry provides biographical information about the poet, and that it is necessary to know about the poet to understand the poem. He focuses on the intrinsic character of a work of literature, rather than extrinsic factors. In reading a poem we look through the poet, rather than at him or her. We see with his or her eyes. We can only see if we do not dwell on the particulars of his or her consciousness. Rather, we indwell them as we attend to a new level of meaning.* The poet's consciousness is a condition of our knowledge, not the knowledge itself.

Lewis' analysis bears remarkable similarities to the insights of Michael Polanyi, who was concerned with the structure of consciousness and the way we participate in knowledge.

This passage from *The Personal Heresy* is characteristic:

> Let it be granted that I do approach the poet; at least I do it by sharing his consciousness, not by studying it. I look with his eyes, not at him. . . . To see things as the poet sees them I must share his consciousness and not attend to it; I must look where he looks and not turn round to face him; I must make of him not a spectacle but a pair of spectacles: in fine, as Professor Alexander would say, I must *enjoy* him and not *contemplate* him.

C.S. Lewis' position here has implications for all the arts (as his late work, *An Experiment in Criticism*,* makes clear). As I understand it, he is saying that art takes us into meanings not normally perceived by us, and perceivable only through the actual arrangement of the artwork. We are reaching meanings which were not accessible to us before the making of the artwork, but which are now available to both the artist and the reader, viewer, or audience. C.S. Lewis claimed, 'If we mean something, we do not mean alone.' His Christian view of the world was that it was full of meaning rather than meaningless (or strictly absurd). An artistic arrangement *means* as part of that world. It follows that artistic value has the value that any part of the world has; but its *special* value for us is that our sense of meaning, our perception, is enlarged. We see with larger eyes than merely our own. Lewis would reiterate the poet Shelley's view, in his brilliant *Defence of Poetry*, that imagination allows us to see quantities as qualities, and to perceive what we know.

See also LITERARY CRITIC, C.S. LEWIS AS A; TRANSPOSITION.

Peter, High King *See* PEVENSIE, PETER, SUSAN, EDMUND AND LUCY.

Pevensie, Peter, Susan, Edmund and Lucy The four brothers and sisters, evacuees from wartime London, who enter Narnia★ in *The Lion, the Witch and the Wardrobe*★ and become Kings and Queens there. Peter, as eldest, is the High King during Narnia's Golden Age (echoes of the biblical St Peter). Edmund had for a time been traitor, but had repented and been restored by the sacrifice of Aslan★ on the Stone Table.★ The children return again to Narnia as told in *Prince Caspian.*★ After that, however, only the two youngest, Edmund and Lucy, are allowed to return, with their cousin Eustace Scrubb,★ in the tale of *The Voyage of the 'Dawn Treader'.*★ While they are enjoying this adventure, Peter is being tutored for an exam by Professor Kirke,★ and Susan has gone to America with her parents for Mr Pevensie's lecture tour.

The Pevensie children, with the exception of Susan, who is no longer a friend of Narnia, return to Narnia after a train crash in the apocalyptic final story, *The Last Battle.*★

Lucy is often the favourite character with young readers of *The Chronicles of Narnia.*★ As Martha C. Sammons puts it: 'Lucy is one of the most clearly depicted characters in all the Narnia books. . . . Lucy seems to be spiritually closer to Aslan than anyone else, and they seem to share a special relationship of love!' Lucy's response to Aslan,★ such as hugging him, is one of the secrets of the lion's success as an imaginative creation. C.S. Lewis achieves a figure of authority, the creator and true sovereign of Narnia, who is eminently approachable by the innocent and good. Those also, like Edmund and later Eustace, who approach him in fear and repentance, find a friend like no other.

Pfifltriggi In *Out of the Silent Planet*,★ one of three intelligent kinds of being on Malacandra.★ These frog-like creatures were the crafts people and engineers of the planet. They were expert in digging Malacandra's abundant gold and making artistic objects from it. They also recorded the history and mythology of their planet on monoliths at Meldilorn.★

Phars In *Till We Have Faces*,★ a kingdom neighbouring Glome.★ After the marriage of King Trunia★ of Phars with Princess Redival★ of Glome the two countries enter an alliance, forcing Essur,★ to the west of Phars, to stay at peace with the two kingdoms.

Phoenix In *The Magician's Nephew*,★ a bird, larger than an eagle, sitting in a tree in the centre of Aslan's garden. The phoenix is a traditional symbol of rebirth and immortality because of its resurrection from the ashes.

The Pilgrim's Regress: An Allegorical Apology for Christianity, Reason and Romanticism (1933; new edition 1943) C.S. Lewis was researching the method of allegorical story-telling for his study, *The Allegory of Love*,★ when he wrote this book. In fictional and more general form, it covers the ground of his later account of his life up to his conversion, *Surprised by Joy*.★ He wrote it during a fortnight's holiday in Ireland.

Twenty years after writing *The Pilgrim's Regress*, Lewis admitted in a letter to a lady: 'I don't wonder that you got fogged in *The Pilgrim's Regress*. It was my first religious book and I didn't then know how to make things easy. I was not even trying to very much, because in those days I never dreamed I would become a "popular" author. . . .'

The Pilgrim's Regress is an intellectual, early twentieth-century version of John Bunyan's great allegory. Instead of Christian, the central figure is John, loosely based on C.S. Lewis himself. Like *The Pilgrim's Progress*, the quest can be mapped. Indeed, Lewis provides his reader with a *Mappa Mundi*, in which the human soul is divided into north and south, the north representing arid intellectualism and the south emotional excess. A straight road passes between them. Needless to say, John's route strays far off the straight and narrow. Like the young Lewis, he tends towards intellectual rather than sensual follies. The story gives a vivid picture of the intellectual climate of the 1920s and early 30s.

John's way is a *regress* rather than a *progress* because he in fact is going away from rather than towards the beautiful island that he seeks. The island is Lewis' equivalent to the Celestial City of Bunyan. When he gains the knowledge of how to achieve his island, through Mother Kirk, he has to retrace his steps.

John's quest for the island is a fine embodiment of the theme of joy★ which is so central in Lewis' auto-biography, *Surprised by Joy*. The quest helps John to avoid the various snares and dangers he encounters.

Born in Puritania, John early was taught to fear the Landlord of the country. From the first moment, however, that he glimpsed the island in a vision he was gripped with an intense longing to find it.

On his journey he encounters characters like Mr Enlightenment from the city of Claptrap, Mr Vertue, who becomes John's companion, and Media Halfways, from the city of Thrill. Later, John is imprisoned by the Spirit of the Age, and rescued by the tall, blue–clad figure of Reason. She teaches him many things and directs him back to the main road.

Upon finding the road abruptly cut off by a vast canyon, John at first refuses the help of Mother Kirk, and has many adventures as he looks for a way down, first to the north and then to the south of the main road. After becoming lost, and calling for help, John is aided by the hermit History and then by Reason once more. He finds Vertue in the presence of Mother Kirk, and both follow her guidance and reach the other side of the canyon. From here John can see the sea, and his island. The two are given a guide to lead them back across the world, for the island, in fact, is the other side of the mountains near Puritania, not an island at all. John's idea of the Landlord has turned out to be false, and the home of the Landlord in those mountains is to be John's as well.

In Lewis' new edition of *The Pilgrim's Regress* he provided a detailed foreword and notes to the chapters to help his readers with the obscurer points of the allegory. It is best to enjoy the book as a story and not be too concerned with the meaning of every allusion. Read as a quest for joy, and in parallel with *Surprised by Joy*, it yields its main meanings. Clyde S. Kilby's study, *Images of Salvation in the Fiction of C.S. Lewis* (1978), provides help with interpretation of the allegory, including its frequent classical references.

Pittencream   In *The Voyage of the 'Dawn Treader'*,★ the sailor left behind at Ramandu's Island★ who eventually went to live in Calormen.★

The planets   In the science fiction trilogy *(Out of the Silent Planet,★ Perelandra,★ and That Hideous Strength★)* the true names of the planets are revealed. These names are in the tongue of Old Solar,★ spoken before the fall of mankind and beyond the moon's orbit.

The sun is properly called *Arbol*, Mercury *Viritrilbia*,

Venus *Perelandra*, Earth *Tellus* or *Thulcandra* (the Silent Planet), Mars *Malacandra*, Jupiter *Glundandra*, and Saturn *Lurga*. *Handra* in Old Solar means 'world'.

Plato A famous Greek philosopher, born about 427 BC in Athens, much admired by C.S. Lewis. He founded idealism* in philosophy. His work provided much imaginative inspiration for C.S. Lewis, though he was not a platonist. Some forms of platonism were deeply influential during the medieval period, which was C.S. Lewis' great love, and which was the object of much of his scholarship. Different aspects of Plato's thought have been emphasised at different periods of Western history, such as his view of existence, or his theory of how we know truth. Belief in the immortality of the soul, as held by C.S. Lewis and the Christian tradition, is not in itself Platonism, nor is imaginative use of the platonic idea of this world as a copy of a more real one. In his essay, *Transposition*,* C.S. Lewis gives a Christian, non-dualistic account of the relationship between spiritual and natural reality.

See also GOD; NATURE; THEOLOGY OF ROMANCE.

Platonism *See* PLATO.

Plummer, Polly Digory Kirke's* next-door friend in Edwardian London, who is drawn with him into other worlds, and eventually Narnia,* in *The Magician's Nephew*.*

***Poems* (1964)** This volume contains most of C.S. Lewis' lyrical verse, with the exception of the early cycle of poems entitled *Spirits in Bondage*,* They reveal a great variety of themes, including 'Narnian Suite', which is in two parts—'a march for strings, kettledrums, and sixty-three dwarfs' and a 'march for drum, trumpet, and twenty-one giants'.

See also *NARRATIVE POEMS*.

Pole, Jill A fellow sufferer with Eustace Scrubb★ at
Experiment House,★ who is taken into Narnia with him
on two occasions to help in time of need. The stories are
told in *The Silver Chair*★ and *The Last Battle*.★

Prayer *See LETTERS TO MALCOLM.*

A Preface to Paradise Lost **(1942)** *Paradise Lost* is John
Milton's great epic, and C.S. Lewis believed that most
recent Milton scholarship had hindered rather than helped
a proper reading of the poem. Following the lead given by
his friend Charles Williams★ in his short preface to an
edition of Milton's poetical works, Lewis attempted
'mainly "to hinder hindrances" to the appreciation of
Paradise Lost.' He defended the epic form of literature that
Milton chose to use, arguing that it had a right to exist, as
does ritual, splendour and joy★ itself. Lewis argued that he
differed from the critics of Milton not over the nature of
his poetry, but over the nature of mankind and even of joy
itself. Qualities that he (and Milton) regard as virtues, the
critics blame him for. Lewis complains: 'It reminds us of
Aristotle's question—if water itself sticks in a man's
throat, what will you give him to wash it down with? If a
man blames port wine for being strong and sweet, or a
woman's arms for being white and smooth and round, or
the sun for shining, or sleep because it puts thought away,
how can we answer him?'

See also LITERARY CRITIC, C.S. LEWIS AS A;
PERELANDRA.

Preston, Marjorie In *The Voyage of the 'Dawn Treader'*,★ a
friend of Lucy Pevensie★ whom she overhears talking
about her to another girl through a spell in Coriakin★ the
magician's book.

Prince Caspian **(1951)** A year after their first adventure in
Narnia,★ the four Pevensie★ children are drawn back to
help Caspian,★ the true heir to the throne, whose life is
in danger from the tyrant, Miraz,★ who holds control

over Narnia. He has suppressed the Old Narnians who remained loyal to the ancient memory of Aslan* and Narnia's long-ago Golden Age, when the children had been Kings and Queens at Cair Paravel.*

This story reveals much about the history of Narnia, the rule of humans over the talking animals,* and the Telmarines* who had stumbled into Narnia long before from our world.

See also NARNIA: History.

The Problem of Pain (1940)   C.S. Lewis' purpose in writing this book was to 'solve the intellectual problem raised by suffering'. He had never felt himself qualified 'for the far higher task of teaching fortitude and patience'. In this respect, he said that he had nothing to offer his readers 'except my conviction that when pain is to be borne, a little courage helps more than much knowledge, a little human sympathy more than much courage, and the least tincture of the love of God more than all'. Years later he was able to offer more. After his wife, Joy Davidman,* died he recorded his reactions and reflections in *A Grief Observed.**

For such a small book, Lewis ranged far and wide, discussing God's control over all human events, including suffering, the goodness of God,* human wickedness, the fall of mankind, human pain, hell, animal pain, and heaven.* He took up similar themes in imaginative form in his science-fiction story, *Perelandra.** Austin Farrer* comments that Lewis presents 'a world haunted by the supernatural, a conscience haunted by the moral absolute, a history haunted by the divine claim of Christ'.

The Problem of Pain, like *Miracles,** is among the best of C.S. Lewis' theological writings, and, though a work of popular theology, is a key text in philosophy of religion. It contains fine passages on heaven, joy,* hell, and the sense of the numinous which is present in so much of Lewis'

fiction. It argues from the starting-point of God's relationship to the universe that he has made, and is uncom-
promising in its supernaturalism.★ It also reveals Lewis'
position when he was an atheist, and why he finds such a
position untenable.

The Dutch title of the book is *God's Megaphone*, taken
from Lewis' memorable claim: 'God whispers to us in our
pleasures, speaks in our conscience, but shouts in our
pains: it is His megaphone to rouse a deaf world.'

Prunaprismia In *Prince Caspian,*★ the red-haired wife of
Caspian's★ uncle, the usurper Miraz.★

Psyche A character whose name means the soul, from
Apuleius' *Golden Ass*, upon which C.S. Lewis based his
character of the same name in his novel, *Till We Have
Faces.*★ In Apuleius' story, Psyche is so beautiful that
Venus becomes jealous of her. Cupid, sent by Venus to
make Psyche fall in love with an ugly creature, himself
falls in love with her. After bringing her to a palace, he
only visited her in the dark, and forbade her to see his face.
Out of jealousy, Psyche's sisters told her that her lover
was a monster who would devour her. She took a lamp
one night and looked at Cupid's face, but a drop of oil
awoke him. In anger, the god left her. Psyche sought her
lover throughout the world. Venus set her various
impossible tasks, all of which she accomplished, except
the last, when curiosity made her open a deadly casket
from the Underworld. At last, however, she was allowed
to marry Cupid.

In *Till We Have Faces,*★ C.S. Lewis essentially follows
the classical myth, but retells it through the narration of
Orual,★ Psyche's sister, who seeks to defend her actions to
the gods as being the result of deep love for Psyche, not
jealousy.

Psyche's palace In *Till We Have Face,*★ the palace of the
god of the Grey Mountains★ in which Princess Psyche★

dwelt after her marriage. It could not normally be seen by mortal eyes, though Orual★ glimpsed it in the swirling mist. As a child, Psyche had dreamed of living in a gold-and-amber castle, married to the 'greatest king of all'. When Orual glimpsed the palace she saw 'wall within wall, pillar and arch and architrave, acres of it, a labyrinthine beauty'. It was like no house she had ever seen. Pinnacles and buttresses seemed to be springing up. They were unimaginably tall and slender, looking as if stone were shooting out into branch and flower.

Puddleglum the Marshwiggle   In *The Silver Chair*,★ the companion of Jill Pole★ and Eustace Scrubb★ in their quest for the lost Prince Rilian.★ He is one of C.S. Lewis' most memorable Narnian creations. Puddleglum is delightfully pessimistic, though never cynical or disloyal to Aslan.★ He is tall and angular, with webbed hands and feet as befits a marshy existence. His character owed something to Lewis' gardener at The Kilns, Fred Paxford.

Puzzle the Ass   A simple donkey duped by Shift★ the Ape into dressing in a lion skin and pretending to be Aslan★ in *The Last Battle*.★

R

Rabadash, Prince   Also called 'The Ridiculous'. In *The Horse and His Boy*,★ the vain Calormene★ Prince who, after being rejected by Queen Susan,★ attempts to conquer Archenland★ and Narnia★ during the reign of High King Peter★ and the other children. After the battle at Anvard★ he is left dangling from a wall-hook. Later he is temporarily turned into a donkey by Aslan.★

Ram the Great   According to *The Horse and His Boy*,★ the popular Narnian tale, he becomes King of Archenland.★ He is the son of Cor★ and Aravis.★

Ramandu   In *The Voyage of the 'Dawn Treader'*,★ a retired star, resplendent in silver clothes, who lives near Aslan's Table on World's End Island,★ far across the Eastern Ocean.★ The voyagers in the *Dawn Treader* encountered him on their way towards Aslan's Country.★ King Caspian★ later married Ramandu's daughter.

Ramandu is undergoing renewal until he once more can return to the skies. The stars of Narnia and its world are not made up of flaming gas but of glimmering people with silver clothes and hair. Ramandu had been brought down to World's End Island when old and fading. The birds each day would bring him a fire berry from the valleys of the sun. These berries were restoring him.

Ramandu's daughter   In *The Voyage of the 'Dawn Treader'*★ the travellers met Ramandu★ and his daughter on World's End Island.★ Later King Caspian★ married her. In the adventure of *The Silver Chair*★ we learn that, one day, many years later, while she was sleeping, she was slain by the Green Witch* in the form of a green serpent. It was while Prince Rilian* was seeking his revenge for his mother's murder that he was bewitched by the Green Witch.

Ransom, Dr Elwin (b 1898?) Hero of C.S. Lewis' science fiction trilogy, later renamed the Fisher King, and partially modelled on J.R.R. Tolkien* and Owen Barfield.* He was a philologist of Cambridge University. Much like C.S. Lewis he had a war wound, and was a 'sedentary scholar'. One of his publications was *Dialect and Semantics*. He was a bachelor who found swimming the only sport he excelled in (a skill which proved useful in watery Perelandra*). Ransom was also an anti-vivisectionist. He combined intellectual and heroic qualities, though he tended to put himself down. Clyde S. Kilby pointed out that Ransom speaks like Lewis himself.

In *Out of the Silent Planet*,* Ransom is kidnapped to the planet Malacandra* (Mars), enabling him to learn Old Solar,* the Great Tongue, and discover the nature of life outside of quarantined planet Earth. On his return he spends three months in hospital recuperating. (It may have been in this period that Lewis described him, in *The Dark Tower*,* as a pale man with grey, distressed-looking eyes.) In *Perelandra* he is transported by the Oyarsa* or ruler of Mars to the planet Venus (Perelandra) to foil a satanic plot against a new Adam and Eve in that paradisal world. Here he suffers a debilitating wound to the heel.

In *That Hideous Strength*,* Ransom is revealed as the latest in the succession of Pendragons of Logres, withdrawn from Cambridge to secretly run a community at St Anne's.* This community is what is left of Logres, the true Britain, and is pitted against the demonic forces of the N.I.C.E.* He may have found The Manor at St Anne's on one of his walking tours—he originally had a country cottage in Worchester. After the routing of the N.I.C.E., Ransom is permitted the rare honour of returning for ever to Perelandra, the Third Heaven, and now dwells with King Arthur and others in Aphallin.★

Elwin Ransom is tall, slightly-built, golden-haired, but a little round-shouldered and weak-eyed, aged about thirty-five to forty in the late 1930s when the events of *Out of the Silent Planet* take place. He did not have much dress sense, and, at first sight, might have been mistaken for a doctor or schoolmaster. His only relation was a married sister in India.

Lewis tells us that 'Ransom' was not (or was no longer?) his real name, though he is told by the Oyarsa that his name literally means 'ransom'. Lewis had known Dr Ransom slightly before the events of the first science fiction tale, corresponding with him on literary and philological subjects, though at that time they seldom met. They became firm friends when Ransom had the idea of asking Lewis to cast his adventures in fictional form. Lewis regarded him as sane, wholesome and honest. We may speculate that some of their conversations and correspondence form the basis of C.S. Lewis' book, *Studies in Words*.★

When Ransom returned from Perelandra after his second planetary adventure Lewis found him glowing with health, rounded with muscle, and seeming ten years younger. He thereafter retained the golden beard that he had grown. This process of rejuvination continued in the story, *That Hideous Strength*, where he at first appeared to Jane Studdock★ to be a boy of twenty, until she noticed his strength and his full beard. She was reminded of her mental picture of King Arthur or Solomon.

Redival   In *Till We Have Faces*,★ the frivolous, golden-haired sister of Orual★ and half-sister of Psyche.★ When Orual becomes Queen of Glome★ she marries Redival off

REHABILITATIONS AND OTHER ESSAYS (1939)

to Trunia★ of the neighbouring kingdom of Phars,★ to improve their alliance. Redival's son, Daaran, becomes heir of Glome's throne on the unmarried Orual's death.

Reepicheep the Mouse A brave and decorous talking mouse of Narnia★ who journeys to Aslan's Country★ in *The Voyage of the 'Dawn Treader'*.★ Mice were granted the privilege of becoming talking animals★ after gnawing through Aslan's★ cords in *The Lion, the Witch and the Wardrobe*.★ Reepicheep, the chief of the mice, is around two feet in height, wears a long crimson feather on his head, and carries a long, sharp sword. In *Prince Caspian*★ he is badly wounded, and his proud tail severed. Lucy★ is able to heal him, and Aslan restores his pride.

Reflections on the Psalms **(1958)** C.S. Lewis disliked the view that the Bible is literature, and could be read as such. If it is taken for what it is, those parts of it that are literature can be properly received as such. The Psalms are an important literary part of the Bible, and Lewis felt that he had something he could say about them as a layperson and literary critic. The Psalms, he considered, are great poetry, and some, such as Psalms 18 and 19, are perfect poems. Unless the Psalms are read as poetry 'we shall miss what is in them and think we see what is not'. The book is particularly good in bringing out how the Hebrews had an appetite and longing for God,★ how they appreciated his Law (which they saw as rooted into nature★ as the very structure of reality), and how they viewed nature. There are three key chapters which deal with the inspiration of Scripture and 'second meanings' within it.

See also THEOLOGY, C.S. LEWIS AND; THE BIBLE, C.S. LEWIS AND; LITERARY CRITIC, C.S. LEWIS AS A.

Rehabilitations and Other Essays **(1939)** In his preface, C.S. Lewis tells us that all the pieces in this collection are written in defence of things that he loves which have been the object of attack. The first two essays defend great romantic poets like Shelley and William Morris against 'popular hatred or neglect of Romanticism'. The third and fourth defend the present (1939) Oxford English syllabus. The fifth supports the reading of many popular books which have, he believes, greatly increased his power of enjoying more serious literature as well as what is called 'real life'. The sixth essay champions Anglo–Saxon poetry.

The full contents are as follows.

I Shelley, Dryden, and Mr. Eliot. A reasoned and powerful defence of Shelley's greatness as a poet, even judged by classical criteria. C.S. Lewis' deep sympathy for the unbeliever is strikingly evident.

II William Morris. This essay is of particular interest for a study of C.S. Lewis' fiction, for he owed a debt to William Morris.

III The Idea of an 'English School'. This piece is of historical interest, because C.S. Lewis, along with J.R.R. Tolkien,★ helped to shape the Oxford University English syllabus for many years.

IV Our English Syllabus. C.S. Lewis reveals his thoughts on the purpose of education.★

V High and Low Brows. This defence of some popular reading as being acceptable as 'good literature' anticipates the ideas which reached mature form in C.S. Lewis' *An Experiment in Criticism.*

VI The Alliterative Metre. Along with this defence of an Anglo-Saxon and Old Norse metre C.S. Lewis includes an example of his own poem employing it, 'The Planets'. In *Narrative Poems,*★ a longer example is included, 'The Nameless Isle'.

VII Bluspels and Flalansferes: a Semantic Nightmare. This is a seminal essay on the relationship between thinking and imagining, truth and meaning,★ metaphor and concept.

VIII Variation in Shakespeare and Others. An essay on Shakespeare's poetic method. He saw Shakespeare's greatness as having 'combined two species of excellence . . . the imaginative splendour of the highest type of lyric and the realistic presentation of human life and character'.
IX Christianity and Literature.★ An early attempt by C.S. Lewis to relate his faith to literature.
See also LITERARY CRITIC, C.S. LEWIS AS A.

Restimar In *The Voyage of the 'Dawn Treader'*,★ he was one of the seven Telmarine★ Lords of Caspian★ IX. The usurper, Miraz,★ had sent them away to search for new lands across the vast Eastern Ocean.★ He was found by the voyagers turned to gold in a bewitched pool on Deathwater Island.★

Revilian In *The Voyage of the 'Dawn Treader'*,★ he was one of the seven Telmarine★ Lords of Caspian★ IX. The usurper, Miraz,★ had sent them away to search for new lands across the vast Eastern Ocean.★ The travellers discovered him sleeping at Aslan's Table on World's End Island,★ along with the two other Lords, Argoz and Mavramorn.

Rhince Drinian's★ ship's mate in the tale of *The Voyage of the 'Dawn Treader'*.★

Rhindon In *The Lion, the Witch and the Wardrobe*,★ the name of the sword given to Peter Pevensie★ by Father Christmas.

Rhoop In *The Voyage of the 'Dawn Treader'*,★ he was one of the seven Telmarine★ Lords of Caspian★ IX. The usurper, Miraz,★ had sent them away to search for new lands across the vast Eastern Ocean.★ He was discovered trapped on the nightmarish Dark Island.★ Later in the voyage he was granted restful sleep at Aslan's Table★ on World's End Island.★

Rilian, Prince The son of Caspian★ X (formerly Prince Caspian). Rilian is kidnapped for ten years by the Green

Witch.★ The tale of his daring rescue by Eustace Scrubb,★ Jill Pole,★ and Puddleglum★ the Marshwiggle★ is told in *The Silver Chair.*★

Rishda In *The Last Battle,*★ a Calormene★ captain who assists Shift the Ape★ and Ginger the Cat★ against King Tirian.★ His fate is to be carried away by Tash, the demon god of Calormen.

Romanticism C.S. Lewis wished for the word 'romantic' to be banned as it now had so many usages as to be virtually useless. He failed to find another term, however, to characterise the central preoccupation he shared with his friends J.R.R. Tolkien★ and Charles Williams,★ or kindred spirits like G.K. Chesterton★ and his mentor, George MacDonald.★

He tells us in his preface to the third edition of *The Pilgrim's Regress*★ that when he wrote that book in the early 1930s, he meant 'romanticism' to mean the special experience of inconsolable longing, or joy.★ He certainly was not in revolt against reason or classicism, which romanticism is sometimes taken to mean. He was not a subjectivist, seeing art as the expression of its maker's soul.

In English literature, the Romantic Movement is often taken to begin with the publication of *Lyrical Ballads* in 1798 by Wordsworth and Coleridge. This was part of a wide reaction against deism and a mechanistic view of nature and mankind. Romanticism gave rise to the Gothic genre, and its offspring, Mary Shelley's remarkable *Frankenstein* (1818) and the rise of science fiction. It also created a vogue for historical romance, as in the novels of Sir Walter Scott. In Germany, Romanticism was connected with the rise of modernist theology, in reaction to rationalism. George MacDonald's rejection of his native Calvinism was part of the same trend.

The subjective link between different aspects of

romanticism, as far as C. S. Lewis and The Inklings★ were concerned, is a preoccupation with the imagination and creative fantasy. This linking thread can be seen in all the main influences upon C. S. Lewis. Indeed, a brief outline of these influences is the best way of characterising the romanticism of C. S. Lewis.

'Romantic' influences upon C.S. Lewis can, for convenience, be divided into four areas: (1) ancient mythologies; (2) older writers; (3) nineteenth-century authors; and (4) contemporary sources. These influences are mentioned by C.S. Lewis, or come through friends and acquaintances like J.R.R. Tolkien, Charles Williams, Dorothy L. Sayers,★ or from his mentor, George MacDonald. Very often, sources are sources of sources, a fact which can provide hours of fun for a literary student.

(1) *Ancient mythologies.* Old Norse mythology deeply influenced Tolkien's fantasies, and affects some features of Lewis' Narnia★ stories. Lewis drew more upon classical mythology, most notably in *Till We Have Faces*★ and in characters such as Mr Tumnus★ in Narnia. Lewis mentions his great love of Irish mythology. Welsh and British mythology—especially 'The matter of Britain' and Merlin★—is found in *That Hideous Strength.*★ Lewis believed that scattered among pagan myths there are certain 'good stories' which prefigure Christian truth. They anticipate and give form to adequate vehicles of truth (*see* MYTH).

(2) *Older writers.* The main sources seem to be the author of *Beowulf* (especially with Tolkien), Dante (particularly with Williams), and Milton, whose influence on *Perelandra*★ is marked. Milton is probably an important root of the science fiction genre, of which, according to Brian Aldiss, C.S. Lewis is an important part. John Bunyan and earlier medieval allegorists deeply influenced C.S. Lewis also. Edmund Spenser was one of Lewis' favourite authors.

(3) *Nineteenth-century writers*. Most important of writers from this period was George MacDonald. MacDonald in turn confesses a debt to the German romanticism of Novalis and others. C.S. Lewis' concept of joy★ or *sehnsucht* is found in German romanticism. (He also discusses the ideas of Rudolf Otto on the numinous in *The Problem of Pain*,★ and seeks to embody that quality in his fantasies, for example in Aslan's Country.★)

C.S. Lewis points out that William Morris (1834–96) influenced his work. While an undergraduate at Oxford,★ C.S. Lewis gave a paper on Morris to *The Martlets*, a university society. Here he compared Morris to Homer and Thomas Malory, but, the minute book records, 'the general sense of the Society was that too high a position had been claimed' for the writer. Lewis later wrote (the piece can be found in *Selected Literary Essays*) that Morris 'seems to retire far from the real world and to build a world out of his wishes; but when he has finished the result stands out as a picture of experience ineluctably true'.

(4) *Contemporary writers*. A number of influences on his work are mentioned by C.S. Lewis, including James Stephens, G.K. Chesterton (his thought, not so much his fiction), E.R. Eddison and David Lindsay.★

Both C.S. Lewis and J.R.R. Tolkien considered E.R. Eddison (1882–1945) an important writer, and he was much discussed by The Inklings. Tolkien disliked his invented names; he felt that they lacked colour and conviction. Eddison's geography of his imaginary three kingdoms—Rerek, Meszria and Fingiswold—bears a superficial resemblance to the geography of Tolkien's Middle-earth. Eddison was appreciated for his attempts at sub-creation.★

The Inklings themselves influenced C.S. Lewis, particularly Tolkien, Charles Williams and Owen Barfield.★

See also THEOLOGY OF ROMANCE; LITERARY CRITIC, C.S. LEWIS AS A; MYTH; MEANING AND IMAGINATION.

Roonwit In *The Last Battle*,★ a great and golden-bearded centaur. He reads of danger in the stars over Narnia★ and warns King Tirian.★ He is slain by a Calormene★ arrow.

For readers interested to learn more of centaurs, Robert Siegal's story, *Alpha Centauri*, is worth reading. Centaurs originate in Greek mythology. The upper part of their bodies is human; the remainder is composed of the body and legs of a horse.

Rumblebuffin In *The Lion, the Witch and the Wardrobe*,★ the giant who assists in the fight against the White Witch.★ In attempting to borrow a handkerchief from Lucy,★ he picked her up by mistake. The giant was a member of the respected Buffin family, a family not very clever, but old and with traditions.

Rush River In *Prince Caspian*,★ we are told that it joins the Great River★ at Beruna.★

See also NARNIA: Geography.

Rynelf In *The Voyage of the 'Dawn Treader'*,★ a sailor on the galleon.

S

Sacramental theology *See* TRANSPOSITION.

St Anne's The country house in *That Hideous Strength*★ in which Dr Elwin Ransom★ formed a community in opposition to the sinister N.I.C.E.,★ and which represented the spiritual Britain (Logres), the remnant of Atlantis.★

Salamander In *The Silver Chair*,★ salamanders dwell in Bism★ in the great river of fire. They are witty and eloquent small dragons.

Sallowpad In *The Horse and His Boy*,★ an old, wise raven who is advisor to King Edmund★ and Queen Lucy.★

Sayer, George (b 1914) A pupil and friend of C.S. Lewis' who in 1988 published a major biography of his one-time tutor, *Jack: C.S. Lewis and his times*. Lewis often stayed in his home in Malvern. George Sayer was head of the English Department at Malvern College from 1949 to 1974. When Sayer first met his tutor he was told by J.R.R. Tolkien, 'You'll never get to the bottom of him.' Sayer's biography particularly dwells on Lewis' early life, his early poetry, his relationship with Mrs Janie Moore,★ his life as a university lecturer, and his domestic life.

Sayers, Dorothy Leigh (1893–1957) Dorothy L. Sayers, best known for her detective stories about Lord Peter Wimsey, was a friend of C.S. Lewis' and later also of his wife, Joy Davidman.★ She was acquainted too with Charles Williams,★ and contributed to *Essays Presented to Charles Williams*,★ the posthumous tribute from The

Inklings.★ Her robust popular theological writings, such as *The Mind of the Maker* (1942), reveal a sharp and brilliant mind which, like those of Lewis and G.K. Chesterton,★ delighted in dogma and orthodoxy. Her series of BBC radio plays, *The Man Born to be King*, was immensely popular in wartime Britain. Towards the end of her life she discovered Dante's *The Divine Comedy*, and translated it into fresh, contemporary English (a task completed after her death by Barbara Reynolds).

C.S. Lewis wrote a panegyric to Dorothy L. Sayers which was read out at the memorial service, concluding, 'Let us thank the Author who invented her.'

Screwtape In *The Screwtape Letters*,★ and its brief sequel, *Screwtape Proposes a Toast*,★ an eminent Under-Secretary to the High Command of hell, and uncle of the junior tempter, Wormwood.★ Lewis deliberately gives Screwtape a certain, twisted eminence, in his belief that greater beings are capable of greater evil. Interestingly, Screwtape admits hell's lack of power against its Enemy, but continues to trust optimistically in its bureaucracy. Screwtape ceased to be a practising tempter in the latter half of the nineteenth century, when he was rewarded with an administrative post.

The Screwtape Letters (1942) The most direct of several books about devilry that C.S. Lewis wrote, and, of all his books, the one he found most unpleasant to compose. It gave him, he says, a sort of spiritual cramp, because of the inverse perspective of hell that it employs. The book is a comic, satirical look at perhaps the most serious subject possible, damnation. The letters first appeared in a religious journal called *The Guardian*. One reader, a country clergyman, wrote in to cancel his subscription on the grounds that much of the advice given in these letters seemed to him not only erroneous but positively diabolical.

The Screwtape Letters consists of letters of advice and warning from a senior devil prominent in the lowerarchy of hell to his nephew, Wormwood, a trainee tempter. Wormwood, fresh from the Tempters' Training College, has been assigned a young man. His task is to secure his damnation. Unfortunately for Wormwood, his client becomes a Christian. Screwtape passes on a number of useful suggestions for reclaiming the young man. These come both from his centuries of experience and from information from hell's Intelligence Department. Screwtape is also in touch with other tempters assigned to the patient's friends, acquaintances, and relations. Wormwood particularly sees great possibilities in the person of the young man's mother, who is very trying. The young man successfully avoids the pull of the inner ring★ of a smart set of people (yuppies, in today's terminology). Wormwood faces hell when, first, his patient falls in love with a Christian girl, and, second, he fails to keep the young man out of the danger of death and he is killed in an air-raid, and is for ever out of the reach of hell's clutches. Screwtape's only consolation lies in devouring his incompetent nephew.

The Screwtape Letters is one of C.S. Lewis' most popular books. C.S. Lewis' view of a personal devil comes over clearly, despite the satirical genre that he employs. Though considered by Lewis not to be among the best of his books, it stands in a long line of books concerned with angels, demons, heaven★ and hell, such as Dante's *Divine Comedy*, Milton's *Paradise Lost*, and John Macgowan's★ *Infernal Dialogues*. The novels of C.S. Lewis' pupil Harry Blamires, including *Highway to Heaven*, continue the same tradition.

Screwtape Proposes a Toast (1965) A collection of literary and theological pieces, including several reprinted from *Transposition and Other Addresses*★ and *They Asked for*

a Paper.★ It contains 'Screwtape Proposes a Toast', 'The Inner Ring',★ 'Is Theology Poetry?', 'Transposition',★ 'On Obstinacy in Belief', 'The Weight of Glory', 'Good Work and Good Works', and 'A Slip of the Tongue'.
See also THE SCREWTAPE LETTERS.

Scrubb, Eustace A cousin of the Pevensie★ children, he is drawn into Narnia,★ along with Lucy and Edmund, in *The Voyage of the 'Dawn Treader'.*★ He returns to Narnia on two occasions with Jill Pole,★ a school friend, as recounted in *The Silver Chair*★ and *The Last Battle.*★ When we first meet him he is self-centred and spoiled by the modern education he is receiving at Experiment House.★ His adventures with the travellers on the *Dawn Treader* give him a wider view of life, particularly after his experience of turning into a dragon★ on Dragon Island.★ This experience, and his undragoning by Aslan,★ provide a powerful image of sin, repentance, and Christian salvation. Unlike his cousins, Eustace is never a monarch in Narnia.

Sea girl In *The Voyage of the 'Dawn Treader'*,★ a girl seen herding fish by Lucy★ as the ship passed over the clear waters of the Last Sea before Aslan's Country.★ She and Lucy became friends simply by seeing each other, even though their worlds could never touch.
See also SEA PEOPLE.

Sea people In *The Voyage of the 'Dawn Treader'*,★ undersea people seen by Lucy★ as the ship passed over the clear waters of the Last Sea before Aslan's Country.★ They ride sea horses, wear no clothes, and have bodies the colour of old ivory, with dark purple hair. Their beautiful submarine land is made up of mountains, hills, forests and parkland. The sea people enjoy hunting, and use small fierce fish as falcons are used in our world.

Sea serpent In *The Voyage of the 'Dawn Treader'*,★ this attacks the ship after the travellers have visited Burnt Island.★

Seven Isles A group of seven small islands a few days' sailing from the coast of Narnia,★ described in *The Voyage of the 'Dawn Treader'*.★ Muil is the westernmost island, separated from Brenn by a choppy stretch of water. On Brenn, the town of Redhaven provides supplies for shipping in the area.

Seven Lords Telmarine★ Lords of Caspian★ IX. The usurper, Miraz,★ had sent them away to search for new lands in the Eastern Ocean★ during his reign, as recounted in *Prince Caspian*.★ In its sequel, the tale of *The Voyage of the 'Dawn Treader'*,★ Caspian seeks the seven missing Lords. The seven are Argoz,★ Bern,★ Mavramorn,★ Octesian,★ Restimar,★ Revilian,★ and Rhoop.★

A Severe Mercy **(1977)** This is an account of love, courtship, marriage and grief in which C.S. Lewis played an important pastoral part, mainly through letters to its author, Sheldon Vanauken. The American movingly records his romance with Jean Davis, whom he calls 'Davy', their conversion, and her subsequent early death. A key discovery of the young couple's is that God's love is stronger than their own deeply romantic love of each other. The 'shining barrier' they had erected around their love was invaded by Christ, who replaced each other as the centre of their lives. At Oxford, where they studied, C.S. Lewis and Christian friends influenced their conversion. Thereafter Lewis is both mentor and friend. After Davy's death, and though Sheldon is in America, Lewis stays close to his suffering by letter. Vanauken's book is particularly important to those for whom C.S. Lewis inspires a sacramental view of Christian faith. Such a view is exemplified well in Leanne Payne's study, *Real Presence: The Holy Spirit in the Works of C.S. Lewis* (1979, 1988, British edition 1989).

See also IDEALISM, C.S. LEWIS AND.

Shadow-brute *See* GOD OF THE GREY MOUNT-AINS.

Shadow Lands In *The Last Battle,*★ the name given to England by Aslan★ to mark its contrast to the real, new England.

Shallow Lands *See* UNDERLAND.

Shasta *See* COR.

Shift the Ape In *The Last Battle,*★ a Narnian★ talking animal★ who deceives many loyal beasts and trees into believing that Aslan★ has returned, and that Puzzle the Ass,★ draped in an ill-fitting lion skin, is he. Shift's treachery knows no boundaries, and he forms an alliance with Narnia's traditional enemy, Calormen.★

Shribble River In *The Silver Chair,*★ a river flowing from east to west near Ettinsmoor.★

The Silent Planet *See* THE PLANETS.

The Silver Chair (1953) This Narnia★ story is a sequel to *The Voyage of the 'Dawn Treader'.*★ It concerns Eustace Scrubb★ and another pupil of Experiment House,★ a 'modern school', a girl named Jill Pole.★ They are brought to Narnia by Aslan★ to search for the long-lost Prince Rilian,★ son of Caspian★ X, the Caspian of the previous adventure, now in his old age. Their search takes them into the wild lands north of Narnia, and eventually into a realm under the earth called Underland.★ The two children are accompanied by one of C.S. Lewis' most memorable creations, Puddleglum★ the Marshwiggle.★ They narrowly escape being eaten by the giants of the city of Harfang,★ for whom mankind is a delicacy, and who even have a recipe for marshwiggle. Later, they encounter and destroy the Green Witch,★ murderer of Rilian's mother.

Silver Sea The reach of ocean covered with lily-like white flowers, found by the travellers in *The Voyage of the 'Dawn Treader'.*★ As they penetrated the dazzlingly bright sea, the voyagers discovered its waters becoming gradually more shallow as World's End was approached. It was necessary to leave the *Dawn Treader* and use a rowing boat instead. Beyond World's End lay Aslan's Country.★

Slubgob   In *The Screwtape Letters*,★ Dr Slubgob is Principal of the Tempters' Training College★ of hell.

Slumtrimpet   The tempter assigned to the fiancée of Wormwood's★ charge in *The Screwtape Letters*.★

Socratic Club   *See* OXFORD UNIVERSITY SOCRATIC CLUB.

Sopespian   In *Prince Caspian*,★ a Lord of the usurper King Miraz★ who turns traitor and plans his death.

Sorlois   In *The Magician's Nephew*,★ a world dead like Charn.★

Sorn   Sorns (or, properly, seroni) are one of three intelligent kinds of being living on the planet Malacandra.★ As befits their nature as the planet's intelligensia, they had long thin legs, top-heavy bodies, and thin faces with long, drooping noses and mouths. They were three times as tall as the earthman Elwin Ransom.★ Sorns had scientific interests, including cosmology and astronomy, and enjoyed metaphysical speculation. Ransom found, in response to their eager probing, that his knowledge of earth geography, history and science was extremely sketchy.

Spear-head   In *The Voyage of the 'Dawn Treader'*,★ Narnia's★ north star, brighter than our own pole star.

Spenser's Images of Life (1967)   C.S. Lewis' longest piece of literary criticism, as opposed to literary history. It is based upon C.S. Lewis' Cambridge lectures on Edmund Spenser's great poem, *The Faerie Queene*. He intended to turn his material into a book, but did not live to do so. Lewis' holograph notes were expanded and edited into this book by Alastair Fowler of Brasenose College, Oxford. Fowler comments: 'The best I hope for is that some may agree with me that if Lewis himself had lived to write the book it might have stood out among his works as a critical new departure. Here I am not thinking of the iconographical interpretations (although these have their interest) so much as of the adumbration of a manner of approach to fiction not suitable for textual analysis.'

C.S. Lewis approaches *The Faerie Queene* as a splendid and majestic pageant of the universe and nature,★ which celebrates God,★ in Lewis' own phrase, as 'the glad creator'. He argues that if the poem is to be fully enjoyed and understood by the modern reader, conventional views of epic and allegory★ need to be modified. He suggests in his introduction: 'We should expect, then, from Spenser's poem, a simple fairy-tale pleasure sophisticated by polyphonic technique, a simple "moral" sophisticated by a learned iconography. Moreover, we should expect to find all of these reacting on one another, to produce a work very different from what we are used to.' Lewis considers *The Faerie Queene* to be perhaps the most difficult poem in English, above the demand of great literature for both a simple and a sophisticated response. His final chapter analyses the story of King Arthur in the poem.

See also LITERARY CRITIC, C.S. LEWIS AS A.

Spirits in Bondage: A Cycle of Lyrics (1919) Written while C.S. Lewis was an atheist, and when he had a strong ambition to be a poet, this collection of poetry was published under the pseudonym of Clive Hamilton (Hamilton was his mother's maiden name). According to Lewis, the poems are 'mainly strung around the idea . . . that nature is wholly diabolical and malevolent and that God, if he exists, is outside of and in opposition to the cosmic arrangements'.

The volume has similarities with his early, long narrative poem, *Dymer*.★ Its opening stanza explains the book's purpose:

> In my coracle of verses I will sing of lands unknown,
> Flying from the scarlet city where a lord that knows no pity
> Mocks the broken people praying round his iron throne,
> Sing about the Hidden Country fresh and full of quiet green,
> Sailing over seas uncharted to a port that none has seen.

See also NARRATIVE POEMS: POEMS; IDEAL-ISM, C.S. LEWIS AND.

Stable Hill   In *The Last Battle*,★ there is a stable here in which Shift★ keeps Puzzle★ the Ass, as he pretends to be Aslan.★ Later, Tash,★ the Calormene★ demon god, enters the stable, followed by Aslan himself. When the great lion takes it over, its inside turns out to be larger than its outside.

Sterk   In *That Hideous Strength*,★ between Stratford and Edgestow★ on the railway line to London. In *Out of the Silent Planet*,★ the deserted country home of Professor Weston★ lay on the far side of the hills a good four miles from Sterk. Elwin Ransom★ came across Weston's home while on a walking tour, and heading for Sterk. The town had industrial areas beyond it, in contrast to the feature-less, desolate countryside in which Ransom was kidnapped.

Stevens, Courtnay E. ('Tom') (1905–76)   A member of The Inklings,★ and Fellow and Tutor in Ancient History at Magdalen College, Oxford,★ from 1934. He acquired the nickname 'Tom Brown Stevens' while a schoolboy at Winchester.

Stone knife   This was used by the White Witch★ to slay Aslan,★ as recounted in *The Lion, the Witch and the Wardrobe*.★ Later in the history of Narnia,★ the travellers discover it kept by Ramandu★ at Aslan's Table in *The Voyage of the 'Dawn Treader'*.★

The Stone Table   In *The Lion, the Witch and the Wardrobe,*★ a table of ancient magic upon which Aslan,★ the great lion, is slain by the White Witch,★ and which is split for ever when he returns to life. It is a slab of grey stone supported by four upright stones. The table is obviously ancient, and covered with engraved lines and figures. A mound called Aslan's How★ is eventually built over it, and plays a significant part in the actions recorded in *Prince Caspian.*★

Strawberry   In *The Magician's Nephew,*★ the horse of London cabby, Frank,★ who is turned into a talking and flying horse by Aslan★ and renamed Fledge.

Studdock, Jane   In *That Hideous Strength,*★ the wife of Mark Studdock.★ Like Damaris Tighe in Charles Williams' novel, much admired by C.S. Lewis, *The Place of the Lion,*★ Jane is a post-graduate student. Six months after her marriage, alone during the day in their tiny flat, she is experiencing a crisis over the meaning of romantic love★ even while she works on John Donne's love poetry.

As a child Jane had given up any belief in the supernatural, along with Santa Claus. She is, however, gifted with unwelcomed second sight, by which the devilish activities of the N.I.C.E. are opened to her. She is the innocent agent who alone can reveal the hidden whereabouts of the sleeping Merlin,★ in a trance since the Dark Ages. As such she is sought both by the N.I.C.E. and the opposing forces of humanity, led by Dr Elwin Ransom.★

As Jane is slowly drawn into the community surrounding Ransom, there is no violation of her personhood like that of her husband Mark as he moves closer to the inner ring★ of the N.I.C.E. at Belbury.★ Gradually her sense of reality, and her commitment to the marriage of love return until she is able to receive back again the undeceived and restored Mark.

Studdock, Mark Gainsby   In *That Hideous Strength,*★ a junior Fellow of Bracton College★ of the Midland university of Edgestow.★ His subject is sociology. Six months before the story opens he married Jane,★ a postgraduate student of English literature. Mark is drawn into involvement with the sinister N.I.C.E.,★ whose headquarters are within a few miles at Belbury.★ There his very soul is endangered by the lure of the N.I.C.E.'s 'inner ring' of members. We learn that the temptation of the inner ring★ has beset Mark throughout his young life.

With daunting self-honesty, C.S. Lewis modelled Mark on aspects of himself as a new lecturer at Magdalen College, Oxford.★ Mark finds himself constantly denying his spontaneous like and dislike of people in order to go deeper into Belbury's inner circle. In fact, naturally he disliked all the core people.

Jane, his wife, provided his connection with reality. Whenever he thought about her, she was a mirror. He imagined her disliking his pretty heavy drinking at Belbury. She would be scathing about its leading lights. He knew that she would not fit in there, despite efforts to persuade him to get her to join Belbury. Her real self would be a living criticism of all that the N.I.C.E. stood for. From Jane's point of view, she considered Mark a person easily taken in. He liked to be liked, opening him to manipulation.

According to the story's narrator, revealed as Lewis himself, Mark's mind held virtually no remnant of noble thought, either Christian or pagan, that could lodge. He had not had either a properly scientific or a classical education,★ merely a modern one. He had bypassed the disciplines of abstract thought and of the traditions of civilisation, the 'literatures of freedom and dignity'. These lacks made him a man of straw. He had done well in academic subjects that required no exact knowledge, being good at essays and general papers. He had typically once written an article on vagrancy though he had no knowledge of the tramp's life of the roads.

Mark experienced 'undeception'★ after being falsely arrested for the murder of Hingest, a Fellow of Bracton disillusioned after a brief flirtation with the N.I.C.E. Painful self-knowledge suddenly enlightened him. He saw himself as always drawn towards odious inner rings, even losing his only real friend at school in his efforts to get into an unpleasant society called Grip. Later, he had left behind his undergraduate friends, like Arthur Denniston.★ In this new state of being undeceived his public self or face fell off him, leaving himself as the person responsible for all his follies. Jane was the only real person he had left, and he had nearly discarded her for the N.I.C.E. and the sinister forces behind it.

Mark's undeception is part of the story of his faltering steps towards Christian conversion. At Belbury, Mark was Wither's pupil for initiation into the satanic inner circle. At the point when he was expected to despoil a figure of a crucified man, he suddenly realised for the first time that there might be something in Christianity. Whereas his wife Jane had abandoned belief in Christianity along with Father Christmas, Mark had never believed.

Studies in Words (1960; 1967) C.S. Lewis became Professor of Renaissance and Medieval Literature at Cambridge University in 1954, setting the pattern of his work with his unaugural address, *De Descriptione Temporum*.★ His book, *Studies in Words*, enlarged for the second edition after his death, is based on lectures he gave at Cambridge, and is mainly addressed to undergraduates studying literature. He warns in his preface that the book is not an essay in linguistics; his purpose is merely lexical and historical. His approach, however, differs greatly from that of a dictionary, with a number of advantages. His studies provide an aid to more accurate reading, and the words studied are selected for the light they shed on ideas and sentiments. The history of ideas, Lewis believes, is intimately recorded in the shifts of meaning★ in words. There is value in considering the relationship between words in a family of meaning, rather than considering words and their roots individually.

The modern reader's natural tendency is to assume that he or she knows the meaning of words in old texts. Lewis confesses that he early cultivated the habit of following up the slightest 'semantic discomfort' he felt with a word, a habit now second nature. Any such discomfort rouses him, like a terrier, to the game of discovering the history of thought and sentiment which underlies the semantic biography of a word.

Though Lewis does not mention it specifically, this habit of first noticing and then discovering the history of certain meanings of thought and feeling lies behind his great studies, such as *The Allegory of Love*★ and *The Discarded Image.*★

The sections of the book are as follows.

(1) Introduction. The effects of ramification. The insulating power of the context. The dangerous sense (ds). The word's meaning and the speaker's meaning. Tactical definitions. The methodological idiom. Moralisation of status-words.

(2) Nature. 'Natura.' 'Kind.' 'Phusis.' 'Nature' and its opposites. 'Natural and unnatural.' The 'natural' and the interfered with. The 'natural' as an element in man. 'Nature' and grace. Nature and the mimetic arts. By 'nature' or by law. The state of 'nature' and the civil state. 'Natural' and 'supernatural'. Physical and metaphysical. The 'natural' as the excusable. 'Nature' in eighteenth- and nineteenth-century poetry.

(3) Sad [with 'Gravis']. 'Gravis' and 'grave'. 'Sad': the 'full'-senses. The 'grave'-senses. 'Sad (ds).' Our Polly is a 'sad' slut.

(4) Wit [with 'ingenium']. Early history. Wits. 'Ingenium.' 'Ingenium' and wit. Early history of the 'dangerous sense'. The afflictions of 'wit-ingenium'. Happy ending.

(5) Free [with 'eleutherios', 'liberal', 'frank' etc].'Eleutheros.' 'Liber.' 'Free.' 'Frank' and 'villain'. An obsolete branch line. 'Liberal' as a cultural term.

(6) Sense [with 'sentence', 'sensibility', and 'sensible']. Introductory. 'Sentire.' The nouns. 'Sententia' and 'sentence'. 'Sensus' and 'sense'. 'Communis sensus' and 'common sense'. 'Sense' and 'sens' in later times. 'Sensible' and 'sensibility'. 'Sensible (ds).' Triumph of 'sensible (ds)'.

(7) Simple. The logical branch. The ethical branch. The semantic sediment.

(8) Conscience and conscious. Preliminaries. The weakened branch. The external witness. The internal witness. Summary. The internal lawgiver. Survival of the sense 'consciring'. The lawgiver. Diversity of consciences. Precariousness of the sense 'lawgiver'. Mixed usages. Conscience as fear. Ramifications of the sense 'synteresis'. Return to the weakened branch.

(9) World. 'World A' and 'World B'. 'World A' as state or period. 'World A' as the common lot or 'things'. 'World' in biblical translation. The confusion of 'kosmos' and 'aion'. 'The other world.' 'World' and 'worldly' (pejorative, depreciative or impure). 'World' and 'worldly' (neutral). 'World B' and 'earth'. 'World B' as a measure of value. Subordinate 'worlds'. 'World' (people).

(10) Life. 'Life' (concrete). 'Life' (chronological). 'Life' (qualitative). 'Life' (the 'common lot of man'). Semantic halo. 'Life': What I like. 'Real' life. 'Life' (biological). The 'tree'. Apology.

(11) I dare say.

(12) At the fringe of language.

See also LITERARY CRITIC, C.S. LEWIS AS A.

Sub-creation Sub-creation is a concept developed by

C.S. Lewis' friend, J.R.R. Tolkien,★ and one which deeply influenced him. It is expressed in Tolkien's contribution to *Essays Presented to Charles Williams*.★

J.R.R. Tolkien believes that the art of true fantasy or fairy–story writing is sub–creation: creating another or secondary world with such skill that it has an 'inner consistency of reality'. This inner consistency is so potent that it compels secondary belief or primary belief (the belief we give to the primary or real world) on the part of the reader. Tolkien calls the skills to compel these two degrees of belief 'fantasy' and 'enchantment' respectively. A clue to the concept of sub–creation lies in the fact that the word 'fairy', or more properly 'faery', etymologically means 'the realm or state where faeries have their being'. A faery story is thus not a story which simply concerns faery beings. They are in some sense otherworldly, having a geography and history surrounding them.

Tolkien's key idea is that Faery, the realm or state where faeries have their being, contains a whole cosmos, a microcosm. It contains the moon, the sun, the sky, trees and mountains, rivers, water and stones, as well as dragons, trolls, elves, dwarves, goblins, talking animals,★ and even a mortal person when he or she is enchanted (through giving primary belief to that other world). Faery is sub–creation rather than either representation or allegorical interpretation of the 'beauties and terrors of the world'. Sub–creation comes, says Tolkien, as a result of a two–fold urge in human beings: first, the wish to survey the depths of space and time, and second, the urge to communicate with living beasts other than mankind, to escape from hunger, poverty, death, and to end the separation between mankind and nature.★ Just as the reason wishes for a unified theory to cover all phenomena in the universe, the imagination also constantly seeks a unity of meaning★ appropriate to itself.

Tolkien took the idea of sub-creation much further than C.S. Lewis, and disliked the lack of genuine sub-creation in Lewis' *The Chronicles of Narnia*,★ which he regarded (relatedly) as too allegorical.

Sunless Sea In *The Silver Chair*,★ the sea crossed by Eustace Scrubb,★ Jill Pole,★ and Puddleglum,★ in order to reach Underland★ in their quest for the lost Prince Rilian.★

Supernaturalism *See* NATURALISM AND SUPER-NATURALISM.

Surprised by Joy: The Shape of My Early Life (1955) This autobiography records C.S. Lewis' life up to his conversion to Christianity at the age of thirty-three. 'Joy'★ is a technical term used by C.S. Lewis to help define a distinct tone of feeling which he discovered in early childhood, and which stayed with him on and off throughout his adolescence and early manhood. This inconsolable longing contradicted the atheism and materialism that his intellect embraced. In first theism and then Christianity both his intellect and his imagination were fulfilled.

See also LEWIS, C.S.

Susan, Queen *See* PEVENSIE, PETER, SUSAN, EDMUND AND LUCY.

Swanwhite In *The Last Battle*,★ a Queen of such beauty that if she looked into any pool, her reflected face shone out for a year and a day afterwards, just like a star in the night sky. She lived in Narnia★ before the days of the ascendancy of the White Witch★ who brought perpetual winter to the land.

T

Talapal In *Till We Have Faces*,★ the name for Ungit★ (or Aphrodite) used in the kingdom of Essur.★

Talking animals C.S. Lewis was constantly fascinated by the gap between humanity and the sub-humanity of beasts. The title of his Narnian★ tale, *The Horse and His Boy*★ tells it all. The pronoun 'his' bridges the gap between animal and human; the boy, Shasta (Cor), belongs as much to the talking Narnian horse, Bree,★ as Bree belongs to Shasta. Lewis' fascination with this gap is evident, also, in his description of the warm inner life of the bear, Mr Bultitude,★ in *That Hideous Strength*,★ and in his magnificent concept of Narnia as a land of talking beasts created by the great talking lion, Aslan.★ Talking animals are normally found only in children's books, such as *The Wind in the Willows*, by Kenneth Graham, a book much admired and quoted by C.S. Lewis. In his science fiction tale, *Out of the Silent Planet*,★ however, Lewis smuggles in talking animals that are palatable to its adult reader. Most notably this is the case with the hrossa,★ who, though personal beings, also retain the qualities of animals.

C.S. Lewis regarded the invention of talking beasts as a feature of what his friend, J.R.R. Tolkien,★ called 'sub-creation'. Lewis once wrote: 'We do not want merely to *see* beauty . . . we want something else which can hardly be put into words—to be united with the beauty we see, to pass into it, to receive it into ourselves, to bathe in it, to become part of it. That is why we have peopled air and earth and water with gods and goddesses and nymphs and elves.' And, we could add, the talking beasts of Narnia and Malacandra.*

See also NATURE, C.S. LEWIS' VIEW OF.

Tarin In the novel, *Till We Have Faces*,* a young officer of the King's Guard at the royal palace in Glome.* After King Trom discovers that he has been flirting with Redival,* his daughter, Tarin is castrated and sold as a slave in Ringal. This was one of Trom's many mistakes, as his father sought revenge. Tarin became great in the south and east of Glome and later visited Queen Orual.* From him, Orual learnt of her selfish neglect of Redival, a factor which helps in the Queen's painful undeception.*

Tash The demon god of Calormen,* who appears in terrifying form in the story of *The Last Battle*.* It had a head of a bird and four arms. The Calormene nobility considered itself descended from Tash. Part of the deception, in the last days of Narnian* and Calormene 'new theologians', led by Shift,* was to syncretise Tash and Aslan* into a mixture they called 'Tashlan'.

Tashbaan The capital of Calormen, named after the country's deity, Tash.* *See* CALORMEN.

Telmar, land of This lies to the far west of Narnia.* It was unpeopled until populated by pirates who accidently stumbled into it from our world.

See also TELMARINES.

Telmarines Descendants of pirates who accidently stumbled into the land of Telmar* after entering a magical cave in a South Sea island. They became a proud and fierce nation. After a famine, the Telmarines, led by King Caspian* I, crossed the western mountains and conquered the peaceful land of Narnia,* long after the reign of High King Peter and the other Pevensie* children. They silenced the talking animals* and trees, drove away dwarves and fauns, and even tried to cover up the memory of such things. Prince Caspian learns of the 'Old Narnia', as it is then called, as told in the book, *Prince Caspian*.★

See also NARNIA: History.

Tempters' Training College   In *The Screwtape Letters*,★ and its brief sequel, *Screwtape Proposes a Toast*,★ the college where junior devils learn their skills in damning human beings, or in attempting to reclaim those who have gone over to the Enemy. After graduation, it appears, novices gain practical experience under the guidance of an experienced devil. Wormwood★ is a recent graduate, advised by letters from his eminent uncle, Screwtape.★ Every year, the Tempters' Training College holds a dinner. One year, Screwtape was the guest of honour, and his speech is recorded in *Screwtape Proposes a Toast*. The college's principal is Dr Slubgob.

Terebinthia   An island visited by the travellers in the tale of *The Voyage of the 'Dawn Treader'*.★ It lies off the coast of Narnia,★ beyond Galma.★ The island, a haunt of pirates, had been plagued by a terrible illness, and its main town was in quarantine. In *The Silver Chair*,★ King Caspian★ seeks Aslan★ there.

That Hideous Strength   **(1945; abridged paperback version 1955)** The final volume of the science fiction trilogy, begun in *Out of the Silent Planet*,★ and *Perelandra*★ (*Voyage to Venus*). It continues C.S. Lewis' presentation of the problem of good and evil. In this 'modern fairy tale for grown-ups', Dr Elwin Ransom★ stays on earth. The setting is the small Midland university town of Edgestow,★ just after the war. The 'progressive element' among the Fellows of Bracton College★ engineer the sale of a piece of property called Bragdon Wood★ to the N.I.C.E.,★ the National Institute for Co-ordinated Experiments. According to Arthurian legend, the magician

Merlin* lay secretly in a trance within the wood, his 'sleeping' body preserved from aging.

The N.I.C.E. was a sinister, totalitarian organisation of technocrats; scientists given over to the pragmatic use of technology for social and individual control. Deeply involved in the Institute was Dick Devine,* now Lord Feverstone, first encountered by Ransom before the war as his kidnapper, along with Professor Weston,* stealing him off to Mars.

Mark Studdock,* a Fellow in sociology at Bracton, is duped into working for the N.I.C.E., whereas his wife, Jane,* a research student, finds herself helping the other side, led by Ransom, now revealed as the great Pendragon of Logres. Her gift of second sight helps to locate Merlin and to provide vital intelligence. Merlin's ancient magic, linked into the power of the eldila* of Deep Heaven,* overcomes the evil of the N.I.C.E. In a satirical climax, Merlin revives the curse of Babel, confused speech, as a fitting judgement on people who have despised ordinary humanity.

This book, as a sequel to the previous stories, set on other planets, brings matters 'down to earth', under the influence of Lewis' friend, Charles Williams.* It is set on Thulcandra, the silent planet Earth, so called because it is cut off by evil from the beatific language and worlds of Deep Heaven. In another sense, matters are brought down to earth because Lewis takes pains in characterising the marriage and personalities of Mark and Jane Studdock. In the style of Charles Williams, the supernatural world impinges upon the everyday world of ordinary people. There are other Williams–like touches also. Jane, like Damaris in *The Place of the Lion*, is engaged upon literary research. More notably, C.S. Lewis makes use of the mythical geography of Logres, the Arthurian matter which is the focus of Williams' unfinished cycle of poems.

As Lewis makes clear in his preface, his story illustrates the point that he made in one of his most forceful studies of ethics, *The Abolition of Man*★ (1943); that a world which rejects objective principles of right and wrong, beauty and ugliness, also rejects what constitutes mankind's very nature, and creates an unhumanity. The new society projected by the N.I.C.E. is the corruption of the Unman★ of *Perelandra* writ large.

As a study of evil, *That Hideous Strength* shows how wickedness sows the seeds of its own destruction. Professor Weston's forays into space with evil intent had allowed the ending of an ancient prohibition: that no inhabitants of Deep Heaven would ever come to the quarantined planet Earth until the very end of things. Now that bent mankind had tried to contaminate unfallen worlds such as Mars and Venus, however, the eldila of Deep Heaven could unlease their good powers through a suitable human agent—Merlin.

The novel has been criticised for being over-complex in structure. It has, for example, an uneasy mixture of satire and serious study of damnation, a mixture that worked in *The Screwtape Letters*.★ Nevertheless, it is one of Lewis' fictions that makes the most impact upon its reader, revealing a power to portray ordinary human beings in a 'realistic' setting. It is plausible as an anti-utopian parable of our times, like Aldous Huxley's *Brave New World* (1932) and George Orwell's *Nineteen Eighty-four* (1949). Furthermore, it was a preparation for probably his best novel, *Till We Have Faces*.★

Theology, C.S. Lewis and   C.S. Lewis, by profession, was a literary critic who also had philosophical interests. Anything that he wrote on theology, such as *Miracles*, *The Problem of Pain*, *Reflections on the Psalms*, or *Mere Christianity* he regarded as the offerings of a layperson. Some of his opinions he presented explicitly as speculation. He tried to set forward an orthodox theology, what Francis Schaeffer called the historic Christian position. A few of the views he held (such as on the inspiration of Scripture), evangelicals could not be entirely happy with. However, many of his views were searingly painful to a liberal Christian—such as his supernaturalism,★ his literal belief in heaven,★ hell, and the devil, and his unflinching emphasis on the demands of truth. (He had no concept of a merely religious truth, separate from reason and historical fact.) His many years as an atheist gave him a deep sympathy for the unbeliever's position.

An important contribution that Lewis made to theology was on the nature of language, and how language pictures reality, including the deep reality of the world that we do not normally see. His work on the relationship between meaning★ and theoretical truth-claims shows it is possible to hold that the Bible has the character of a propositional revelation from God. This is even though most of the Bible is made up of historical narrative, with other sections of poetry, and only a relatively small proportion of didactic material. Biblical history provides the meaning of the terms of the biblical propositions of the nature of God, sin, salvation, the atonement, and the like. Biblical history, epitomised in the Gospels, combined the qualities of a good story with being factual. This kind of approach will bring more joy to evangelicals, and other orthodox groups, than to liberals.

C.S. Lewis' great dislike of liberal theology is expressed in an essay greatly admired by Austin Farrer,★ 'Fern seeds and elephants' (also called, 'Modern theology and biblical criticism'), first published in *Christian Reflections*.★ His orthodoxy was a traditional Anglican kind, and like Dorothy L. Sayers★ and G.K. Chesterton,★ he delighted in dogma.

See also THEOLOGY OF ROMANCE.

Theology of romance   Like his friends J.R.R. Tolkien★
and Charles Williams,★ C.S. Lewis worked in his fiction
according to a theology of romanticism★ which owed
much to the nineteenth-century writer who was Lewis'
mentor, George MacDonald.★ The term 'romantic theologian', Lewis tells us, was invented by Charles Williams.
What Lewis says about Williams in his introduction to
Essays Presented to Charles Williams★ applies also to himself.

'A romantic theologian,' C. S. Lewis points out, 'does
not mean one who is romantic about theology but one
who is theological about romance, one who considers the
theological implications of those experiences which are
called romantic. The belief that the most serious and
ecstatic experiences either of human love or of imaginative
literature have such theological implications and that they
can be healthy and fruitful only if the implications are
diligently thought out and severely lived, is the root
principle of all his [Williams'] work.'

Whereas a key preoccupation of Charles Williams was
romantic love, C.S. Lewis was 'theological' about romantic longing or joy,★ and Tolkien reflected deeply on the
theological implications of fairy tale and myth,★ particularly the aspect of sub-creation.★

In a doctorial thesis, *Romantic Religion in the Works of
Owen Barfield, C.S. Lewis, Charles Williams, and J.R.R.
Tolkien*, R.J. Reilly saw C.S. Lewis as an advocate of
'romantic religion'. This was the 'attempt to reach
religious truths by means and techniques traditionally
called romantic, and ... to defend and justify these
techniques and attitudes of romanticism by holding that
they have religious sanction'.

C.S. Lewis was not doing anything new in this. Rather,
he was presenting in modern terms what seemed to be a
normal attitude of mind a few centuries ago. It was
perhaps beginning to be lost in the seventeenth century,

when John Bunyan was forced to defend what now could be called 'romantic religion' in his author's apology at the beginning of *The Pilgrim's Progress*. Bunyan's reasoning in that prologue follows lines similar to Lewis' defence of the imagination.★

In *Surprised by Joy*,★ C.S. Lewis reported some of his sensations—responses to natural beauty, and literary and artistic responses—in the belief that others would recognise similar experiences of their own.

J.R.R. Tolkien was fascinated by several structural features of fairy tales and other stories that embodied myths. These features are all related to a sense of imaginative decorum, a sense that imagining can, in itself, be good or bad, as rules or norms apply strictly in fantasy, as they do in thought. Meaning★ can only be created by skill or art, and plays an essential part in human thought and language. As Tolkien said, 'The incarnate mind, the tongue, and the tale are in our world coeval.' As Barfield has shown in his introduction to the new edition of *Poetic Diction*, the ideal in logical positivism and related types of modern linguistic philosophy is, strictly, absurd; it systematically eliminates meanings from the framing of truths, expecting thereby to guarantee their validity. In Tolkien's view, the opposite is the case. The richer the meanings involved in the framing of truths, the more guarantee is there of their validity.

G.K. Chesterton★ once wrote that we should sometimes take our tea in the top of a tree, as our perceptions tend to get dulled. One of the essential features of the fairy tale or mythopoeic fantasy is the sense of 'recovery'—the regaining of health or a clear view of things. Tolkien pointed out that we too often get caught in the specific corridor of daily, mundane life, and lose a view of 'things as we are (or were) meant to see them'. Entry into a imaginary world 'shocks us more fully awake than we are for most of our lives'. C.S. Lewis said the latter of myth, but it applies to this feature of recovery. Part of this recovery is a sense of imaginative unity, a survey of the depths of space and time. The essential patterns of reality are seen in a fresh way.

Charles Williams' 'romantic religion', though concerned with romantic love, took the form of what he characteristically called the Way of the Affirmation of Images. In *The Allegory of Love,*★ much admired by Williams, C.S. Lewis pointed out that there are basically two ways in which the mind may develop an essential equivalence between material and immaterial, natural and spiritual. When a person begins with immaterial fact—such as qualities like beauty or joy—and invents *visibilia* to express them, he is *allegorising*. It is possible, however, to reverse this process, and to view the material world as itself a copy of the invisible world. When a person attempts to read something else through the sensible—to discover the idea or meaning in the copy—he is engaged in *symbolism* or *sacramentalism*. 'The allegorist,' argues Lewis, 'leaves the given—his passions—to talk of that which is confessedly less real, which is a fiction. The symbolist leaves the given to find that which is more real.' Later, C.S. Lewis was to write that allegory in its highest form approaches myth.

The neo-platonic idea of sacramentalism applies to Charles Williams; except that when he leaves behind the given to find its meaning, he retains the importance of the given. It has a greater reality which can now be seen. Thus in romantic love (as when Dante saw Beatrice) the beloved is both an image of divine beauty and important in him or herself. To care for divine beauty is to care for the ordinary yet transfigured mortal before you. This is Philip's experience in Williams' novel, *Shadows of Ecstasy*:

Now, suddenly, he understood Rosamond's arm when she leant forward to pass a plate to her sister; somehow that arm always made him think of the Downs against the sky. There was a line, a curved beauty, a thing that spoke to both mind and heart; a thing that was there for ever. And Rosamond? Rosamond was like them, she was there for ever. It occurred to him that, if she was, then her occasional slowness when he was trying to explain something was there for ever. Well, after all, Rosamond was only human; she couldn't be absolutely perfect. And then as she stretched out her arm again he cried out that she was perfect, she was more than perfect; the movement of her arm was something frightfully important, and now it was gone.

This interplay between the reality of the image (here the image of perfection) and the reality pictured by the image is captured in Williams' distinctive doctrine of the two-fold Way of the Affirmation and Rejection of Images. Here we say of any created person or thing in reference to the Creator: 'This also is Thou; neither is this Thou.' In his *The Descent of the Dove*, Williams described the principle like this: 'The one Way was to affirm all things orderly until the universe throbbed with vitality; the other to reject all things until there was nothing anywhere but He. The Way of Affirmation was to develop great art and romantic love and marriage and philosophy and social justice; the Way of Rejection was to break out continually in the profound mystical documents of the soul, the records of the great psychological masters of Christendom. All was involved in Christendom. . . .' The validity of both aspects of the two-fold Way was con-nected in Williams' thinking with another key doctrine of Christianity—co-inherence. This doctrine was captured for him, characteristically, in the beautiful image of the city. This social image brings out, for Williams, the dependence of each of us upon others' labours and gifts, and the necessity of bearing one another's burdens.

They Asked for a Paper (1962)   A collection of literary and theological pieces, including several reprinted from *Transposition and Other Addresses*.★ It contains *De Descriptione Temporum*,★ 'The Literary Impact of the Authorised Version', 'Hamlet: The Prince or the Poem?', 'Kipling's World', 'Sir Walter Scott', 'Lilies that Fester', 'Psychoanalysis and Literary Criticism', 'The Inner Ring',★ 'Is Theology Poetry?', 'Transposition',★ 'On Obstinacy in Belief', and 'The Weight of Glory'.

They Stand Together   Walter Hooper was briefly C.S. Lewis' acting secretary during the last months of his life, and spent ten years editing Lewis' letters before *They Stand Together* appeared in 1979. In an interview, Mr Hooper told the author that this correspondence would easily run into fifteen volumes. From this vast output he decided to select letters to one man, Arthur Greeves, a close friend of Lewis' over a period of almost fifty years; that is, from his atheistic mid-teens to literally days before Jack Lewis died. These letters give rich insight to Lewis' life and to the development of his Christian thought and imagination.★

As Mr Hooper pointed out to the author, this selection makes up a more complete autobiography than *Surprised by Joy*,★ where he tells his life from a particular point of view—his awareness of joy,★ the longing that no earthly philosophy or bodily pleasure could satisfy, and how only Christian theism made sense of it. Also, that story finishes at C.S. Lewis' conversion at the age of thirty-three. Walter Hooper's collection contains 296 letters.

A factor which fascinated Mr Hooper in compiling the letters was the sheer detective work involved. He told the author, 'I like detective work very much. I like details and

I like mysteries. I knew that I was up against something extremely difficult in dating these letters. But they do not make sense, perfect sense, unless they are in the right order.' At the end of his life, Arthur Greeves had tried to put the correct dates on the letters from Lewis, but was often confused. 'Greeves notices, say, that Lewis had taken a holiday in Cornwall, so he assumes that a letter also from Cornwall was written at the same time. There are really two visits, and the letters are years apart. When you put them together you have to stretch the sense in them. Once you put them in their right place the sense comes through—you get so much more out of them.'

The biggest mystery was why there were originally so few letters towards the end of the correspondence. It was solved by accident. Walter Hooper says that in 1974, 'I wrote on other business to the headmaster of Campbell College, Belfast, about one of Lewis' friends. He wrote back and told me that Greeves' cousin, Lisbeth Greeves, had had put in her keeping by Arthur a number of letters that dealt with his brother's alcoholism.' As Major W.H. Lewis★ was dead, and his alcoholism was now well known, Mr Hooper felt that these letters, with their first-hand accounts, should be included. His brother's alcoholism 'was a very great problem for C.S. Lewis', and one of the many that he shared with Arthur Greeves in the letters. This is why, in one place, C.S. Lewis speaks of him as 'my father confessor'. One letter vividly recounts his conversion to Christianity.

We also learn much about the Ulsterman Arthur Greeves from these letters, though Lewis kept little of Arthur's side of the correspondence. The foundation of their friendship★ was a common insight into the joy,★ with its longing, that was the main constant theme of Lewis' life and writings. This basis of friendship is revealed in a poem to Arthur that Jack Lewis wrote in 1917:

That we may mark with wonder and chaste dread
At hour of noon, when, with our limbs outspread
Lazily in the whispering grass, we lie
To gaze out fully upon the windy sky—
Far, far away, and kindly, friend with friend,
To talk the old, old talk that has no end,
Roaming—without a name—without a chart—
The unknown garden of another's heart.

See also LETTERS OF C.S. LEWIS.

Thulcandra   The name for planet Earth in the language of Old Solar★ in *Out of the Silent Planet*★ and the others of C.S. Lewis' science fiction trilogy.

See also THE PLANETS.

Till We Have Faces **(1956)**   At different times, C.S. Lewis regarded *Till We Have Faces* or *Perelandra*★ as his best book. He retells an old classical myth, that of Cupid and Psyche,★ in the realistic setting of a historical novel. It is set several hundred years BC in the imaginary and barbaric country of Glome,★ somewhere to the north of the Greeklands.

The story is told through the eyes of Queen Orual★ of Glome. Having heard a legend in the nearby land of Essur★ similar to the myth of Cupid and Psyche, she seeks to set the record straight. The gods, she claims, have distorted the story in certain key respects. She recognises herself and her half-sister Psyche in the newly sprung-up legend.

The gods, she said, had called her deep love for Psyche jealousy. They had also said that she saw Psyche's palace,★ whereas Orual had only seen shapes in a mist, a fantasy that momentarily resembled a palace. There had been no evidence that Psyche had married a god and dwelt in his palace.

Orual therefore recounts her version of the story, being

as truthful as possible. She had a reader in mind from the Greeklands, and agreed with the Greek demand for truth and rational honesty. She has to tell her life story to do this properly.

Orual is a Princess, the daughter of a barbarian and callous King, Trom,★ and has a sister, Redival.★ Her mother having died young, Trom marries again, and the stepmother dies giving birth to the beautiful Psyche. Psyche's outstanding beauty contrasts with Orual's ugliness (in later life she wore a veil). The King engages a Greek slave, named The Fox,★ to teach his daughters. The Fox is able to pass on his Greek Stoicism and rationalism to Psyche and Orual, though the daughters never reject the paganism of their land.

In Glome the goddess Ungit,★ a deformed version of Venus, is worshipped. After a drought and other disasters, a lot falls on the innocent Psyche to be sacrificed on the Grey Mountains to the Shadow-brute or West-wind,★ the god of the mountain.

Some time afterwards, Orual, accompanied by Bardia,★ a faithful member of the King's Guard, seeks the bones of Psyche to bury her. Finding no trace of Psyche, Bardia and Orual explore further and find the beautiful and sheltered valley of the god. Here Psyche is living, wearing rags but full of health. She claims to be married to the god of the mountain, whose face she has never seen. Orual, afraid that the 'god' is a monster or outlaw, persuades Psyche, against her will, to shine a light on her husband's face, while he is sleeping. As in the Greek myth, Psyche as a result is condemned to wander the earth, doing impossible tasks. In the terrible storm, which disfigures the valley, Orual seems to see a beautiful god who tells her, 'You also shall be Psyche.'

Orual's account goes on to record the bitter years of her suffering and grief at the loss of Psyche, haunted by the fantasy that she can hear Psyche's weeping. Succeeding King Trom, she reforms the kingdom, and does her best to rule justly, applying civilised principles learned via The Fox from the Greeks. She becomes a great Queen and a renowned warrior.

Late in life she decides to travel the wider world, and it is then she hears what she believes to be the warped story of Orual, Psyche and the god, causing her to write her account. Most of *Till We Have Faces* is made up of this narration.

The short second part of the novel—still in Orual's voice—continues a few days later. Orual has undergone a devastating undeception,★ whereby, in painful self-knowledge, she discovers how her affection for Psyche had become poisoned by possessiveness. Her clinging and impossible love for Bardia had also blighted his life. In this discovery, which allowed the restoration of a true love for Psyche, was the consolation that she had also been Psyche, as the god had said. She had suffered on Psyche's behalf, in a substitutionary manner, bearing her burdens and thus easing her tasks. By what Charles Williams★ called 'the Way of Exchange', Orual had thus helped Psyche to be reunited with her divine husband. With the curing of her poisoned love, Orual in a vision sees that she has become herself beautiful. She has gained a face in becoming a full person. After this reconciliation, the aged Queen Orual dies, her narration ending with her.

This novel is unlike Lewis' other fiction and is consequently less easy to interpret. It in fact repays several readings. One key to *Till We Have Faces* is the theme of love. It is helpful to see Lewis' study, *The Four Loves*,★ as parallel to it, in the way that *The Abolition of Man*★ is parallel to *That Hideous Strength*.★ The loves of affection and eros are particularly explored. Another key is that of substitution and atonement. Psyche is prepared to die for the sake of the people of Glome. Orual is a substitute for much of Psyche's suffering and pain.

Psyche herself represents a Christ-likeness, though she is not intended as a figure of Christ. Lewis wrote in explanation to Clyde S. Kilby: 'Psyche is an instance of the *anima naturaliter Christiana* making the best of the pagan religion she is brought up in and thus being guided (but always "under the cloud," always in terms of her own imagination or that of her people) towards the true God. She is in some ways like Christ not because she is a symbol of Him but because every good man or woman is like Christ.'

This limitation of the imagination of paganism comes out in the ugly figures of Ungit and the Shadow-brute, deformed images of the brighter Greek deities of Venus (Aphrodite) and Cupid. The truth that these poor images are trying to glimpse is even more beautiful, free of the vindictiveness of the Greek deities. Psyche is able to see a glimpse of the true God himself, in all his beauty, and in his legitimate demand for a perfect sacrifice.

A further key to this novel lies in the theme of the conflict of imagination★ and reason, so important to Lewis himself throughout his life, and vividly portrayed in *Surprised by Joy*.★ The final identification of the half-sisters Orual and Psyche in the story represents the harmony and satisfaction of both reason and imagination made fully possible, Lewis believed, only within Christianity.

See also THE FOUR LOVES.

Timeless at heart   *See UNDECEPTIONS.*

Tirian, King   In *The Last Battle*,★ he is the final King of Narnia★ who, along with his dear friend, Jewel★ the Unicorn, makes a heroic last stand against the Calormene★ and other forces of darkness. Eustace Scrubb★ and Jill Pole★ come to help him in answer to his prayer to Aslan.★

See also NARNIA: History.

211

Tisroc   The Calormene★ sovereign.

Toadpipe   Secretary to Screwtape★ in *The Screwtape Letters*.★

Tolkien, J.R.R. (1892–1973)   John Ronald Reuel Tolkien was one of C.S. Lewis' closest friends, and like him valued friendship★ highly. Until the 1950s, Professor Tolkien was known mainly to a few learned scholars. Now, in the post-hobbit era, he has been read by many millions of people. BBC radio successfully dramatised his *The Lord of the Rings* over thirteen hours. Since his death, *The Silmarillion* has been published. This is set in the fictitious Middle-earth and related worlds of an earlier age than that of the adventures of the Bagginses.

J.R.R. Tolkien, whose name is Germanic, was born in South Africa in 1892, but his family soon moved to England. He attended King Edward VI Grammar School, on the outskirts of Birmingham, and was familiar with Worcestershire and the Vale of Evesham. It is said that the Malvern Hills helped to inspire the mountains of Gondor in Middle-earth. After graduating from Exeter College, Oxford, he saw bitter action in World War I, losing all but one of his best friends.

It was during the Great War years that Tolkien began working on *The Silmarillion*, writing 'The Fall of Gondolin' in 1917 while convalescent. In fact, in general plot, and in several major episodes, most of the legendary cycle of *The Silmarillion* was already constructed before 1930—before the writing and publication of *The Hobbit*, the forerunner of *The Lord of the Rings*. In the latter books there are numerous references to matters covered by *The Silmarillion*: ruins of once-great places, sites of battles of long ago, strange and beautiful names from the deep past, and elvish swords made in Gondolin, before its fall, for the Goblin Wars.

Tolkien's lifelong study and teaching of languages was

the spring and nourishment of his imaginative creations. Just as science fiction writers generally make use of plausible technological inventions and possibilities, Tolkien has used his deep and expert knowledge of language in his fantasies. He created in his youth two forms of the elvish tongue, starting a process which led to a history and geography to surround these languages, and peoples to speak them (and other tongues). He explains: 'I had to posit a basic and phonetic structure of Primitive Elvish, and then modify this by series of changes (such as actually do occur in known languages) so that the two end results would have a consistent structure and character, but be quite different.'

The imaginative possibilities of an invented language were also explored by his friend C.S. Lewis, under his influence. Lewis acknowledges a great debt, especially to his idea of sub-creation.* Lewis makes use of the possibilities of his own imagined language, Old Solar,* in *Out of the Silent Planet*,* and its sequels. The debt was mutual: it is unlikely that Tolkien would have completed *The Lord of the Rings* for publication without Lewis' fervent encouragement.

After the Great War, Tolkien began university teaching. After a few years he moved to Oxford to become Rawlingson and Bosworth Professor of Anglo-Saxon; this was in 1926. It was in this year that he met C.S. Lewis. Their long friendship was soon to begin. Lewis had then been an English Don at Magdalen College for one year. They met at the English Faculty Meeting on 11th May 1926, and Lewis was not amused, recording in his diary: 'He is a smooth, pale, fluent little chap. Can't read Spenser because of the forms—thinks language is the real thing in the English School—thinks all literature is written for the amusement of *men* between thirty and forty—we ought to vote ourselves out of existence if we are honest. . . . No harm in him: only needs a smack or two.'

Any initial antipathy, however, was soon forgotten. Within a year or so they were meeting in each other's rooms and talking far into the night. These conversations proved crucial both for the two men's writings, and for Lewis' conversion to Christianity. As the Ulsterman Lewis remarked in *Surprised by Joy*:★ 'Friendship with . . . J.R.R. Tolkien . . . marked the breakdown of two old prejudices. At my first coming into the world I had been (implicitly) warned never to trust a Papist, and at my first coming into the English Faculty (explicitly) never to trust a philologist. Tolkien was both.'

A typical note of the time occurs in a letter from C.S. Lewis to his Ulster friend Arthur Greeves★ in December 1929: 'Tolkien came back with me to college and sat discoursing of the gods and giants of Asgard for three hours.'

Tolkien himself recalled sharing with Lewis his work on *The Silmarillion*, influencing his science fiction trilogy. The pattern of their future lives, including the later Inklings,★ was being formed. Tolkien remembered: 'In the early days of our association Jack used to come to my house and I read aloud to him *The Silmarillion* so far as it had then gone, including a very long poem: Beren and Luthien.'

The gist of one of the long conversations between Lewis and Tolkien was fortunately recorded by Lewis in another letter to Arthur Greeves in October 1931. It was a crucial factor in his conversion, as he moved from mere theism to Christianity. Tolkien argued that human stories tend to fall into certain patterns, and can embody myth.★ In the Christian Gospels there are all the best elements of good stories, including fairy stories, with the astounding additional factor that everything is also true in the actual, primary world. It combines mythic and historical, factual truth, with no divorce between the two. C.S. Lewis' conversion deepened the friendship.

Tolkien's academic writings were sparing and rare. In 1937 he published an article entitled, '*Beowulf:* the Monsters and the Critics', which, according to Donald K. Fry, 'completely altered the course of *Beowulf* studies'. It was a defence of the artistic unity of that Old English tale. In 1938 he gave his Andrew Lang lecture at St Andrews University, 'On Fairy Stories', which was later published in *Essays Presented to Charles Williams*★—The Inklings' tribute to the writer who had a great deal in common with Tolkien and Lewis. It sets out Tolkien's basic ideas concerning imagination,★ fantasy, and sub-creation.

The Professor's famous children's story, *The Hobbit*, came out in 1937. He continued with its adult sequel, *The Lord of the Rings*, more and more leaving aside his first love, *The Silmarillion*. It was a long, painstaking task, undertaken in the book-crammed study in his Northmoor Road home in Oxford. At one point, he did not touch the manuscript for a whole year. He wrote it in the evenings, for he was fully engaged in his university work. During the World War II years, and afterwards, he read portions to The Inklings, or simply to Lewis alone. He attended almost all The Inklings' meetings, even though his time was so fully occupied.

In 1945 Tolkien was honoured by a new Chair at Oxford, Merton Professor of English Language and Literature, reflecting his by now wider interests. He was not now so cool to the idea of teaching literature at university as he had been previously. Tolkien retained the Chair until his retirement in 1959. With C.S. Lewis' marriage to Joy Davidman★ the relationship between the two friends was not sustained so deeply, and Tolkien grieved over the estrangement.

The scholarly story-teller's retirement years were spent revising the *Ring* trilogy, brushing up and publishing some shorter pieces of story and poetry, and working on various drafts of *The Silmarillion*. Tolkien also spent much time dodging reporters and youthful Americans, as the 1960s marked the exploding popularity of his fantasies, when his readership went from thousands to millions.

An interviewer at the time, Daphne Castell, tried to capture his personal manner: 'He talks very quickly, striding up and down the converted garage which serves as his study, waving his pipe, making little jabs with it to mark important points; and now and then jamming it back in, and talking round it. ... He has the habits of speech of the true story-teller. ... Every sentence is important, and lively, and striking. ...'

Further reading

Humphrey Carpenter, *J.R.R. Tolkien: A Biography* (1977) and *The Inklings: C.S. Lewis, J.R.R. Tolkien, Charles Williams and their friends (1978)*; H. Carpenter (ed), *The Letters of J.R.R. Tolkien* (1981); Daphne Castell 'The Realms of Tolkien' *New Worlds SF.* Vol 50, No 168, (1966).

Tombs of the ancient kings   In the tale of *The Horse and His Boy*,★ tombs north of the great city of Tashbaan, capital of Calormen.★ They are reputed to be haunted, and look like giant beehives. Shasta (Cor★) spends the night there. He had agreed to rendezvous at the tombs with Aravis,★ and the two Narnian★ talking horses, Bree★ and Hwin.★

Transposition   C.S. Lewis' name for a concept he explained in one of the most important addresses he gave, published in *Transposition and Other Addresses.*★ The talk was originally preached as a sermon on Whit Sunday in Mansfield College, Oxford,★ 28th May 1944.

C.S. Lewis' theory of transposition has affinities with

the ideas of another Oxford Christian thinker, Michael Polanyi (1891–1976). Transposition, says Lewis, is an 'adaptation of a richer to a poorer medium'. No denigration of the poorer medium is implied, only an assessment of its necessary limits. In a Christian universe, as understood by C.S. Lewis, all parts have value in themselves.

To explain the idea of transposition, C.S. Lewis begins his address considering the phenomenon of speaking in tongues at Pentecost. Looking from below, in a purely naturalist way, one would say that the phenomenon was 'merely' or 'nothing but' an affair of the nerves and sensations, resulting in gibberish. Seen from above, however, both the fact and the meaning are clear—this event is a supernatural act of the Holy Spirit. The spiritual is transposed into physical language.

In a similar way, in our emotional life we can reduce emotion to mere sensation if we refuse to see its meaning on a higher level. An identical sensation can stand for a variety of emotions, as the emotions are a richer medium translating into a poorer one.

This point about the danger of reduction came home vividly to C.S. Lewis during his conversion to Christianity. In his quest for joy,* he suddenly realised that he had made the basic mistake of identifying the quality of joy, or inconsolable longing, with the sensation that it aroused. When his attention focused on the sensation, joy itself vanished, leaving only its traces. He had to focus outside of himself, on the object of the joy. This dramatically changed the nature of his quest, which helped to lead him eventually to God himself.

C.S. Lewis illustrated the principle of transposition in language and music. He points out, 'If you are to translate from a language which has a large vocabulary into a language which has a small vocabulary, then you must be allowed to use several words in more than one sense. If you are to write a language with twenty-two vowel sounds in an alphabet with only five vowel characters then you must be allowed to give each of those five characters more than one value. If you are making a piano version of a piece originally scored for an orchestra, then the same piano notes which represent flutes in one passage must also represent violins in another.'

C.S. Lewis found the concept of transposition very helpful in understanding the incarnation of Christ. The insight of one of the creeds is that the incarnation worked 'not by conversion of the Godhead into flesh, but by taking of the Manhood into God'. The idea of humanity being veritably drawn into Deity seemed to C.S. Lewis a kind of transposition. It was like what happened, for example, 'when a sensation (not in itself a pleasure) is drawn into the joy it accompanies'.

The idea of transposition also helped him understand the bodily resurrection. It underpins his discussion of nature★ and supernature in *Miracles*.★ He did not conceive of the natural and spiritual, or think of the mind and the body, in a kind of platonic hierarchy, where the natural and the bodily is less real than the spiritual and the mental. Rather, he saw the relationship as transpositional, with the spiritual and natural worlds as equally parts of God's creation. In a fine passage, C.S. Lewis speculates that there may be many natures in a transpositional relationship with each other.

There cannot, from the nature of the case, be evidence that God never created and never will create, more than one system. Each of them would be at least extra-natural in relation to all the others: and if any one of them is more concrete, more permanent, more excellent, and richer than another it will be to that other *super*-natural. Nor will a partial contact between any two obliterate their distinctiveness. In that way there might be Natures piled upon Natures to any height God pleased, each Supernatural to that below it and Sub-natural to that which surpassed it. But the tenor of Christian teaching is that we are actually living in a situation even more complex than that. A new Nature is being not merely made out of an old one. We live amid all the anomalies, inconveniences, hopes, and excitements of a house that is being rebuilt. Something is being pulled down and something going up in its place (*Miracles*, Chapter 16).

Michael Polanyi develops ideas rather similar to Lewis' transposition into a theory of how we know and what we know. His theory has the value of avoiding subjectivism (as in existentialist thinking) and objectivism (as in positivism). We know, and grow in knowledge, by indwelling and being committed to what we know, not by artificially trying to stand outside our knowledge and neutrally observing it. It is from a vantage point that we see truth. If our attention becomes focused on our vantage point, we are no longer attending to the truth. Our point of vantage provides clues that can never be fully expressed, and we have skills that we have to rely on. For Polanyi, the meaning of the particulars of a lower level resides in a higher level. We could say that the higher level has been transposed into the lower level. If we take the genetic code, the meaning of biological life cannot be reduced to the physics and chemistry of that code. It would be like saying that the meaning of a tape recording of Beethoven's Fifth Symphony could be reduced to a description of the magnetic patterns on the tape.

C.S. Lewis' notion of transposition has led some to see his theology as sacramental. Lewis does write: 'The word *symbolism* is not adequate in all cases to cover the relation between the higher medium and its transposition in a lower. . . . If I had to name the relation I should call it not symbolical but sacramental.' However, the term 'sacramental' does not seem entirely adequate either to Lewis, at least as it is understood by Roman Catholics, Lutherans, or Orthodox theologians, all of whom use it in different senses. Lewis regarded transposition as most like incarnation, rather than as most like transubstantiation or consubstantiation. In his theory of transposition, C.S. Lewis is making a metaphysical case which (as the thought of Polanyi seems to show) has important consequences for theories of knowledge. He is not, I think, making a theological point about the means of grace and salvation. The incarnation in itself is not the means of grace, rather Christ's death on the cross.

That C.S. Lewis was aware of the consequences of his view of transposition for knowledge is clear from his ideas on meaning and imagination.* Like his friend Owen Barfield,* he believed that mankind has moved away from a unitary consciousness into a division of subject and object. Theoretical reasoning abstracts from real things, real emotions, real events. In his theory of transposition, Lewis is revealing his tangible vision of how all things— especially the natural and the supernatural—cohere. He saw this desirable unity, for example, in the Gospel story, where the quality of myth* is not lost in the historical facticity of the events. There is no separation of story and history.

There is . . . in the history of thought, as elsewhere, a pattern of death and rebirth. The old, richly imaginative thought which still survives in Plato has to submit to the deathlike, but indispensable, process of logical analysis: nature and spirit, matter and mind, fact and myth, the literal and metaphorical, have to be more and more sharply separated, till at last a purely mathematical universe and a purely subjective mind confront one another across an unbridgeable chasm. But from this descent, also, if thought itself is to survive, there must be re-ascent and the Christian conception provides for this. Those who attain the glorious resurrection will see the dry bones clothed again with flesh, the fact and the myth remarried, the literal and the metaphorical rushing together (*Miracles*, Chapter 26).

See also THE PERSONAL HERESY.

Transposition and Other Addresses (1949)   A selection of addresses given by C.S. Lewis during the war years and immediately afterwards, including a famous sermon, one of the outstanding of such documents in the history of Christianity. The contents are 'Transposition',★ 'Learning in War-Time',★ 'Membership', 'The Inner Ring',★ and the sermon, 'The Weight of Glory'.

Trom   In *Till We Have Faces*,★ the bullying and insensitive King of Glome,★ father of Orual,★ Redival,★ and Psyche.★ His savage temper led him on impulse to beat his daughters (usually Orual, whose ugly face he despised), send a faithful servant to certain death in the silver mines, and castrate Tarin,★ a young officer who had flirted with Redival. When the lot fell on Psyche to be the atoning sacrifice, his feeling was of relief that he was spared rather than sorrow for his daughter. Later, his conscience troubled him as he lay dying, and he mistook the veiled Orual for Psyche, come back to haunt him.

Trufflehunter   In the story of *Prince Caspian*,★ a badger and loyal Old Narnian who helps Caspian★ against the tyrant King Miraz.★

See also TALKING ANIMALS.

Trumpkin the Dwarf   In *Prince Caspian*,★ Trumpkin is the dwarf rescued by the Pevensie★ children from some of

221

the men of King Miraz.★ He is a loyal Old Narnian, and leads them to the hideout of Prince Caspian★ in Aslan's How.★

Trunia In *Till We Have Faces*,★ a Prince of Phars,★ neighbouring Glome.★ He was at war with his surly brother, Argan,★ and the old King, their father. After Orual★ kills Argan in single combat, Trunia is proclaimed King of Phars, and marries Redival. Their son, Daaran,★ is pronounced heir to her throne by the virgin Queen, Orual.

Mr Tumnus A faun first encountered by Lucy Pevensie★ as she stepped through the wardrobe into the land of Narnia,★ as told in *The Lion, the Witch and the Wardrobe*.★ For not handing Lucy over to the White Witch,★ Tumnus is punished by being turned to stone. He is later restored by Aslan,★ the great lion. In the tale of *The Horse and His Boy*,★ set in the same period, Mr Tumnus is with the visiting Narnian party in Tashbaan, the capital of Calormen.★

C.S. Lewis tells us that the story of *The Lion, the Witch and the Wardrobe*, and thus the entire *Chronicles of Narnia*,★ began with Mr Tumnus. 'The *Lion* all began with a picture of a Faun carrying an umbrella and parcels in a snowy wood. This picture had been in my mind since I was about sixteen. Then one day, when I was about forty, I said to myself: "Let's try to make a story about it."'

Tynan, Kenneth (1927–80) Drama critic Kenneth Tynan was one of C.S. Lewis' most famous pupils at Magdalen College, Oxford.★ He was there from 1945 to 1949. In an interview given shortly before he died he confessed: 'Lewis was undoubtedly the most powerful and formative influence of my whole life up to that point. I found him the most impressive mind I had ever seen in action.' Like others, he compared Lewis to Dr Samuel Johnson: 'He had the breadth and clarity of mind ... he had the same swiftness to grasp the heart of a problem and the same sort of pouncing intelligence to follow it through to its conclusion. I found him immensely invigorating, stimulating and inspiring.'

As a teacher Tynan found Lewis 'incomparable'. His study, *English Literature in the Sixteenth Century*,★ was regarded by Tynan as 'the most brilliant book of any literary criticism to have been published in my adult lifetime'. Most of the opinions in it he heard expressed when Lewis was his tutor. His greatest quality was his ability as a teacher to 'take you into the mind of a medieval poet and make the man seem a living being'. No other teacher could do this. Tynan felt that he had been in Chaucer's mind after talking to C.S. Lewis.

U

Ulvilas In *Prince Caspian*,★ a Lord of Caspian★ IX whom the usurper Miraz★ had shot with arrows during a hunting party.

Undeception A favourite theme of C.S. Lewis', for whom a characteristic of the human condition is the state of being deceived by others, by sin, or by oneself. He refers to the concept of undeception in his essay, 'A Note on Jane Austen', in *Selected Literary Essays*. He finds the theme in her novels, which were favourite reading for him. Many of Lewis' fictional characters experience undeception, usually associated with salvation. Such characters include Mark Studdock,★ in *That Hideous Strength*,★ and Queen Orual★ in *Till We Have Faces.*★ Lewis regarded the purpose of his fiction as helping to undeceive modern people, who are separated from the past, with its knowledge of perennial human values, and from an acquaintance with even basic Christian teaching about the realities of sin, redemption, immortality and divine judgement and grace.

***Undeceptions: Essays on Theology and Ethics* (1971)** Published in the United States under the title, *God in the Dock*. A large collection of C.S. Lewis' pieces written over a period of many years. Subsequently, much of the content of *Undeceptions* has been republished in two small paperback collections, *God in the Dock* (1979) and *Timeless at Heart* (1987).

Undeceptions includes a number of articles of interest,

including Lewis' account of the founding of the Oxford University Socratic Club,★ 'Vivisection', 'Cross-Examination' (an interview for *Decision* magazine), and 'The Humanitarian Theory of Punishment'.

Underland In *The Silver Chair*,★ the realm of the Green Witch,★ where she kept Prince Rilian★ in enchanted imprisonment. Underland was known by the even deeper world of Bism★ as the Shallow Lands. Gnomes under the Green Witch's rule had been forced to dig tunnels to be used in an invasion of Narnia.★ Eustace Scrubb★ and Jill Pole,★ with the lugubrious help of Puddleglum★ the Marshwiggle,★ enter Underland and rescue Prince Rilian after his undeception.★ Underland, with the death of the Green Witch, is destroyed, but not before the party escape and the gnomes joyfully return to Bism.

Ungit In *Till We Have Faces*,★ the deity worshipped in Glome,★ a paganised form of Aphrodite or Venus. She is the mother of the god of the Grey Mountains★ (or Cupid in Greek myth).

Un-man *See* WESTON, EDWARD ROLLES.

V

Valley of the God   In *Till We Have Faces*,★ the secret
and beautiful valley beyond the Grey Mountains where
Psyche★ dwelt in the palace of the god.
 See also PSYCHE'S PALACE; GOD OF THE GREY
MOUNTAINS.

The Voyage of the 'Dawn Treader' (1952)   The sequel
to *Prince Caspian*,★ this is the story of a double quest, for
seven Lords★ of Narnia★ who disappeared during the
reign of the wicked King Miraz,★ and for Aslan's
Country★ at the end of the world over the Eastern
Ocean.★ Reepicheep★ the Mouse is particularly seeking
Aslan's Country, and his quest embodies Lewis' characteristic theme of joy.★ During the sea journey of the
Dawn Treader various islands are encountered, each with
its own kind of adventure. Of the original Pevensie★
children, only Edmund and Lucy return to Narnia in this
story. Their spoilt cousin, a 'modern boy' called Eustace
Scrubb,★ is also drawn into Narnia. At one stage he turns
into a dragon,★ and is sorry for his behaviour. Only
Aslan,★ the great lion, is able to peel off his dragon skin
and restore him.
 The children join the ship on its journey between
Narnia and the Lone Islands.★ Here they fall into the hands
of slave traders. Beyond the Lone Islands they encounter a
great storm, and the bedraggled *Dawn Treader* limps into
the haven of Dragon Island,★ where Eustace becomes a
better boy. Pursuing their quest eastward, and beyond

Burnt Island,★ they are endangered by a great sea serpent. Nearby, at Deathwater Island,★ they find a missing Lord turned to gold, and narrowly avoid the same fate. Yet further east they come across the mysterious Island of Voices,★ where Lucy reads a great magician's book of magic, in one of the most delightful episodes in *The Chronicles of Narnia*.★ Further on, after the nightmare adventure at Dark Island,★ they find refreshment at World's End Island.★ Here they meet Ramandu★ and his beautiful daughter, who later becomes Caspian's Queen. After sailing across the final Silver Sea,★ they reach Aslan's Country,★ the end of Reepicheep's quest.

Voyage to Venus (1943)   *See PERELANDRA.*

W

Wain, John (b 1925)   A famous pupil of C.S. Lewis', and member of The Inklings.★ His autobiographical *Sprightly Running* records his experiences in wartime Oxford:★ 'Once a week, I trod the broad, shallow stairs up to C.S. Lewis' study in the "new building" at Magdalen. And there, with the deer-haunted grove on one side of us, and the tower and bridge on the other, we talked about English literature as armies grappled and bombs exploded.' In 1947 John Wain became Lecturer in English at Reading University, staying there until 1955. His novel *Hurry on Down* (1953) was followed by further novels, as well as books of criticism and poetry. From 1973 to 1978 he was Professor of Poetry at Oxford.

Water rat   In *The Last Battle*,★ Tirian★ and Jewel★ come across a water rat on a raft on the river, carrying logs destined for Calormen.★ Thus Tirian learns that something is gravely wrong in Narnia.

Western Wild   A region of high hills and broken mountain ranges to the far west of Narnia.★ In the story of *The Magician's Nephew*,★ Digory Kirke★ and Polly Plummer★ travel there on the back of Fledge★ the Flying Horse in their quest for the magic apple.

See also NARNIA: Geography.

Weston, Edward Rolles (1896–1942)   In *Out of the Silent Planet*★ and *Perelandra*,★ a scientist who represents all that C.S. Lewis dislikes about the modern world. He embodies the destruction of universal human values as set out in Lewis' book, *The Abolition of Man.*★ Rather than true science, of which Lewis approved, Weston represented scientism, the idolatry of science. With him, science becomes totalitarian, as a means of guaranteeing the survival of mankind at any cost.

In the first story, Weston has invented a spacecraft capable of reaching Mars (Malacandra★). He and Devine★ kidnap Dr Elwin Ransom.★ In the later story, Ransom again encounters him, this time on the planet Venus (Perelandra★). Weston is increasingly demonised as he allows a satanic possession of his faculties, and eventually becomes an Un-man.

West-wind   *See* GOD OF THE GREY MOUNTAINS.

White Witch   Another name for Jadis, the destroyer of the exhausted world of Charn,★ visited by Digory Kirke★ and Polly Plummer★ in the story of *The Magician's Nephew.*★ Through foolish curiosity, and despite Polly's reservations, Digory rings a bell which awakens her. Jadis is drawn with them first back to Edwardian London and then to Narnia,★ just as it is being created. As the Narnian ages flow on she grows in power and puts the land under a curse of perpetual winter but never Christmas. Finally, as told in *The Lion, the Witch and the Wardrobe,*★ she is slain by Aslan.★ Jadis is the progenitor of a line of witches, including the Green Witch★ who tries to dominate Narnia during the time of King Caspian★ X, as recounted in the tale of *The Silver Chair.*★

Williams, Charles (1886–1945)   Equally enigmatic as an author and a person, Charles Williams became a firm friend of C.S. Lewis' during the war years. He was admitted into the literary circle surrounding Lewis, The Inklings,★ and exerted a deep and lasting influence on him. J.R.R. Tolkien describes Lewis as being under Williams' 'spell', and did not entirely approve of this, feeling that Lewis was too impressionable a man.

Charles Williams' writings—encompassing fiction, poetry, drama, theology, church history, biography, and literary criticism—become more accessible in the light of the writings of C.S. Lewis, who was influenced by him. There are many elements consciously drawn from Williams in Lewis' *That Hideous Strength*,★ *The Great Divorce*,★ *Till We Have Faces*,★ and *The Four Loves*.★ Lewis was particularly influenced by Williams' novel *The Place of the Lion*,★ his Arthurian cycle of poetry (including *Taliesin Through Logres*), and his theological understanding of romanticism,★ especially the experience of falling in love★—romantic love.

Anne Ridler captured the essence of Charles Williams when she wrote: 'In Williams' universe there is a clear logic, a sense of terrible justice which is not our justice and yet is not divorced from love.' George MacDonald similarly spoke of God's 'inexorable love'. For Anne Ridler, 'the whole man . . . was greater even than the sum of his works'. Similarly T.S. Eliot—who greatly admired Charles Williams—said, in a broadcast talk: 'It is the whole work, not any one or several masterpieces, that we have to take into account in estimating the importance of the man. I think he was a man of unusual genius, and I regard his work as important. But it has an importance of a kind not easy to explain.'

Like C.S. Lewis and J.R.R. Tolkien, Williams' thought and writings centred on the three themes of reason, romanticism and Christianity. Like Lewis, he was an Anglican, but much higher, an Anglo-Catholic. His interest in romanticism comes out, in a literary way, in his interest in and use of symbols—or 'Images', as he preferred to call them. In the business of living, he was interested in the experience of romantic and other forms of love, and the theological implications of human love. As regards reason, he rejected the equation of rational abstraction with reality, and helped to introduce the writings of Søren Kierkegaard to English readers. Yet he felt passionately that the whole human personality must be ordered by reason to have integrity and spiritual health. His least satisfactory novel, *Shadows of Ectasy* (1933), concerns a conflict between the over-intellectualised European races and the deeply emotional, intuitive approach to life of the Africans. Charles Williams constantly sought the balance between the abstract and the 'feeling' mind, between intellect and emotion, between reason and imagination.★

Charles Williams was in his early forties when his first novel, *War in Heaven*, was published in 1930. Prior to this he had brought out five minor books, four of which were verse, and one a play. His important work begins with the novels; it is after 1930 that his noteworthy works appear, packed into the last fifteen years of his life. During these final years twenty-eight books were published (an average of almost two a year) as well as numerous articles and reviews. The last third of these years of maturity as a thinker and writer were spent in Oxford. They involved Williams' normal editorial duties with Oxford University Press, lecturing and tutorials for the university, constant meetings with C.S. Lewis and The Inklings, and frequent weekends in his London home. His wife stayed behind to look after the flat when Williams was evacuated to Oxford with Oxford University Press.

Islington, London, was the birthplace of Charles Williams on 20th September 1886. His father was a foreign correspondence clerk in French and German to a firm of importers until his failing eyesight forced the family to move out of London to the countryside at St Albans. There they set up a shop selling artists' material, and his father contributed short stories to various periodicals. He guided his son's reading, and they went on long walks together. Charles Williams dedicated his third book of poems to 'My father and my other teachers'.

The talented boy gained a County Council scholarship to St Albans Grammar School. Here he formed a friendship that lasted many years with a George Robinson, who shared his tastes, pursuits, and literary inventions. With Williams, and his sister Edith, the friend sometimes acted plays to the family circle. The two friends gained places at University College, London, beginning their studies at the age of fifteen. The family unfortunately were not able to continue paying the fees, and Charles Williams managed to get a job in a Methodist bookshop.

His fortunes changed through meeting an editor from the London office of the Oxford University Press, who was looking for someone to help him with the proofs of the complete edition of Thackeray which, in 1908, was going through the press. Williams stayed on the staff until his death, creating a distinctive atmosphere affectionately remembered by those who worked with him, particularly women. He married, was considered medically unfit for the wartime army, and lost two of his closest friends in the Great War. In 1922 his only son, Michael, was born.

In the autumn of that year Charles Williams began what was to become a habitual event—giving adult evening classes in literature for the London County Council to supplement the modest family income. He wrote his series of seven supernatural thrillers, including *The Place of the Lion*, for the same reason.

When Williams was evacuated with the OUP to Oxford he brought a distinctive atmosphere there, vividly captured in John Wain's★ autobiography, *Sprightly Running*. He comments: 'He gave himself as unreservedly to Oxford as Oxford gave itself to him.'

Oxford University recognised Charles Williams in 1943 with an honorary MA. In his *Preface to Paradise*

Lost,★ C.S. Lewis publically acknowledged his debt to Williams' interpretation of Milton. T.S. Eliot praised his work on Dante, as did Dorothy L. Sayers★ (who made a vivid translation of *The Divine Comedy*). After his unexpected death, Lewis published a commentary on Williams' unfinished cycle of Arthurian poetry, *Arthurian Torso*.★ This poetry has continued to be an influence today in Stephen Lawhead's *Pendragon* cycle of stories. Several of The Inklings—including Lewis, Tolkien, Owen Barfield,★ and W.H. 'Warnie' Lewis★—contributed to a posthumous tribute, *Essays Presented to Charles Williams*.★ *See also* THEOLOGY OF ROMANCE.

Further reading

Alice Hadfield, *Charles Williams: An exploration of his life and work* (1983); Humphrey Carpenter, *The Inklings: C.S. Lewis, J.R.R. Tolkien, Charles Williams and their friends* (1978); Glen Cavaliero, *Charles Williams: Poet of theology* (1983); John Wain, *Sprightly Running: Part of an autobiography* (1962, 1965).

Wimbleweather A giant, and one of the loyal Old Narnians in the tale of *Prince Caspian*.★ He is a marshall in the combat between Peter Pevensie★ and the usurper, King Miraz.★ Like most giants he is not at all clever, at one stage muffing a strategic battle move. His tears of misery after that occasion soaked some sleeping talking mice in the hideout of Prince Caspian★ in Aslan's How.★

World's End Island An island encountered by the travellers in the story of *The Voyage of the 'Dawn Treader'*.★ It is so far to the east of Narnia,★ across the Eastern Ocean,★ that it is close to Aslan's Country.★ The island is carpeted with a fine, springy turf, sprinkled with a plant like heather. On it there is a roofless wide space paved with smooth stones and surrounded by grey pillars. A long table is to be found on this space, covered with a crimson cloth, and known as Aslan's Table, as he placed it there. The table is stocked with food each day by flocks of great white birds. As they swoop towards the island, the birds sing an unknown human language.

Ramandu,* an elderly star, and his beautiful daughter, live here. Three of the missing seven Lords* lie asleep at Aslan's Table.

Wormwood   An incompetent junior tempter, and nephew of the eminent Screwtape,* high in hell's bureaucracy, in *The Screwtape Letters.** Wormwood is a recent graduate of the Tempters' Training College,* and fails to make the grade on his first assignment, despite guidance by letter from Screwtape, and the frequent progress reports demanded by him. Wormwood's charge successfully stays in the clutches of the Enemy.

Books by C.S. Lewis

Spirits in Bondage: A Cycle of Lyrics. William Heinemann: London, 1919. Reprinted with an introduction by Walter Hooper, Harcourt Brace: New York, 1985.

Dymer. J.M. Dent: London, 1926; E.P. Dutton: New York, 1926. Reprinted with a new preface, Macmillan: New York, 1950.

The Pilgrim's Regress: An Allegorical Apology for Christianity, Reason and Romanticism. J.M. Dent: London, 1933; Sheed & Ward, 1935. Reprinted, with a new preface, footnotes, and running headlines, Sheed & Ward: London, 1944; Eerdmans: Grand Rapids, Michigan, 1958.

The Allegory of Love: A Study in Medieval Tradition. Clarendon Press: Oxford, 1936.

Out of the Silent Planet. John Lane: London, 1938.

Rehabilitations and Other Essays. Oxford University Press: London, 1939.

The Personal Heresy: A Controversy. Oxford University Press: London, 1939. (With E.M.W. Tillyard.)

The Problem of Pain. Geoffrey Bles, Centenary Press: London, 1940.

The Screwtape Letters. Geoffrey Bles: London, 1942. Reprinted as *The Screwtape Letters and Screwtape Proposes a Toast.* Geoffrey Bles: London, 1961.

A Preface to Paradise Lost. Oxford University Press: London, 1942.

Broadcast Talks. Geoffrey Bles: London, 1942.

Christian Behaviour: A Further Series of Broadcast Talks. Geoffrey Bles: London, 1943.

Perelandra. John Lane: London, 1943. Reprinted in paperback as *Voyage to Venus*. Pan Books: London, 1953.

The Abolition of Man: Reflections on Education with Special Reference to the Teaching of English in the Upper Forms of Schools. Riddell Memorial Lectures, fifteenth series. Oxford University Press: London, 1943.

Beyond Personality: The Christian Idea of God. Geoffrey Bles, Centenary Press: London, 1944.

That Hideous Strength: A Modern Fairy-Tale for Grown-Ups. John Lane: London, 1945. A version abridged by the author was published as *The Tortured Planet* (Avon Books: New York, 1946) and as *That Hideous Strength* (Pan Books: London, 1955).

The Great Divorce: A Dream. Geoffrey Bles, Centenary Press: London, 1945.

Miracles: A Preliminary Study. Geoffrey Bles: London, 1947. Reprinted, with an expanded version of Chapter 3, Collins-Fontana Books: London, 1960.

Arthurian Torso: Containing the Posthumous Fragment of the Figure of Arthur by Charles Williams and A Commentary on the Arthurian Poems of Charles Williams by C.S. Lewis. Oxford University Press: London, 1948. Reprinted with an introduction by Mary McDermott Shideler, Eerdmans: Grand Rapids, Michigan, 1974.

Transposition and Other Addresses. Geoffrey Bles: London, 1949. Published in the United States as *The Weight of Glory and Other Addresses*. Macmillan: New York, 1949.

The Lion, the Witch and the Wardrobe. Geoffrey Bles: London, 1950.

Prince Caspian: The Return to Narnia. Geoffrey Bles: London, 1951.

Mere Christianity. Geoffrey Bles: London, 1952. A revised

and expanded version of *Broadcast Talks, Christian Behaviour,* and *Beyond Personality.*

The Voyage of the Dawn Treader. Geoffrey Bles: London, 1952.

The Silver Chair. Geoffrey Bles: London, 1953.

The Horse and His Boy. Geoffrey Bles: London, 1954.

English Literature in the Sixteenth Century Excluding Drama. Volume 3 of *The Oxford History of English Literature.* Clarendon Press: Oxford, 1954.

The Magician's Nephew. Bodley Head: London, 1955.

Surprised by Joy: The Shape of My Early Life. Geoffrey Bles: London, 1955.

The Last Battle. Bodley Head: London, 1956.

Till We Have Faces: A Myth Retold. Geoffrey Bles: London, 1956; Harcourt, Brace & World: New York, 1956.

Reflections on the Psalms. Geoffrey Bles: London, 1958.

The Four Loves. Geoffrey Bles: London, 1960.

Studies in Words. Cambridge University Press: Cambridge, 1960.

The World's Last Night and Other Essays. Harcourt, Brace & Co: New York, 1960.

A Grief Observed. Faber & Faber: London, 1961.

An Experiment in Criticism. Cambridge University Press: Cambridge, 1961.

They Asked for a Paper: Papers and Addresses. Geoffrey Bles: London, 1962.

Letters to Malcolm: Chiefly on Prayer. Geoffrey Bles: London, 1964.

The Discarded Image: An Introduction to Medieval and Renaissance Literature. Cambridge University Press: Cambridge, 1964.

Poems. Edited by Walter Hooper. Geoffrey Bles: London, 1964.

Screwtape Proposes a Toast and Other Pieces. Collins-Fontana Books: London, 1965.

Studies in Medieval and Renaissance Literature. Edited by Walter Hooper. Cambridge University Press: Cambridge, 1966.

Letters of C.S. Lewis. Edited, with a memoir, by W.H. Lewis. Geoffrey Bles: London, 1966. Revised edition, edited by Walter Hooper, 1988.

Of Other Worlds: Essays and Stories. Edited by Walter Hooper. Geoffrey Bles: London, 1966.

Spenser's Images of Life. Edited by Alistair Fowler. Cambridge University Press: Cambridge, 1967.

Letters to an American Lady. Edited by Clyde S. Kilby. Eerdmans: Grand Rapids, Michigan, 1967; Hodder and Stoughton: London, 1969.

Christian Reflections. Edited by Walter Hooper. Geoffrey Bles: London, 1967.

A Mind Awake: An Anthology of C.S. Lewis. Edited by Clyde S. Kilby. Geoffrey Bles: London, 1968. Harcourt, Brace & World: New York, 1969.

Narrative Poems. Edited and with a preface by Walter Hooper. Geoffrey Bles: London, 1969.

Selected Literary Essays. Edited and with a preface by Walter Hooper. Cambridge University Press: Cambridge, 1969.

God in the Dock: Essays on Theology and Ethics. Edited and with a preface by Walter Hooper. Eerdmans: Grand Rapids, Michigan, 1970. A paperback edition of part of it was published as *God in the Dock: Essays on Theology* (Collins–Fontana Books: London, 1979) and as *Undeceptions: Essays on Theology and Ethics* (Geoffrey Bles: London, 1971).

Fern-Seed and Elephants and Other Essays on Christianity. Edited and with a preface by Walter Hooper. Collins–Fontana Books: London, 1975.

The Dark Tower and Other Stories. Edited and with a preface by Walter Hooper. Collins: London, 1977; Harcourt Brace Jovanovich: New York, 1977.

The Joyful Christian: Readings from C.S. Lewis. Macmillan: New York, 1977.

They Stand Together: The Letters of C.S. Lewis to Arthur Greeves (1914–1963). Edited by Walter Hooper. Collins: London, 1979; Macmillan: New York, 1979.

Boxen: The Imaginary World of the Young C.S. Lewis. Edited by Walter Hooper. Collins: London, 1985; Harcourt Brace Jovanovich: San Diego, 1985.

Books about C.S. Lewis

Interest in C.S. Lewis' writings and thinking has continued unabated since his death in 1963. The following list of secondary studies shows the variety of interest.

Adey, Lionel. *C.S. Lewis's 'Great War' with Owen Barfield*. University of Victoria: Canada, 1978.

Aeschlimas, Michael D. *The Restitution of Man: C.S. Lewis and the Case Against Scientism*. Eerdmans: Grand Rapids, Michigan, 1983.

Arnott, Anne. *The Secret Country of C.S. Lewis*. Hodder: 1974.

Beattie, Sister Mary J. *The Humane Medievalist: A Study of C.S. Lewis' Criticism of Medieval Literature*. Unpublished dissertation. University of Pittsburgh: 1967.

Beversluis, John. *C.S. Lewis and the Search for Rational Religion*. The Paternoster Press: Exeter, 1985.

Boss, Edgar W. *The Theology of C.S. Lewis*. Unpublished ThD dissertation. Northern Baptist Theological Seminary: Chicago, 1948.

Carnell, Corbin S. *Bright Shadows of Reality*. Eerdmans: Grand Rapids, Michigan, 1974.

Carpenter, Humphrey. *The Inklings*. George Allan and Unwin: 1978.

Christensen, Michael J. *C.S. Lewis on Scripture*. Hodder: 1980.

Christopher, Joe R. *C.S. Lewis*. G.K. Hall and Co: Boston, 1987.

Christopher, Joe R. and Ostling, Joan K. *C.S. Lewis: An Annotated Check List of Writings About Him and His Works*. Kent State University Press: Ohio, 1974.

Como, James T. (Ed). *C.S. Lewis at the Breakfast Table and Other Reminiscences*. Macmillan: New York, 1979.

Cunningham, Richard B. *C.S. Lewis, Defender of the Faith*, The Westminster Press: Philadelphia, 1967.

Derrick, Christopher. *C.S. Lewis and the Church of Rome*. Ignatius Press: USA, 1982.

Ford, Paul F. *Companion to Narnia*. Harper and Row: San Francisco, 1980.

Fuller, Edmund. *Books with Men Behind Them*. Random House: New York, 1962.

Gibb, Jocelyn (Ed). *Light on C.S. Lewis*. Geoffrey Bles: London, 1965.

Gibson, Evan. *C.S. Lewis: Spinner of Tales*. Christian University Press: Washington, DC, 1980.

Glover, Donald E. *C.S. Lewis: The Act of Enchantment*. Ohio University Press: USA, 1981.

Green, R.L. and Hooper, Walter. *C.S. Lewis: a Biography*. Collins: 1974.

Gresham, Douglas. *Lenten Lands: My Childhood with Joy Davidman and C.S. Lewis*. Collins: 1989.

Griffin, William. *Clive Staples Lewis: A Dramatic Life*. Harper and Row: San Francisco, 1986. *C.S. Lewis: The authentic voice*. Lion: Tring, 1988.

Haigh, John D. *The Fiction of C.S. Lewis*. Unpublished PhD dissertation. University of Leeds: 1962.

Hannay, Margaret. *C.S. Lewis*. Ungar: New York, 1981.

Hart, Dabney A. *Through the Open Door: A New Look at C.S. Lewis*. University of Alabama Press: Alabama, forthcoming.

Hillegas, M.R. (Ed). *Shadows of Imagination*. Feffer & Simons Inc: London and Amsterdam, 1969.

Hoey, Sister Mary A. *An Applied Linguistic Analysis of the Prose Style of C.S. Lewis*. Unpublished PhD dissertation. University of Connecticut: 1966.

Holmer, Paul L. *C.S. Lewis: The Shape of his Faith and Thought*. Sheldon Press: 1977.

Howard, Thomas. *The Achievement of C.S. Lewis: A reading of his fiction*. Harold Shaw: Wheaton, Illinois, 1980.

Hutter, Charles (Ed). *Imagination and the Spirit*. Eerdmans: Grand Rapids, Michigan, 1971.

Karkainen, Paul A. *Narnia Explored*. Revell: Old Tappan, New Jersey, 1979.

Keefe, Carolyn (Ed). *C.S. Lewis: Speaker and Teacher*. Hodder: 1974.

Kilby, Clyde S. *The Christian World of C.S. Lewis*. Marcham Manor Press: 1965; Eerdmans: Grand Rapids, Michigan, 1965.

Kilby, Clyde S. and Douglas Gilbert. *C.S. Lewis: Images of His World*. Eerdmans: Grand Rapids, Michigan, 1973.

Kilby, Clyde S. *Images of Salvation in the Fiction of C.S. Lewis*. Harold Shaw: Wheaton, Illinois, 1978.

Kilby, Clyde S. and Meade, Marjorie Lamp (Ed). *Brothers and Friends: The Diaries of Major Warren Hamilton Lewis*. Harper and Row: San Francisco, 1982.

Kranz, Gisbert. *C.S. Lewis: Studien zu Leben un Werk*. Bouvier: Bonn, 1974.

Kreeft, Peter, *C.S. Lewis*. Eerdmans: Grand Rapids, Michigan, 1969.

Lawlor, John (Ed). *Patterns of Love and Courtesy: Essays in Memory of C.S. Lewis.* Edward Arnold: 1966.

Lindskoog, Kathryn. *The C.S. Lewis Hoax.* Multnomah Press: 1988 (not available in the United Kingdom).

Lindskoog, Kathryn. *C.S. Lewis: Mere Christian.* Gospel Light: Glendale, California, 1973.

Lindskoog, Kathryn. *The Lion of Judah in Never-Never Land: God, Man and Nature in C.S. Lewis's Narnia Tales.* Eerdmans: Grand Rapids, Michigan, 1973.

Lochhead, Marion. *The Renaissance of Wonder in Children's Literature.* Canongate: Edinburgh, 1977.

Manlove, C.N. *Modern Fantasy.* Cambridge University Press: Cambridge, 1975.

Meilander, Gilbert. *The Taste for the Other: The Social and Ethical Thought of C.S. Lewis.* Eerdmans: Grand Rapids, Michigan, 1978.

Montgomery, John W. (Ed). *Myth, Allegory and Gospel.* Bethany Fellowship: Minneapolis, 1974.

Moorman, Charles. *Arthurian Triptych: Mythic Materials in Charles Williams, C.S. Lewis and T.S. Eliot.* University of California Press: Berkeley, 1960.

Moorman, Charles. *The Precincts of Felicity: The Augustinian City of the Oxford Christians.* University of Florida Press: Gainesville, 1966.

Norwood, William D., Jr. *The Neo-Medieval Novels of C.S. Lewis.* Unpublished PhD dissertation. University of Texas: 1965.

Payne, Leanne. *Real Presence: The Holy Spirit in the Works of C.S. Lewis.* Monarch Publications: Eastbourne, 1989.

Peters, John. *C.S. Lewis—The Man and his Achievement.* The Paternoster Press: Exeter, 1985.

Purtill, Richard. *C.S. Lewis's Case for the Christian Faith.* Harper and Row: 1982.

Purtill, Richard. *Lord of the Elves and Eldils: Fantasy and Philosophy in C.S. Lewis and J.R.R. Tolkien.* Zondervan: Grand Rapids, Michigan, 1974.

Reddy, Albert F. *The Else Unspeakable: An Introduction to the Fiction of C.S. Lewis.* Unpublished PhD dissertation. University of Massachusetts: 1972.

Reilly, Robert J. *Romantic Religion in the Work of Owen Barfield, C.S. Lewis, Charles Williams and J.R. Tolkien.* Unpublished PhD dissertation. Michigan State University: 1960.

Sammons, Martha C. *A Guide Through Narnia.* Hodder: 1979.

Sayer, George. *Jack: C.S. Lewis and his times.* Macmillan: 1988.

Schakel, Peter J. *Reading with the Heart: the Way into Narnia.* Eerdmans: Grand Rapids, Michigan, 1979.

Schakel, Peter J. *Reason and Imagination in C.S. Lewis: A Study of 'Till We Have Faces'.* Paternoster Press: Exeter, 1984.

Schakel, Peter J. (Ed). *The Longing for a Form: Essays on the Fiction of C.S. Lewis.* Kent State University Press: Ohio, 1977.

Schmerl, Rudolf B. *Reason's Dream: Anti-Totalitarian Themes and Techniques of Fantasy.* Unpublished PhD dissertation. University of Michigan: 1960.

Schofield, Stephen (Ed). *In Search of C.S. Lewis.* Bridge Publications: USA, 1984.

Sibley, Brian. *Shadowlands.* Hodder: 1985.

Smith, Robert H. *Patches of Godlight: The Pattern of Thought of C.S. Lewis.* University of Georgia Press: Athens, USA, 1981.

Urang, Gunnar. *Shadows of Heaven*. SCM Press: 1970.

Vanauken, Sheldon. *A Severe Mercy*. Hodder: 1977; Harper and Row: New York, 1979.

Wain, John. *Sprightly Running*. Macmillan: 1962.

Walsh, Chad. *C.S. Lewis: Apostle to the Skeptics*. Macmillan: New York, 1949.

Walsh, Chad. *The Literary Legend of C.S. Lewis*. Harcourt Brace Jovanovich: New York, 1979.

White, William L. *The Image of Man in C.S. Lewis*. Hodder: 1970.

Willis, John. *Pleasures For Evermore: The theology of C.S. Lewis*. Angel Press/Loyola University Press: 1989.

Wright, Marjorie E. *The Cosmic Kingdom of Myth: A Study in the Myth-Philosophy of Charles Williams, C.S. Lewis and J.R.R. Tolkien*. Unpublished PhD dissertation. University of Illinois: 1960.

Reference guide

This guide provides a handy reference by grouping together the titles of some of the related articles in *A C.S. Lewis Handbook*. The sections are as follows:

1 The life of C.S. Lewis
2 The works of C.S. Lewis
3 The literary criticism of C.S. Lewis
4 The themes of C.S. Lewis
5 The thought of C.S. Lewis
6 Science fiction
7 *The Screwtape Letters*
8 *Till We Have Faces*
9 Narnia
    (i) *The Lion, the Witch and the Wardrobe*
    (ii) *The Magician's Nephew*
    (iii) *Prince Caspian*
    (iv) *The Voyage of the 'Dawn Treader'*
    (v) *The Silver Chair*
    (vi) *The Horse and His Boy*
    (vii) *The Last Battle*

1   The life of C.S. Lewis

Annie, Aunt
Barfield, Owen
Baynes, Pauline
'Belsen'
Bennett, J.A.W.
Boxen
Brothers and Friends

2 The works of C.S. Lewis